Living in Time

Living in Time

The Philosophy of Henri Bergson

BARRY ALLEN

Oxford University Press is a department of the University of Oxford. It furthers
the University's objective of excellence in research, scholarship, and education
by publishing worldwide. Oxford is a registered trade mark of Oxford University
Press in the UK and certain other countries.

Published in the United States of America by Oxford University Press
198 Madison Avenue, New York, NY 10016, United States of America.

© Oxford University Press 2023

All rights reserved. No part of this publication may be reproduced, stored in
a retrieval system, or transmitted, in any form or by any means, without the
prior permission in writing of Oxford University Press, or as expressly permitted
by law, by license, or under terms agreed with the appropriate reproduction
rights organization. Inquiries concerning reproduction outside the scope of the
above should be sent to the Rights Department, Oxford University Press, at the
address above.

You must not circulate this work in any other form
and you must impose this same condition on any acquirer.

CIP data is on file at the Library of Congress
ISBN 978-0-19-767161-0

DOI: 10.1093/oso/9780197671610.001.0001

The manufacturer's authorised representative in the EU for product safety is
Oxford University Press España S.A. of El Parque Empresarial San Fernando
de Henares, Avenida de Castilla, 2 – 28830 Madrid (www.oup.es/en or
product.safety@oup.com). OUP España S.A. also acts as importer into Spain
of products made by the manufacturer.

For Jeanne and Niko,
who made the time

Wherever anything lives, there is, open somewhere, a register in which time is being inscribed.

—Henri Bergson

Contents

List of Abbreviations   ix

   Introducing Henri Bergson   1
1. Taking Time Seriously   6
2. Making Memory Matter   64
3. *Élan Vital*   113
4. Open and Closed   170
   Conclusion   202

Notes   211
Index   243

Abbreviations

for works by Bergson

CE   *Creative Evolution*, trans. Arthur Mitchell (1907; Mineola, NY: Dover, 1998).

CM   *The Creative Mind: An Introduction to Metaphysics*, trans. Mabelle L. Andison (1934; Mineola, NY: Dover, 2007).

DS   *Duration and Simultaneity*, trans. Leon Jacobson (1922; New York: Bobbs-Merrill, 1965).

L   *Laughter: An Essay on the Meaning of the Comic*, trans. Cloudesley Brereton and Fred Rothwell (1900; New York: Macmillan, 1911).

ME   *Mind-Energy*, trans. H. Wildon Carr (1919; New York: Henry Holt, 1920).

MM   *Matter and Memory*, trans. Nancy Margaret Paul and W. Scott Palmer (1896; Mineola, NY: Dover, 2004).

TFW   *Time and Free Will*, trans. F. L. Pogson (1889; Mineola, NY: Dover, 2001).

TS   *The Two Sources of Morality and Religion*, trans. R. Ashley Audra and Cloudesley Brereton (1932; Notre Dame, IN: University of Notre Dame Press, 1977).

Introducing Henri Bergson

Henri Bergson (1859–1941) was for a time the most famous philosopher in the world and one of the few to receive a Nobel Prize for his work. Among Anglophone philosophers, however, he is mostly forgotten, which is a loss, since Bergson was a great philosopher and understanding his ideas would enhance our philosophy with new problems and concepts.

Bergsonism became controversial in the early twentieth century, though from our distance it can be difficult to comprehend the animosity Bergson drew upon himself.[1] His work is elegant and analytical, the writing limpid, precise, unmarred by ideology or polemic, all beside introducing important innovations to classical problems of philosophy. Yet he ignited violent emotion on all sides: from the right and the left, the church and the positivists, materialists and spiritualists. Julian Benda and Jacques Maritain made their reputations with attacks on Bergson. Conservatives welcomed Bergson's vindication of spirit and despised his naturalization of the divine; progressives applauded his idea of technologically mediated social advance while dismissing *élan vital* as mystical drivel.

Ensconced at the Collège de France, Bergson endured the unremitting animosity of Émile Durkheim and the Sorbonne, where Durkheim was preeminent. It did not help that critics of Sorbonne philosophy (Charles Péguy, for instance) pointed to Bergson as an alternative. By 1914, at the outbreak of the First World War, Bergson had antagonized France's entire educational and political establishment, yet by the end of the war, in 1919, the issues that made him controversial were resolved or had collapsed.

His activity during the war as a diplomat, prominent intellectual, and propagandist contributed to coolness from young postwar intellectuals, who "turned against the philosopher of duration and *élan vital*, whom they had admired in their youth," and began to find his thought "bourgeois, romantic, and self-involved."[2] In 1921, Bergson retired from his academic position and in 1927 was awarded the Nobel Prize for Literature. He died in 1941, a Jew in Paris under German occupation.

At the height of his prestige there was respectable attention to Bergson's work among Anglophone philosophers, and William James was an early admirer, though here again interest collapsed after the First War, and it became fashionable positivist signaling to reject Bergson out of hand. Critics with nothing more in common than visceral dislike of Bergson's philosophy competed to reduce his ideas to a mystical farrago.[3] Since then, little has changed.

Living in Time explains, analyzes, defends, and enlarges upon a selection of philosophical arguments in Bergson's work in a way that I hope may attract the interest of Anglophone readers of philosophy. These include his theories of time as duration and panpsychic consciousness, highly original ideas on perception and memory, and his concept of virtual existence.

Chapter 1 is about time, which is the ground motif of Bergson's philosophy. He criticizes theories that "spatialize" time and unfolds an alternative understanding of time as duration. Bergson, Einstein, and their acolytes had an acrimonious dispute about space and time. Closely considered, though, they disagree on little, and Einstein shares Bergson's concern about spatializing time. We'll see Bergson make unexpected use of conclusions about time to refute determinism, a unique argument that does not merit the neglect of philosophers for whom determinism remains a problem. His promise in *Time and Free Will* is to show that on analysis, the objections to freedom lose all their force, and for the same reason. They treat time like space.

The themes of Chapter 2 draw mostly from *Matter and Memory*, where Bergson introduces theories of perception and memory that feature his concept of virtual existence. Perception is virtual action and memory is virtual experience. Virtual existence is the mode of being shared among tendencies, dispositions, generalities, and habits, as well as memories, and the past itself, and is among Bergson's most valuable innovations. Another is his unique theory of memory, which is an alternative to practically everything psychology and philosophy have said on this topic since Aristotle.

Chapter 3 pursues questions from *Creative Evolution*, Bergson's most widely read and controversial book. In his first book, *Time and Free Will*, he argued (against Zeno) that movement does not instantaneously halt at the points of its trajectory. In *Matter and Memory*, movement is defined as an indivisible duration, then *Creative Evolution* says the same thing about organisms. They are not complex mechanisms composed of ultimate elements, no more than movement is put together from geometrical points. Organisms *are* movements, life cycles, temporal entities like a symphony sounding through their material.

Evolution, philosophically considered, includes cosmology, and among theories in the fledgling science, Bergson's ideas are closest to those of Georges Lemaître and a prototype Big Bang theory. This cosmology is finitistic in time and space and does not allow the universe to come into existence instantaneously or *ex nihilo*, emerging instead by evolution in a process with a physical sequence. Discussing time and evolution opens a context for comparing Bergson and Nietzsche, as both were pioneers of evolutionary epistemology. Several themes suggest their comparison, including reversing the Platonic priority of being over becoming, and ideas on the human future. Following a hint from Gilles Deleuze, I'll show how Bergson's idea of time as duration illuminates Nietzsche's enigmatic "eternal return of the same."

Chapter 4 takes up Bergson's theme of open and closed, chiefly in his final book, *The Two Sources of Morality and Religion*, though also drawing on the earlier opuscule *Laughter*. Closed society, with its closed morality and static religion, is dedicated to the preservation of one group among other, excluded groups. Open society is a cosmopolitan society of humanity with an ethos of aspiration. Bergson regards laughter as an instrument of closed society, which it certainly can be, though it would be wrong to think it is no more than that. Nietzsche is again helpful. Bergson sees practically nothing to laughter but an instrument of social exclusion. Listening to the laughter in *Thus Spoke Zarathustra*, we hear something more and different and not easy for Bergson to accommodate or even acknowledge.

Complaints have been raised against interpretations that attribute to Bergson an "ontological" conception of the virtual.[4] Deleuze is the chief offender and then those (like me) who read Bergson with gratitude to Deleuze. I do not heed the call to deontologize Bergson's virtual, and in the Conclusion I summarize the ontology of the virtual that unfolds through the chapters. The reason for retaining an ontological virtual, aside from understanding Bergson, is to accommodate tendencies, capacities, generalities, and habits. None of these are actual, yet all are physically discernable vectors, qualitatively as distinct as their different finalities. They exist, they are effective, but are not actual, nor are they mere logical possibilities. They are virtual tendencies which, like all beings, strive with all their power to exist. This interpretation situates Bergson in a line of thought running from Chrysippus and the Old Stoa to Leibniz.

Bergson is well informed, even accomplished in science, and his philosophy takes science seriously, though he is not an advocate of philosophical naturalism and does not think that philosophy is or should be continuous with the natural sciences.[5] Bergson's philosophy is emphatically not continuous with science. This stand is required by two principles he holds on the relation between science and philosophy. The first enjoins philosophers never to neglect the value of science as a check on speculation. It is science, specifically evolutionary biology, that confirms the utilitarian character of mental functions, which are tuned by natural selection to adaptive action. In a statement that merits the admiration of any philosophical naturalist, Bergson writes, "In the labyrinth of acts, states, and faculties of the mind, the thread which one must never lose is the one furnished by biology" (CM 38). He means evolutionary biology, biology after Darwin. Mental no less than physical powers are evolved adaptations: "the orientation of our consciousness toward action appears to be the fundamental law of our psychical life" (MM 234). By "action" he means useful, adaptive, practical, utilitarian action, action in the service of life. We can rise above such ends, but they are the default setting.

Bergson offers this first principle as a check on the temptation to consider a concept absolutely valid simply because it does useful work in science. Philosophers have a habit of this error and Bergson's second principle warns against it. Practical ways of thought, especially spatial and quantitative thought, introduce an unconscious utilitarian bias into philosophy that creates pseudo-problems. We come to think concepts are more than contrivances advancing our interest, that instead they disclose nature's own order. This is unconscious anthropocentrism and a flattering fallacy. It is the intellectualism, the rationalism, the metaphysical narcissism with which we reify the cognitive preferences of our contingently evolved neurology. The same qualities that make intellect adaptive make this anthropocentric rationalism a mistake in philosophy.

As a prestigious critic of rationalism, Bergson endured denunciation as an irrationalist and antiintellectual, though he refused to take his designated place in the critics' dichotomies. They are for intellect and think he is for intuition; they are for reason and think he is irrational; they urge clarity and think he is mystical. Everything positive and creative in Bergson's thought militates against these dichotomies. He does not want philosophy that is intuitive instead of intellectual. He wants an intellect that is more intuitive and intuition that knows how to think.

1
Taking Time Seriously

The philosophy of time does not have to be a specialist topic suitable only for those with technical training in mathematical physics. Bergson is critical of what these specialists have concluded about time, especially when they say that time is just another dimension of space. One still hears this said, although we'll see that even Einstein, whose authority is usually invoked for the claim, thought this spatialization of time was a mistake.

Bergson's argument is that time is real and really different from space. To say time is real means two things. First, that time is not an abstraction, like a mathematical entity; second, that time is effective, a power of tendency and change. To say something is real is to say it has effects, acting and changing things, and time does that, geology and the evolution of life being the best evidence. If time is real and real means effective, then the past must be real and effective too. Memory is a term for the effectiveness of the past. Memory is not a trace, a record of the past; it is how the past remains effective, that is, real. Rather than pass directly to Bergson's ideas about time, however, I follow the path by which he led his first readers to them. Why did time become a problem for him? The answer begins with a question about the intensity of mental states.

Mental Intensity

Bergson's way to a philosophy of time passes through his analysis of the error he identifies in conceptualizing consciousness in spatial terms. We do that when we regard mental states as composed of elements placed in inner space, where they can be counted, even if only in terms of more or less; for instance, "The pain is more than yesterday," or "The Sun is brighter than the Moon." Statements such as these seem to describe quantitative degrees of sensory intensity. We can only quantify what we can count, however roughly, and we can count only what reduces to a unit and repeats. So, if intensive mental states really have magnitude, there must be a unit of which their differences are compounded.

Herbert Spencer introduced a theory on this in his influential *Principles of Psychology*. Even the most strongly contrasted sensations are said to be aggregates of a single primordial consciousness-element: "Such homogeneous units of feeling may, by integration in diverse ways, give origin to different though relatively simple feelings; by combination of which with one another more complex and unlike feelings may arise."[1] What is the unit? At this dramatic point Spencer's account gets thin. He alludes to nervous shock but says no more about it. The lacuna was overlooked because Spencer spoke for many who wanted a quantitative science of psychology in the day when psychology was still defined as the science of consciousness. Bergson's counterargument is that a homogeneous unit does not exist, nor do quantitative differences of magnitude exist in consciousness.

We use a body to measure a body, as when a ruler is laid on something and used to quantify length. Nothing like that is possible with consciousness, whose moments cannot be juxtaposed like bodies. Something spatially greater than another can contain it, but mental containment does not make sense. Tiny flakes of gold add up to an estimable lump, but how could lots of barely conscious pains add up to migraine, or explain its difference from charley horse? No simple relation exists between the intensity of mental states and a measurable magnitude in their cause, as if light would seem twice as bright with twice the luminous energy. Sensation is not so simple. Anyway, we go by feeling in decisions on sensory quality, not by an intellectual surmise about the cause.

No verifiable connection relates the intensity of mental states to quantifiable neurological parameters, as if a more intense pain activated more T-cells, energized more c-fiber, drew down more phosphorous ions, something like that. The neurological connection, if it exists, is hypothetical and would have to be verified. To test it we would have to correlate neurological parameters with changing mental intensity. How could we determine that doubling some neurological parameter produced a sensation twice as intense? Before researchers could correlate changes in the neurological parameter with more painful pain, they would require a measure of pain magnitude. So, the only way to verify the neurological correlation requires that we already have the result we need to verify. The appropriate conclusion is that this mind–brain correlation, though widely credited, is imaginary and incapable of being scientifically established.

Another example of specious quantification is mental effort. Bergson recounts investigations by William James of paralytics asked to try to move their disabled limbs (TFW 22–24). James observed that while the affected limb did not move, other parts of the body moved a lot. Muscles contracted all over, breathing changed, more sensitive measures would detect additional small movements. James proposed that our consciousness of effort is an awareness of this whole-body mix of direct and associated muscle movements, and Bergson agrees. The magnitude of mental effort, trying harder and harder, is a specious quantitative interpretation of an enlarging series of sympathetic muscular contractions spreading over a flexible expanse of the body's surface, creating constantly renewed sensations of tension, pressure, and fatigue.

Bergson extends the account to affective sensations of pleasure and pain, which have most attracted the quantifiers' attention. He explains a greater pleasure as a pleasure more preferred, where magnitude of preference is magnitude of anticipatory corporeal response to the prospect of enjoyment: more organs, more muscle groups, more glands and secretions, the whole body anticipating the treat. As for pain, it is partly the feeling of bodily damage, though there is more to it. In many animals the reaction to damage is reflexive and without sensation. Drop acid on a microbe and it reacts to preserve itself. The reaction is automatic, mechanical, determined. There is no sensation, no pain, which would be superfluous. The organism has no alternatives, no choice to make, hence no pain.

We do not *have* to have pain for an organism to respond adaptively to damage, so why the sensation at all? Bergson thinks it indicates the evolutionary emergence of choice. What we feel as an intensity of pain is consciousness of involuntary reactions under preparation, providing an opportunity to suppress, select, or modulate them. Feeling the sensation, one is aware of the looming requirement to act. There is an interval during which memory comes to bear and a preferable response can be selected from alternatives remembered or imagined. Here is the humble beginning of the feeling of freedom: "Either sensation has nothing to do, or it is nascent freedom" (TFW 34).

A more intense heat is a different heat, though the feeling of moving one's body near and away from a source suggests a quantitative interpretation. Physics tells us there are more vibrations in a high pitch than a lower one, but we do not hear their quantity, which is abstract information and cannot explain our impression of high and low. What Bergson thinks does account for it are differences of effort in the musculature of the throat and chest. We interpret the intensity of sound by imagining the effort we would have to expend to mimic it. We know from the experience of our own voice that high notes require more energy. When we hear a pitch "rise," we imagine feeling the effort our voice would have to make to imitate the tone.

Terms of intensity can still apply to mental states provided we understand that there are no magnitudes and nothing to quantify: "The intensity of a simple psychic state is pure quality" (TFW 225). When desire grows greater, nothing doubles or triples like voltage in a circuit. A stronger desire is a different desire, a worse pain is a different one. No matter how finely sliced, every conscious moment is qualitatively different, the heterogeneity never finally diminishing into Spencer's hypothetical homogeneous unit. Bergson's term for this definitively temporal quality is "pure heterogeneity" (TFW 104). I will also call it original or primitive heterogeneity. This is not the heterogeneity Spencer thought evolution was advancing toward as a cosmic *telos*. It is the opposite, a heterogeneity at the beginning, an originally given multiplicity of qualitative difference. Original heterogeneity means there is no end to the differences. Divide and distinguish all you will, there is always more and different. Consciousness is an example of this heterogeneity, difference within difference endlessly. Original heterogeneity is also characteristic of time understood with Bergson as duration. Divide any duration and the result is always a different present with a different past.

Consciousness is continuous, not divided into blocks or states. It is language that breaks up consciousness this way. Language can only express thoughts whose parts are as distinct as words, and reasoning with words is like arranging blocks in space. That makes language clumsy with the filigree of feeling the impersonal designations of ordinary usage ("love," "fear") convey. "Love" is one word but the emotion is as different as people are. We use this psychological vocabulary less for information than ritual, confirming assumptions about ourselves and others. The use of common nouns to describe consciousness is required for smooth social life, but philosophically, each moment of consciousness has a singular past, which makes it qualitatively different from every other. To express such differences with language is hopeless and poetry is its art.

Intelligence meticulously distinguishes and separates, decreeing sharp edges, discovering dichotomies, savaging continuity. Such analysis can be useful, in science it is indispensable, but philosophy has misunderstood its utility in a way that has created pseudo-problems, including the problem of determinism. Bergson's promise in *Time and Free Will* is to show that on analysis, the objections to freedom lose all their force. His conclusion is not a proof of free will, something he considers superfluous, as no one would wonder whether their will was free without the bugbear of determinism to trouble them. It is enough to know that putative proofs of determinism are fallacious and all for the same reason. They fail to take time seriously.

Spatial Thought

By regarding consciousness as if it had magnitude, we treat it like a body in space. To quantify, even roughly, is to render countable and to count things is to juxtapose them in space if only imaginatively. Quantity is a spatial concept, promoted by experience with bodies in space, including their movement. We think in terms of number because things move, and they move in space, which is where we count them. We can generate numbers by successive construction: 1 + 1 + . . . will produce any (whole) number. The operation may seem temporal, as it did to Immanuel Kant: "Arithmetic attains its concepts of number by the successive addition of units in time."[2] This is inadequate, however, because in time we perceive only the succession, not the addition, not a succession that culminates in a sum. We have to imagine mentally holding each unit as we add another to it, and that is a spatial operation, an analogy with bodies in space.

Bergson thinks the fundamental intuition of number or quantity is spatial juxtaposition, which expresses space's most spatial quality, the mutual externality of its points. He does not identify number with space (as Bertrand Russell fallaciously assumed).[3] Instead, he observes that a condition on quantification is for elements to be denumerable, which presupposes spatial qualities of distinctiveness, separability, and discontinuity, even if it does not require that the elements be laid out in space. Spatial points cannot blur into each other or interpenetrate; every point excludes every other, consequently every line, every surface, every volume, every body in space, is external to every other. There is no continuity of spatial bodies, only juxtaposition. That no two bodies occupy the same space has been attributed to a so-called principle of impenetrability. One body cannot penetrate another; it can displace it, divide it, or shatter itself on it, but it cannot interpenetrate and cohabit one space.

Spinoza and Leibniz thought impenetrability was a metaphysical insight into the essence of body, though even if it were, we should be able to imagine multiple bodies in the same place, as we imagine other physical impossibilities, like a frictionless surface, a laminar flow, or a spherical star. That does not work with impenetrability. Imagine two bodies exactly the same size and shape, together in one place, each having exactly the same coordinate relations to everything around them. Why speak of two? Could one be red and the other blue, one electrically positive, the other negative? No, we cannot think this multiplicity.[4] Rather than a metaphysical power of bodies, impenetrability is an implication of number's spatial logic. You cannot have two bodies in one space because *one* is what we count in *one place*. We have two of anything only in two places.

When we think of mental states as intensive magnitudes, we think of them quantitatively and that means spatially, treating consciousness as if it were a space in which particles (successive mental states) circulate. Bergson uses the technical word *endosmosis* to describe this psychological tendency (TFW 109). Endosmosis is a term for the passage of a chemical across a membrane from a region of lower to higher concentration. What happens to space is like that. It is drawn inside consciousness to reappear as an inner space of particulate ideas or impressions. The use of language entrenches spatialization by suggesting unities corresponding to words, ignoring unnamed differences, and assimilating disparate feelings under the same word. I'm angry and so are you. We use the same word but can't mean the same feeling, which would be impossible given our

different histories. Every moment of sensation is qualitatively different, which we do not notice when the differences are irrelevant to the business at hand. We substitute the word for the thing and reduce experience to cliches. In his philosophy of art (in *Laughter*) Bergson argues that the value of art is its capacity to penetrate the veil of cliche and apprehend the individuality of things (Chapter 4).

The cost associated with this social adaptation is not merely to be misled about consciousness, our own and others'. It promotes the decay of freedom. Human evolution endows us with the requirement of social life and with social instincts that smooth the way. One of these is to habituate to a social self enacting ritualized behavior and cliche responses, a self captured by conformity and adapted to social life. Freud called this *das Ich*, Ego. On Bergson's account, it arises when a "profound self," profoundly individuated (and without Freudian analogue), becomes overlain by cliches, submersed in common sense, and habituated to a regimen others find reassuring, banishing remnant individuality to dreams. Spatialized consciousness is practically homogeneous, described and enacted as homogeneous, which tends to make *us* homogeneous. It makes our minds more alike than they might be, expressing what Nietzsche called our herd instinct. As a result, less and less of what we choose is truly free, not because of mechanical determinism, but from regimentation and conformity. The threat to freedom lies here and not in metaphysics.

It is not an accident that we favor the spatial mode of thought, as we may suppose that such thinking was adaptive for evolutionary ancestors. Concepts of space and number are tools for coping with change. We attend to the immobile, static, and changeless because it is at such points that we can act on matter. If you want to act on water you have to contain it, give it shape, make it somewhat solid. As long as it flows, we cannot act on it or even calculate it, given the chaotic tendency to turbulence.

We plan and act from point to point, following a line of means to ends. The habit of point-to-point thinking encourages the idea of any movement as passing from one state to another—[state$_1$] *click* [state$_2$] *click*. . . . That happens in computers, though before computers Bergson saw it in cinema. He says he worked out his ideas on cinematography in 1902–03, which is well before narrative cinema (CE 272). He was chiefly aware of the use of cinema for the analysis of motion in the work of Étienne-Jules Marey and Eadweard Muybridge. A series of instantaneous snapshots generates the illusion of movement. There is no movement in the images, each being a changeless synchronic state. The only movement is in the apparatus, where a motor conveys a series of snapshots past a projector with insensible speed.[5]

In a 1914 discussion of cinema, Bergson says, "When I first saw the cinematograph I realized it could offer something new to philosophy. Indeed, we could almost say that cinema is a model of consciousness itself. Going to the cinema turns out to be a philosophical experience."[6] Bertrand Russell says he made his first visit to a cinema to verify Bergson's statement, which he found to be "completely true": "The cinema is a better metaphysician than common sense, physics, or philosophy."[7] However, it was not without irony that Bergson recommends cinema as a model of consciousness, for it is a model of misperception and the tendency of consciousness to objectify and externalize itself. The cinematographic analogy that works for machines and planetary systems is wrongly applied to organisms simply because nothing can *live* cinematographically. We cannot pass in and out of existence so rapidly that no one notices, ourselves least of all, as room-lighting insensibly flickers at 60Hz. Life is real continuity, which implies temporal interpenetration and succession without separation. Cinematography offers real separation and succession without interpenetration; next does not grow from former but is merely juxtaposed, external, like points in space.

Russell is under the influence of the unconscious utilitarianism I mentioned in the Introduction, equating the convenience of calculation with a principle of reality. If you want to control moving bodies, think like Russell and consider them cinematographically. The cinematographic tendency of thought is the tendency to conceive of change as a series of potential halts where action might intervene, and that is how we usually perceive our environment; we see not "things" but rather what psychologists call affordances, meaning stabilities suitable for interaction.[8] Cinematographic thought, which analyzes processes in terms of potential halts, is good for the adaptive challenges an animal like us faced half a million years ago. It is no mistake to use it; a tool may be inefficient but not wrong. A mistake arises only when we think that our tool is so useful it must express the truth of nature.

The slide into cinematographic thinking is perhaps the gravest error philosophy has suffered from unconscious pragmatism. We can act only on discontinuous bodies, and it is such action that intelligence and concepts aim to enhance, which makes movement's cinematographic representation appealing. That is how we like to think of movement in pursuit of mastery over it, and that is how we *will* think of movement unless prodded from unconscious bias. The cinematographic tendency of perception and thought is a biased interpretation of practices by which people have lived from before the first stone tool. Bergson calls it "the natural metaphysic of the human intellect" (CE 326). The Greeks did not need our experience of cinema to think cinematographically about nature, as Zeno demonstrates with his famous paradoxes of motion.

Zeno of Elea was a fifth-century BCE follower of Parmenides who made a famous defense of the master's monism. Parmenides had argued that Being is. Only Being is, nonbeing is not. Among the wonderful consequences of these seeming platitudes is the impossibility of movement, which requires void, for nothing can move to a place that is full. But since nonbeing cannot be, every place *is* full; so there is no void and no motion. The logic is impeccable and still people laugh. Zeno thought he might enhance the teaching by exposing contradictions in the popular idea of motion. Apparently, he developed many arguments, though accounts of only a few survive. One is called the Arrow.[9]

An archer lets an arrow fly. Many in Zeno's audience would have muscle memory of performing this very action, though now Zeno tells them they were dreaming, their arrows did not move, they didn't even draw their bow. An arrow cannot move in the place where it is not—if it is not there, it assuredly is not in motion there. Neither can it move in the place where it is; for this place is precisely equal to the arrow's dimensions, and a thing at a place equal to its dimensions is at rest there. The arrow is always at the place where it is, and cannot move where it is not, so it is always at rest. The argument may have been more dizzying to an ancient audience because we think of velocity as a conserved quantity, the principle of inertia. If something is moving, it might move to a place where it currently is not. The ancient philosophers did not have this principle or its intuitions, which must enhance the specious rationality of Zeno's argument. How could the arrow be where it is not? How could it *get* there from where it is? Surely it never leaves where it is!

The argument exposes the difficulty of conceptualizing continuity. The discrete and discontinuous are appealing to practical reason, which pursues distinctions and discovers dichotomies, transforming the continuous into analytical discontinuity and pronouncing it clear and distinct. When we treat movement that way, however, we lose it. Zeno's argument makes the same mistake by conflating a movement, which is a phenomenon of duration, with a geometrical line, a spatial concept. The geometrical properties of a line are not properties of the movement, which is a temporal, not spatial entity. The *trajectory* that a movement, now finished, passed through is an infinitely divisible line, but that does not mean *the movement* was divisible or had parts. A line can be divided and put together any way we like, but not a movement: "Though we can divide at will the trajectory once created, we cannot divide its creation, which is an act in progress and not a thing" (CE 336).

Zeno assumes that the arrow coincides with the instantaneous positions of its trajectory, even though it never *is* at any of those points. The most we can say is that it could be stopped there, which is a statement about us and how we might act on the arrow. Zeno's mistake is everybody's mistake and it is not entirely a mistake. We think of motion geometrically because doing so enhances action. We analyze movement in terms of potential interaction, attending to where it can be halted, prolonged, or redirected. Geometry makes such thinking efficient: "Homogeneous space concerns our action and only our action, being like an infinitely fine network which we stretch beneath material continuity in order to render ourselves masters of it, to decompose it according to the plan of our activities and our needs" (MM 308). That is a useful result, but to impute the conventions of a convenient calculus to the movement it describes makes a fetish of our symbolism, as if its utility could only be explained by adequacy to the inner nature of bodies.

Why is thought so tenaciously spatial? Bergson's explanation is evolutionary: "Our tendency to form a clear picture of this extensity of things and the homogeneity of their medium is the same as the impulse which leads us to live in common and to speak" (TFW 138). Spatialization may appear to be something we learn, but Bergson thinks "it is native to the human mind; we practice it instinctively. Its recipe is deposited in language" (DS 54). He is not the only one to notice the relation between language (hence sociality) and spatialization, though he may have been the first. German linguist Walter Porzig observes that "language translates all nonvisual relationships into spatial relationships. All languages do this without exception, not just one or a group. This is one of the invariable characteristics of human language."[10]

French philosopher of science Émile Meyerson, a young contemporary of Bergson, thought that spatialization expresses an "eternal and immutable tendency of the human mind," namely, to shun novelty and crave identity and repetition.[11] He thinks the prestige of rational explanation in European philosophy arises from reason's power to eliminate diversity by discovering identity everywhere. This animus against difference is not empiricism or pragmatism, which on the contrary favor discrimination and foresight. It is irrelevant to practice to be told that fundamentally nothing changes, but rationalists find it sublime.[12]

Duration

Worse than spatializing consciousness is spatializing time. We do that when we assume that like space, time is a continuous series of mutually external points. This is a mistake because it eliminates the interpenetration and temporal anisotropy that are characteristic of time and its difference from space.

I should ensure that we understand Bergson's term *duration* (*durée*). This is the time of consciousness, the time of experience, the time of waiting, expecting, and delay. It is the time that prevents everything from happening all at once, the time that makes nature processual and the cosmos evolutionary. Bergson's idea is that time has no other concrete, primary reality than duration, which is time's mode of being, whether in consciousness or in the cosmos: "*Real duration* is what we have always called *time*, but time perceived as indivisible" (CM 124); "the more or less lengthy changes we witness within us and in the external world take place in a single identical time" (CM 125). The facile distinction between subjective psychological time and objective scientific time exasperated Bergson. He encountered it in Einstein's testy reply at their Paris meeting. "The time of the philosopher," Einstein said, "is both physical and psychological at once, [and assumes that] physical time can be derived from the time of consciousness. . . . [But] the philosopher's time does not exist; there is only a psychological time, different from the time of the physicist."[13]

In *Duration and Simultaneity*, from later that year, Bergson argues that psychological and physical time intertwine no matter how methodologists strain to segregate them. A later philosopher of time (and no Bergsonian) confirms Bergson's point: "If what we mean by 'time' when we talk of the time order of events in the physical world has nothing to do with the meaning of 'time' as meant when we talk about the order of time in our experiences, then why call it time at all?" Why indeed, especially since, "if the 'time' of physics is not real, perceived time, then the 'causation' of physics is not real causality."[14]

Another unhelpful idea to set aside is the distinction between so-called A-series and B-series time. In *The Nature of Existence*, British philosopher J. M. E. McTaggart introduced these two temporal series, two formally different orders of events.[15] The A-series is a tensed order of past and future with an ever-new *now*. Since the past is always growing, relations among events in the A-series are always changing, with yesterday's tomorrow becoming tomorrow's yesterday. To McTaggart that was a problem, as one event cannot be both tomorrow and yesterday. He decided that A-series time is inconsistent and unreal. The B-series is time for classical physics: a linear order represented by a line on which each point is an instant and an event. No *now*-moment hovers over the series, and any event that occurs before another always does so by an unchanging interval.

Replies have been made on behalf of A-series time, but even if some A-series theory were made consistent, it is not a good theory of time and for a simple reason. A-series time does not express or model temporal passage. McTaggart's idea is that time, all time, can be conceptualized in his two ways. All the events of time are already given in their order of succession and the question is how best to describe their series, whether in tensed or tenseless terms. However, to assume that all the events of time are given assumes that future events are already on the line and waiting for us to reach them. B-series time makes the same assumption, namely, that events take position in time independently of their having occurred. This is fallacious because future and past events do not exist in the present. The existence of events is their existence at the time of their occurrence.[16]

Without passage, time may as well not exist. How do events occur if they never succeed each other? To say that passage is mere appearance is no avail since, as Hermann Lotze observed, "We must either admit becoming or else explain the becoming of an appearance of becoming."[17] Arthur Eddington thought it was "absurd to pretend that we have no justifiable conception of 'becoming' in the external world." With consciousness, he says, "We have a direct insight into 'becoming' that sweeps aside all symbolic knowledge as on an inferior plane."[18] I agree with the philosopher who writes that "a century spent evaluating the relative merits of the A-series and the B-series has, in my view, yielded meager understanding of time, at least in part because it has not been widely enough recognized that passage does not fall with the narrow A-theory."[19] In other words, taking passage seriously does not incur commitment to an A-series theory. Passage is characteristic of time and no spatial analogue exists.

Bergson apparently never commented on McTaggart's idea, though he could hardly avoid disapproving. Both series assume what for Bergson is insupportable, namely, that time is timelessly given. Duration is unrecognizable in the A-series, whose changing *now* moments are external, juxtaposed, without temporal interpenetration. In either series, events are ordered sets of mutually external elements, sets that are closed, which makes them unsuitable to describe duration's open wholeness. Instead, as Deleuze explains, time "is that which prevents each set, however big it is, from closing in on itself, that which forces it to extend itself into a larger set. The whole is therefore like thread which traverses sets and gives each one the possibility, which is necessarily realized, of communicating with another, to infinity. Thus, the whole is the Open." Continuing, he observes that the nature of this whole (time) "is to change constantly, or to give rise to something new, in short, to endure (*durer*).... Each time we find ourselves confronted with a duration, or in a duration, we may conclude that there exists somewhere a whole which is changing, and which is open somewhere."[20]

To endure therefore does not mean to remain changeless. Duration does not merely tolerate change, it requires it; duration is a way of changing, namely, continuously. Every moment of duration is transitional, a phase in a process, the passage to a new condition. Duration is therefore dense, a line, a plane, never a point. No matter how finely cut, duration is thickened by the past and its difference from the present. This is the primitive heterogeneity we noticed earlier. Every present has lodged within it the ever-changing multiplicity and difference of the past.

The best analogy for thinking about duration is music. Melody is a familiar and convincing example of a temporal entity that exists only in duration. A melody has no being at an instant; at any instant there is only silence. The very sounding of a melody is intrinsically a duration, with duration's quality of interpenetrating succession without separation. A melody is not generated from tones one by one. It pulses through them, like a moving body pulses through points of a trajectory. Each tone retains individuality while melding with others before and after. A tone followed by silence has a different quality from the same tone in a succession. The first three notes of "Three Blind Mice" are the same as the second, third, and fourth notes of the slow movement of J. S. Bach's Double Violin Concerto.[21] They do not sound the same when surrounded by their respective melodies.

Another melodic quality of duration is primitive passage, that is, passage without self-identical beings undergoing it. Music flows more radically than a river, with no floating bodies like molecules in a stream. Duration is original and self-sufficient; its flow requires nothing but itself. Solely this mode of time is justly described as *given*. What we call "thing" or "state" are sampled invariants selected by perception from an original continuity and answering to perspective and interest. A thing or a body is a synchronization, the temporary stability of resonant energies; not a changeless substance but many interpenetrating events changing together, orchestrated like a symphony.

No music resounds in the lifeless inane. Only consciousness can hold past and present together in the tense contraction music requires. That is why time (as duration) is another name for consciousness: "We cannot speak of a reality that endures without inserting consciousness into it" (DS 207). Time and consciousness are the same because any passage, any before and after, requires a bridge, a hyphen, a stitch, a contract, or contraction. That is the simplest function of memory, an impersonal memory that belongs to time itself, inducing passage: "It is impossible to imagine or conceive a connecting link between the before and after without an element of memory and, consequently, of consciousness" (DS 207). Impossible, because "it is impossible to distinguish between the duration, however short it may be, that separates two instants and a memory that connects them." Duration is this connective continuity and is another name for consciousness: "Duration therefore implies consciousness; and we place consciousness at the heart of things for the very reason that we credit them with a time that endures" (DS 48–49).

Interpenetrating continuity defeats quantification, yet any duration has a manyness, a qualitative multiplicity, despite being uncountable. It is meet that multiplicity is many, with more ways than one to be multiple. Numerical multiplicity is the manyness we count in bodies spatially juxtaposed. Qualitative multiplicity is the uncountable many- or fewness of a continuous process or an enduring event, for example embryonic ontogenesis. Animal development from zygote to maturity is a complicated process and has a kind of manyness (many phases, many parameters), yet the phases enfold each other in a melodious movement that resists the state-by-state juxtaposition thoroughgoing quantification presupposes. Melody is another example of qualitative multiplicity. There is a manyness to melody without anything to count. Counting notes won't do, because the beginning interpenetrates all that follows, which is the unfolding development of a quality and not a series of discrete occasions. Consciousness too is an example of qualitative, uncountable multiplicity, each moment interpenetrating every other and none discontinuously excluding others despite being flush with difference.

Difference is indelible from duration, there is no end to it; no matter how finely divided we never reach a homogeneous phase. This is the heterogeneity we have noticed, an original or as Bergson says pure (i.e., unconditioned) heterogeneity: "Duration might well be nothing but a succession of qualitative changes, which melt into and permeate one another, without precise outlines, without any tendency to externalize themselves in relation to one another, without any affiliation with number . . . pure heterogeneity" (TFW 104). That means differences *ab initio*, original difference and multiplicity. Plato began the argument that difference is secondary, depending on the primitive self-identity of an original being. The primitive heterogeneity of duration overturns the ancient ontology. Differences of duration are an original, auto-differentiating manyness, ontologically prior to beings and identity.

Duration eludes measurement because we cannot stipulate a unit or locate a point where changes stop: "As soon as we try to measure it we unwittingly replace it by space" (TFW 106). One might think clocks measure time, though it is a mistake and for an interesting reason. Any measurement involves a presupposition that looks innocent. To measure a given property the standard must itself exemplify that property. Only a volume can measure volume, only a length a length, and so on. So, a clock measures duration only if it is an enduring temporal entity, which it is not. Any machine-state of the clock is as external to every other as points on a line—state @ t_1, state @ t_2, and so on. These states are juxtaposed positions in space, each external to the other, with no continuity or interpenetration. Every machine-state is new, as if the past did not exist. A clock is no more an enduring entity than is a cloud, and if care were removed, the clock's deterioration would resemble the slow-motion dissipation of a cloud. So a clock is not an enduring entity and does not measure duration.

Time measurement is a comparison of two clocks, as a philosopher of chronology writes: "No time reckoner can in itself reckon time; one needs at least two of them."[22] This is not a mere inconvenience; it means in effect that *consciousness* measures time, clocks do not. A clock displaying 9:00 and then 9:01 is not measuring time. *Looking* at the clock showing 9:00 and *noticing* the change to 9:01 might be a measurement, but then it is consciousness that measures, correlating a felt, conscious change with the change of the clock and counting on memory. We have to measure time by time and that is impossible without memory, which is therefore a condition on consciousness, duration, and the very being of time.

Any present moment is alive, an egg, a densely heterogeneous multiplicity of developments. The presence of a present is relative to form and scale of life. What we feel as "the present" is an attitude to the immediate future, a memory of the immediate past, a preparation for interaction, and the kinesthetic feeling of muscular and metabolic adjustments coordinated with perception. In other words, *now* is not a structural component of time; it is an expression of animal duration, or what Bergson calls attention to life: "The distinction we make between our present and past is, therefore, if not arbitrary, at least relative to the extent of the field which our attention to life can embrace" (CM 152). There is no such thing as *the* present; one can only ask, Whose present? The presence of a present depends on the quality of attention, the tension or dilation of temporal contraction, which is relative to a metabolic scale of life.

Consciousness is always consciousness of the present, but this present has no reality apart from its remembered past. "However you try, you cannot draw a line between the past and the present, nor consequently between memory and consciousness.... There is no exact moment when the present becomes the past, nor consequently when perception becomes recollection" (ME 69). This interval, which varies with form and scale of life, defines the duration of the present. The present does not disappear into the past, it emerges from it, as a former present becomes past. The presence of the present is the passing of a former present and cannot be perceived until it passes into the past. The *perceived* present is an immediate past: "We never perceive anything but our own immediate past" (MM 195).

Bergson characterizes this retention of the past in the present as *contraction*. This is a properly temporal version of what Stoics spatialized as *tonos* or (pneumatic) tension. A portion of the past contracts with a present, becoming one duration with it, a continuous interpenetration. Duration contracts any portion with any intensity and each present contracts the entire past. Past existence is virtual existence, an idea I take up in the next chapter. Cognition is greatly enhanced by the timely recollection of an intelligently selected portion of the past, though in dreams we are less selective. Personal character condenses all this past and each moment modifies the entire personality. "For conscious beings, to exist is to change, to change is to mature, to mature is to go on creating oneself endlessly" (CE 7).

Movement is the content of duration, with modes of movement defining different phenomena of duration, such as passage, development, and evolution. Common sense locates movement in space: you walk, run, or raise your hand. We say these are movements *in space*, though Bergson might express the point differently. The successive positions through which a movement passes are in space, being points of space, but the moving, the passage, does not exist in, or occur in, or occupy any space at all. Movement, like all phenomena of duration, is a temporal being, more like music than like an accident of a substance.

A prominent opponent of Bergson's philosophy of time is Gaston Bachelard, who in *The Dialectic of Duration* writes disarmingly that "of Bergsonism we accept everything but continuity."[23] But without continuity nothing remains of Bergsonism. "The nearer we draw to the ultimate elements of matter," Bergson said, "the better we note the vanishing of that discontinuity which our senses perceived on the surface" (MM 266). Discontinuity is an analytical abstraction applied to what is intrinsically continuous. "Pure time has no separate or distinct moments, none of its parts begins or ends properly speaking, but each of them prolongs and continues in all the others, like the successive shades of the solar spectrum."[24] Against this continuity, Bachelard advances a dialectical conception of duration, comprising moments of action and moments of repose, which fracture duration and introduce voids. Time is not continuous duration but rhythm, dialectical alteration, pulses of action, and repose, which Bachelard glosses in terms of being and nothingness.

Why is Bachelard's ontologically punctuated rhythm superior to Bergson's continuity? I find four arguments.

(1) We never experience unbroken continuity. Consciousness has gaps, duration as experienced is fragmentary. Bachelard rejects Bergson's "metaphysical extrapolation" of a continuous in itself, "when we at all times face the discontinuity of our experience."[25] An example he develops is the attitude of pretense (pretending to be a licensed physician, say). Such pretense can be lived only as detached from the continuity of life, a temporal superimposition riddled by voids. Successful pretense requires making what is really discontinuous (physician) appear continuous, which is done by making what is really continuous (you) discontinuous, punctuated by voids when the continuity shifts back to pretense.

As this argument shows, Bachelard thinks that continuity means sameness, while for Bergson it means interpenetration and memory. Even when living the pretense, one *remembers* who one is, as when the mask is off one remembers the role and when to recommence. I have the impression that Bachelard does not want to acknowledge interpenetration, which cannot be reconciled with geometry. What he calls temporal lacunae are not intrusions of nonbeing or dialectical negation and can be redescribed in terms of gap-free interpenetration and ever-shifting attention to life.

For Bergson, duration is primitive and given; for Bachelard it derives from rhythm, which is dialectical, entailing instants and void: "To have duration we must entrust ourselves to rhythms—that is to say, to systems of instants."[26] He says that "in order to think, to feel, to live, we must bring order into our actions by holding instants together through the reliability of rhythm."[27] He evidently thinks that rhythm presupposes instantaneity, that rhythm is a system of instants. Why do rhythmic changes have to be instantaneous? Why can rhythm not be interpenetrating? When we hear it, rhythm *sounds* more like interpenetration than a system of instants, which is how sound sounds to a computer.

As if foreseeing Bachelard's argument, Bergson refers to philosophers "antagonistic to the idea of duration," who "are drawn to the point of view of the multiple," that is, the discontinuous, and "set up as concrete reality the distinct moments of a time which they have, so to speak, pulverized" (CM 157). This foresees Bachelard's analysis of rhythm as a system of instants. Interruption and fragmentation are facts, but their occurrence does not pivot on instantaneous change. Bergson identifies two sources of fragmented duration, both more apparent than true challenges to continuity. One is the constantly shifting quality of attention. "Attention places clean-cut states side by side, where actually there is a continuity which unfolds" (CE 4). Another force of fragmentation is multiplicity and difference. There are as many durations as there are forms of life, or forms at all, that is, enduring forms, and if our duration is interrupted, it is by *their* duration soliciting interpenetration, and not an implosion of abyssal nonbeing in dialectical sublation.

(2) Bachelard criticizes the imagery of music, "a metaphor which is often misleading for a metaphysical study of duration."[28] He explains that melody has duration only when sound is experienced as recommencing. When for the first time we hear what we later appreciate is a melody, we did not expect it and only retrospectively recognize that we ought to have expected it. What gives melody its

seeming continuity is a "wholly virtual expectation which is real only in retrospect"; hence, melody "gives us not really duration but the illusion of duration."[29] To virtual expectation he adds an emotional response, which makes a sequence of instants surrounded by void feel continuous. He claims there is no continuity in the melodic line itself, but only imagined in our emotional response to the tones: "Music's action is discontinuous; it is our emotional resonance that gives it continuity."[30]

The analysis seems tone deaf. Melody does not owe its seeming duration to repetition. The quality that makes music an image of duration is interpenetration, moment by moment, phase by phase of the playing, whether we listen for the first or fiftieth time. Bergson speaks of the "indivisible and indestructible continuity of a melody where the past enters into the present and forms with it an undivided whole which remains undivided and even indivisible in spite of what is added at every instant, or rather, thanks to what is added" (CM 53). It is this interpenetration, the accumulating memories of a passing past, that make music an image of duration.

(3) Bachelard assigns priority to the instant, which he thinks is necessary to account for revolutionary commencements. The advance of science is not assured by any positive quality, no perfection of method or experimental rigor. Science does not change until someone says *No*. Not until then do new possibilities appear. That's dialectics. Bergson's philosophy is delinquent in dialectics, dismissing the dialectical power of the negative: "No idea will come forth from negation" (CE 290); "it is absurd to attribute to negation the power of creating ideas" (CE 297). Max Horkheimer also criticized Bergson's dialectical deficiency, saying that he refuses to "let the negative act."[31] These arguments equate negation, saying no, with some contribution of nullity or nonbeing to a creative outcome. Later, we'll see that "nothing" is always *something*, just not something relevant or expected. As for the history of science, isn't the effectiveness of saying *no* the product of a lot of saying *yes*? The

creative effect of that *no* is not independent of the experience that stands behind it, evincing not a power of dialectic but of the will, which is positive and wills only life.

(4) "The thread of time has knots all along it," and "the easy continuity of trajectories has been totally ruined by microphysics."[32] It would be wrong to suggest that Bergson is stuck in Newton's physics and comes to wreck with quantum theory. Bergson followed the new physics and at least one prominent contributor was convinced that quantum physics offers a veritable lesson in Bergson's philosophy. Louis de Broglie was impressed by "the analogy between certain new conceptions of contemporary physics and some of the astounding intuitions of the philosopher of duration," referring specifically to quantum indeterminacy.[33] Bachelard thinks indeterminacy proves ultimate discontinuity, while de Broglie thinks it confirms Bergson's idea that physical entities are ceaselessly in progress: "If Bergson could have studied the quantum theories in detail, he would have noted certainly with joy that, in the images that they offer us of the evolution of the physical world, they show us nature in all its occasions hesitating between several possibilities, and he would have undoubtedly repeated, as in *La pensée et le mouvant* that 'time is that very hesitation or it is nothing at all' " (CM 75).[34]

In sum, Bachelard does not so much criticize Bergson's conception of duration as elaborately contradict and refuse it. He wants instants, temporal voids, and the dialectical power of negation, and makes a show of refuting Bergson with arguments that presuppose everything they are supposed to justify.

Since I have made temporal heterogeneity prominent in the idea of duration I attribute to Bergson, I should take account of an argument that this interpretation harbors a mistake:

> Duration is not quite the "pure heterogeneity" that Bergson posits hypothetically, for *as he will write* in an 1891 review of Jean-Marie Guyau's posthumous 1890 *La genèse de l'idée de temps*

(*The Genesis of the Idea of Time*), although "duration begins only with a certain variety of effects," "absolute heterogeneity, if it was possible, would exclude time, whose principal character is continuity."[35]

The first thing to say about this argument is that the words of the quotation attributed to Bergson are not his but rather those of Guyau, whose book Bergson is reviewing. It is Guyau who writes, "a complete and absolute (*trop absolue*) heterogeneity, if it was possible, would also exclude the idea of time, which includes continuity among its principle characteristics, that is, unity within variety."[36] The words misattributed to Bergson were the opening lines of the review and not placed within quotation marks, although after the next sentence there is a parenthetical reference to the range of Guyau's pages that Bergson has been quoting-paraphrasing to begin his review, including the words misattributed to him.

Bergson's own words in the rest of the review make it clear that he does not agree with Guyau on all points, including the one in contention, namely, whether duration is heterogeneity *trop absolue*. Guyau denies it, with the argument that bottomless heterogeneity would eliminate continuity. In other words, he thinks temporal continuity presupposes ultimate homogeneity, which is not an argument Bergson can approve. His review is generous with praise but ends by observing that Guyau treats time too much like space, against which Bergson affirms the necessity always

> to dissociate pure succession, the immediate intuition of time, from the forms in which we envelop it for the greater convenience of discursive thought and language. From this point of view, we would find that pure time has no separate or distinct moments, that none of its parts begins or ends properly speaking, but that each of them prolongs and continues in all the others, like the successive shades of the solar spectrum.[37]

In other words, duration is pure, that is, unconditioned and original heterogeneity, combined, as always, with continuous interpenetration.

Endless heterogeneity is no obstacle to continuity because the continuity that matters to time is the qualitative continuity of interpenetration. Pure or original heterogeneity is a qualitative multiplicity, and its differences are endless. Any portion, any sample, is an interval and differentiated by its past. The samples never lose their multiplicity and never stop presenting different differences, never terminating in a unit that simply repeats. Continuity is not the most important quality of duration or consciousness. A line is mathematically continuous without being interpenetrating; every point of its extension being external to every other. The heterogeneity of duration poses no threat to temporal continuity because the continuity of time, process, and consciousness is interpenetration, not ultimate homogeneity. Deleuze was right. Duration is original difference, pure heterogeneity.[38] This is time's positive, nondialectical productiveness, ceaselessly producing differences.

An Effective Past

In this part of the chapter, I discuss Bergson's ideas about the existence of time. To forestall misunderstanding I should explain that Bergson's thinking underwent a decisive change on this point, so that certain arguments which he once advanced are withdrawn in favor of new ones. It must be borne in mind that *Time and Free Will*, despite its evocative title, is *not* the proof text for Bergson's philosophy of time.

The argument of that work is expressly dualistic, a dualism not of substances but of space and time. Space is in no way time-like nor time like space: "Within our ego, there is succession without mutual externality; outside the ego, in pure space, mutual externality without succession" (TFW 108). That is not to say physical nature is timeless, but rather that time in nature is a present without a past, a present that is always starting over. Time does not bite into things: "Of the simultaneities which have proceeded them nothing remains" (TFW 227). Imagine watching an oscillating pendulum. Bergson says that if we withdraw the ego that thinks successive movements, then "there will never be more than a single oscillation, and indeed only a single position, of the pendulum, and hence no duration" (TFW 108). While "the successive positions of the moving body really do occupy space," the *passage* from one position to another "has no reality except for a conscious spectator." Temporal passage is "a mental synthesis, a psychic and therefore unextended process" (TFW 110–11): "Succession exists solely for a conscious spectator who keeps the past in mind" (TFW 108–09), and "the interval of duration exists only for us and on account of the interpenetration of our conscious states" (TFW 116).

This is the argument that Bergson drops, and the passages I have quoted, quotable as they are, cannot stand as epitomes of Bergson's philosophy of time.

What matter lacks is not time per se; it lacks an effective past and any form of memory. Without memory, the past is virtual only, without actual effect. A body in space *tends* to develop an individuated past and *tends* to an individuating future, but the tendencies are swamped by countervailing tendencies everywhere, so all that actually happens is the present starting over again. In space, the only time is *now*, the past is the same as the present, and the future the same as the past. Matter in space "unfolds a series of moments of which each is the equivalent of the preceding moment and may be deduced from it: thus, its past is truly given in its present" (MM 297). Rather than no duration, we have the immanent limit of duration, a virtual duration that never breaks into actuality, stymied before it can evolve, and thus only ever restarting, as if the past made no difference, which it does not although it tends to. This tendency, the virtual past, becomes active and effective with the emergence of life and memory. The past exists virtually in a world without life, but it is with life that the past breaks into act and becomes effective, the terrestrial evolution of species being the effect. I revisit this argument in Chapter 3. The point is that the phenomena of duration are phenomena of memory, which is the effectiveness of the past.

Let me return to the change I mentioned in Bergson's thinking about time. Beginning with his second book (*Matter and Memory*) and continuing through the later work, he eliminates the dichotomy of space and time and introduces duration into extensity, which makes consciousness and matter continuous, eliminating the mind-body problem with a new panpsychism, as I discuss in Chapter 2. The universe endures, though solely on the scale of the whole, the "duration immanent to the whole of the universe," bearing in mind Deleuze's point that wholeness does not entail closure. Systems marked off by science as relatively isolated can be said to *endure* "only because they are bound up inseparably with the rest of the universe." In other words, their timelessness is an artifact of stipulation, not insight into physical temporality. A duration can be "attributed to the systems that science isolates, provided such systems are reintegrated into the Whole" (CE 11). Never again will Bergson write such words as "succession exists solely for a conscious spectator" or "duration exists only for us."

In place of the earlier distinction between space (external) and time (internal), he develops a distinction between concrete and abstract time. Time as represented by the variable t in mechanical calculations applies only to abstractly or artificially isolated systems, which stipulate a discontinuity that cannot be concretely realized. Concrete time is the duration of the whole, the evolution of the universe. Time in isolated systems is abstract; any state of a system that is *entirely* a function of its immediate past is *ipso facto* isolated and artificial: "Science can work only on what is supposed to repeat itself—that is to say, on what is withdrawn, by hypothesis, from the action of real time" (CE 29). That entails abstraction from the concrete time of the whole, for which, as an evolution, time is *never* an independent variable: "The systems science works with are, in fact, an instantaneous present that is always being renewed; such systems are never in the real, concrete duration in which the past remains bound up with the present" (CE 22).

Bergson proposes a distinction between our own duration (*notre propre durée*) and what he calls "time in general" (*temps en général*; MM 273). Time in general is duration, but a duration out of all proportion to our existence, a duration that "goes beyond all our imagination" (MM 274). This is not a universal duration, flowing equitably, external to all that endures, which Bergson dismisses as "an idol of language." What he calls "time in general" is not time universalized but rather endlessly differentiated and multiplied: "There is no one rhythm of duration"; many durations exist, faster, slower, tenser, more relaxed, each correlated with "different kinds of consciousness" and occupying "their respective places in the scale of being" (MM 275). Inorganic matter enjoys the least tense duration, yet duration percolates down to atoms if the scale is cosmological. Matter resolves "into elementary vibrations, the shortest of which are of very slight duration, almost vanishing, but not nothing" (CE 201).

The quality of effective duration rises with forms of life, microbial, vegetable, animal. Forms of life rise in the scale of individuality and freedom by growing "the distance between the rhythm of their duration and that of the flow of things" (MM 331). Brownian motion is nothing to us but to bacteria it's a perfect storm. The time of life beats to the rhythm of an organism's potential for action, and with memory it discerns those invariances or synchronies that afford an adaptive response, becoming the first of many discontinuities introduced by perception for the sake of vital action.

Ultimately there is no difference between duration and temporal content; movements are not "in" a generalized duration, rather movement's many qualitatively different durations make up what Bergson called "time in general." If we set aside the abstract time of mathematical mechanism and return to concrete existence, then time is no longer an independent variable but an effective duration.

Its passage makes a difference. Arthur Lovejoy, who rarely admired anything in Bergson, called this recognition of time's "dynamic effectiveness" Bergson's "most significant personal *aperçu* about time . . . his truly fundamental insight."[39]

Extension is Tension Interrupted

Descartes identified matter with geometrical extension, making space and matter coextensive terms. The space of Cartesian coordinates is homogeneous, hence featureless and imperceptible, and isotropic or without intrinsic orientation. The space of perception could not be more different. It is a space of bigness without number and over-there-ness without location, qualitatively inflected in terms of near and far, up and down, left and right, front and back, as well as bearing primitive spatial qualities—too big to carry, too small to see, taller than me, and so on. "That which is given," Bergson says, "that which is real, is something intermediate between [Descartes's] divided extension and [Berkeley's] pure inextension." Bergson calls it the *extensible* and regards it as "the most salient quality of perception" (MM 326); "*All* sensations partake of extensity" (MM 288).

Kant decided that Cartesian geometrical intuitions are a condition on experience, a ruling Bergson sets aside to begin a new precedent. Perceptual extensity is not the infinite, homogeneous space of Cartesian coordinates. Extensity is aesthetic, a felt quality, not space, which is a concept. Geometrical space is like graph-paper on which to plot a trajectory. Thinking in geometric terms makes action efficient, but Cartesian intuitions are not a condition on spatial experience, and geometry tells us nothing about nature, being fit only for our convenience.[40] "Extensity is prior to space," prior perceptually and existentially (MM 308). "It is space that we thrust into extensity" (MM 289), thrusting Cartesian coordinates into primitive extensity like a measuring stick in a well, disciplining naive perception with an infinitely divisible grid. Once we appreciate the merely diagrammatic use of geometry, thought can "transcend space without stepping out from extensity" (MM 245). We transcend space when we understand that geometrical space is an artifact of our notation and not the mental perception of an ideal reality. We should not feel fatally cast into geometric space, where everything is mechanically determined. It is we who introduced this abstraction from the concrete time of duration, and we did so not the better to *know* nature (what it is), but the better to *interact* with its interactions.

In place of the former dichotomy of pure space and pure time, Bergson substitutes a continuum of tensed *tension*, a mnemic, contractile power, and a consistently temporalized version of the Stoic *tonos*, a pneumatic tension that penetrates all things and binds them in cosmic unity. For Bergson, tension is the tendentious energy of tendency, propagated through an interpenetrating duration. In duration there is always the tension or contraction of a past, but how intense that is, how deep or penetrating the mnemic synthesis, varies with scale of action and draw on attention. The greater the tension, the more lucid the interpenetration; with less tension, interpenetration becomes slack and consciousness oneiric. Suppose we could dilute duration, distending the interval between the present and its immediate past. As the present becomes less tensely interpenetrated by the past, the immediate past itself recedes and at some point flickers in and out of the present and eventually remains external.

At this limit, duration becomes space-like, its parts external to each other. Time becomes spatial as it loses interpenetration with the past, and space becomes temporal as it loses externality and begins to interpenetrate. A pure space of purely external relations is an imaginary limit-case of duration, and all real extensity is a mix of space and time. For Bergson in 1907, as for Einstein in 1905, there is no purely spatial distance; space is temporalized, spatial being is a mode of temporal being: "Matter is a relaxation of the inextensive [i.e., time] into the extensive" (CE 218). A body is "a *tension* which is interrupted" (CE 245). This is a notable formulation: *Extension* (i.e., body) is *tension* (i.e., temporal interpenetration) *interrupted* (i.e., punctuated by perception). Milič Čapek insightfully describes this reduction of extension to an interruption of temporal continuity as "the most delicate, the most difficult, and the least known aspect of Bergsonism."[41]

Space and time are ideal endpoints of a continuum and pass into each other: "Concrete extensity is not really divided, any more than immediate perception is in truth unextended" (MM 308–09). Matter is maximally dilute duration, a present reduced to endlessly starting over. Pure space "would consist in a perfect externality of parts in their relation to one another." But that is imaginary. Nothing in space is really external when every point acts on every other, and "matter *extends* itself in space without being absolutely *extended* therein" (CE 203). Something remains nonspatial, tending, and virtual.

Writing in 1907, Bergson observed a trend in physics to efface the individuality of bodies and dissolve them in universal interaction. A body is a center of forces; it *is* where it acts or makes a difference, which at some level must implicate every particle in the universe: "There is no material point that does not act on every other" (CE 203). That was already Michael Faraday's understanding of the new physics of fields. "Matter is not merely mutually penetrable, but each atom extends, so to say, throughout the whole of the solar system, yet always retaining its own center of force." John Venn thought astronomy perturbs its object merely by observing it: "Every motion to or from his instrument, nay the very calculations he writes down on paper or the words he utters by his voice, are motions of matter, and therefore react on the motions of every other natural thing in the universe, including the planets themselves."[42] In 1912, mathematician Émile Borel published a calculation concerning the Earth's relation to Sirius, the brightest star in our night sky, 8.6 light years distant. He calculated that the displacement of one gram of this star's matter by one centimeter would change the Earth's gravitational field by 10^{-100}.[43]

Obviously, that is a small quantity, though the wonder is that it can be calculated at all. These rapports exist and make virtually everything interact; it is just a question of scale. All the baryonic matter (protons and neutrons) in the universe has a history of interaction, and the effects of one body propagate to the end of time. No system is isolated, no particles are external. Pure space, Cartesian coordinates infinite in all directions is a concept, a diagram, a method, but nothing concretely real, and the same goes for pure time, which makes Bergson's understanding of time consistent with possible temporal minima at the Planck scale.

A Little Fact

In the opening pages of *Creative Evolution*, Bergson describes a toy experiment. He wants to dissolve a cube of sugar in his hot water, but the sugar takes time to melt and he has to wait. That imposed delay is a "little fact" which, he says, "is big with meaning" (CE 9). He waits for the sugar, waits for the water; the particles take their time and there is nothing to do but wait. From this little fact Bergson infers that "the universe endures" (CE 11), that is, duration reaches into extensity, into space and matter, contrary to his assumption in *Time and Free Will*. This is a brilliant and consequential change of view in Bergson's philosophy. Explaining elsewhere he says, "the material universe in its entirety *keeps* our consciousness *waiting*; it waits itself. Either it endures, or it is bound up in our duration" (CM 21).

He returns to the experiment in the book's closing pages (CE 340). Why must he wait? Because time is real, because the universe endures, because nothing happens (or exists) instantaneously. Since nothing changes in matter at one place that does not touch matter everywhere, and since there is no purely spatial distance, change takes time. He refers to the experiment a third time fifteen years later. The necessity of waiting "shows that if one can cut out from the universe the systems for which time is only an abstraction, a relation, a number, the universe itself becomes something different. If we could grasp it in its entirety, inorganic but interwoven with organic beings, we should see it ceaselessly taking on forms as new, as original, as unforeseeable as our states of consciousness" (CM 10).

Waiting implies that the future does not exist and has to be created. It takes time. It is the universe, an open whole, that takes this time, and not our imagination. Time exists in the universe, that "time in general" comprising our and every duration. Conceptually, Bergson has moved from "time is in us" to "we are in time," a transposition required for an evolutionary philosophy.

According to Heisenberg's uncertainty principle, measuring energy leaves location uncertain and vice versa. Given a value for energy, I know that something will happen but not where, and given a location, I know where something will happen but not what. A philosopher of Heisenberg's generation commented on this uncertainty: "If the instantaneous cut of the temporal flow according to Heisenberg's formula leaves energy completely undetermined, does not this prove that the universe needs a certain time to take on precise forms?"[44] No enduring process can be pinned down to an instant, because nothing, not matter or form, exists at an instant. Homogeneity, simple presence, and self-identity may be serviceable abstractions, like laminar flow or a spherical star, but considered concretely, the cosmos is an enduring, moving, multiplicity with no being at an instant.

Bergson and Einstein

Although Bergson's major works were published in advance of Einstein's Theory of Relativity, his ideas are admirably consistent with the new scientific thinking. Einstein stipulates that the velocity of light is finite yet unsurpassable, and the limit character of this velocity precludes instantaneous space. There is no now-everywhere or a simultaneous present-everywhere for the simple reason that light cannot be everywhere at once, which would require the infinite velocity nothing has. These conclusions pose no difficulty for Bergson, who never assumed that the universe is a simultaneous (i.e., closed) whole. He is even more skeptical of simultaneity than Einstein, objecting to the latter's supposedly unproblematic local simultaneity: "The distinction between 'small' and 'large,' 'not far apart' and 'very far apart,' has no scientific validity" (DS 55).

Einstein concluded that space in itself, Cartesian coordinates infinite in all directions, does not exist. Space and time merge into each other in an indivisible space–time continuum. Contrary to what is suggested typographically, this space–time continuum does not *unify* time and space; it does not make them poles of a continuous dimension as Bergson did in *Matter and Memory*. Instead, the spatial character of the continuum is all that matters for scientific thought and time's asymmetry is ignored. That is fallacious because future and past events do not timelessly exist; the existence of events in time is their existence at the time of their occurrence. The future does not exist until it comes to pass, and passage, being anisotropic, cannot be modeled by a line in space.

In 1922, Bergson published *Duration and Simultaneity*, which includes his analysis of Relativity's philosophical implications for time. Einstein's Nobel Prize (1921) was awarded for work on the photoelectric effect and not for Relativity, even though the work had been published. In an extraordinary statement that indicates Bergson's prestige in Europe at this time, the President of the Nobel Committee explained that Einstein's Theory of Relativity did not merit the prize, citing among other reasons that "it will be no secret that the famous philosopher Bergson in Paris challenged this theory," which established to the Committee's satisfaction that Relativity "pertains to epistemology" rather than physics.[45]

Einstein knew about Bergson's book and had studied at least part of it, as he records in a diary entry, October 9, 1922: "Yesterday I looked into Bergson's book on relativity and time... he does seem to grasp the substance of relativity theory and doesn't set himself in opposition to it."[46] Fair and correct. Bergson criticizes not the physics, but rather a philosophical gloss grafted to it according to which Relativity proves that "coming into being is only coming into awareness," that "the world simply exists, it does not happen," that time is really a dimension of space.[47]

Émile Meyerson was also exasperated by such misstatements (which continue to this day): "The relativistic exaggerations in this area have usually been accepted without too much protest."[48] Einstein himself used the occasion of a review of Meyerson's *Relativistic Deduction* to add his voice to the critics. He says the tendency Meyerson denounces, "although often latent, is nevertheless real and profound in the mind of the physicist, as is unequivocally shown by the extravagances of the vulgarizers and even of many scientists in their expositions of Relativity." He says Meyerson "rightly insists on the error of many expositions of Relativity which refer to the 'spatialization of time.' Time and space are fused in one and the same continuum, but this continuum is not isotropic. The element of spatial distance and the element of duration remain distinct in nature"—precisely Bergson's argument.[49]

In *Matter and Memory*, he argued that extension is tension interrupted, making pure space and pure time ideal ends of a tensed spatio-temporal continuum. Confronting Relativity, however, he seems to relapse into the old dualism. He says space and time remain "separate from one another, incapable of mingling except as the result of a mathematical fiction" (DS 155). I suggest he means *geometrical* space and *duration*. These are tuned to different scales, quantitative and qualitative. They can be coordinated and harmonized, but their timbre is different, and they don't make the same sound. His earlier point was that Cartesian space—infinite mutually external points—is an idealization, and the same goes for pure time. The space and time that are continuous are primitive extensity and duration. His point in *Duration and Simultaneity* is that time cannot be made geometrical and remain temporal. Relativity does not eliminate the difference between space and time; it eliminates their isolation, which was Bergson's argument too. Time remains time and not a kind of space, but differences of time cannot be isolated from differences of space. The passage of time is an intrinsic asymmetry in space-time itself, an asymmetry without spatial counterpart. The succession of causally determined events is preserved in all frames of reference; for example, if in my frame of reference A causes B, no observer in any frame will observe B preceding A. But Relativity does eliminate the simultaneity of distant events and purely spatial distance, though the result is not to spatialize time but rather to temporalize (dynamize) space. Relativity's space-time continuum does not prove the timeless block universe; instead, it affirms objective becoming. Čapek again writes, "The future, unreal for any present Here-Now, is intrinsically unobservable, that is, physically unreal for any other conceivable frame of reference. . . . Relativistic space-time, currently interpreted, far from implying the elimination of becoming, reintroduces it into the physical world."[50]

Exploring some implications of Relativity, French physicist Paul Langevin proposed what became known as the Twins Paradox. One of a pair of twins departs Earth on a rocket traveling at a very great velocity. The ship travels for an interval, then returns to Earth. Langevin proposed that due to velocity, the traveling twin experiences less time than the Earthbound brother and therefore returns younger than his twin. The argument had already been widely discussed when Bergson delved in. He thought the terms of the paradox imported an adventitious philosophical gloss on the physics which he tried to sort out, arguing that the twins experience the same single lived time (DS 74–80). This is probably a mistake.[51] The path-dependence of time is not an adventitious gloss on the physics but a necessary implication of it, and in 1972 a version of the Twin scenario was experimentally carried out, confirming path-dependence.⁵²

There seems no reason why Bergson could not acknowledge these results and retract his argument about the twins. His idea was never that duration is universal time. What he called time in general is not time universal but rather time endlessly differentiated and multiplied. "There is no one rhythm of duration" (MM 275). He could then readily accept, even require duration on all world lines, with the attractive conclusion that Minkowski space-time, far from representing a static, block universe, teems with temporal dynamism.⁵³

Time and Free Will

I do not know how Bergson's first book came by its English title, *Time and Free Will*. The original title was *Essai sur les données immédiates de la conscience*, which sounds more like what it was, a polished doctoral thesis. The new title is striking and apt, though, and he must have approved it as he did the entire translation. Never before (or since) has the question of "free will" been linked to considerations about time. Bergson's argument is that once we have the right understanding of time, all the supposed proofs of determinism fail. He does not explain what freedom is, and logically his argument requires no such explanation. The problem of free will is really a problem of determinism and its putative proofs. It has been said that without the threat of determinism, the free will problem "would float away." Bergson would agree, and also that the problem "is far more an artifact of traditional methods and preoccupations of philosophers than has been recognized."⁵⁴

Proofs of determinism come in two types. One is psychological, invoking the determination of action by antecedent psychological states (beliefs, desires, trauma, and so on). The other is physical, invoking fundamental mechanical properties of matter, as expressed in the principles of causality, sufficient reason, and the conservation of energy. Kant states the psychological argument:

> If it were possible to have so profound an insight into a man's mental character as shown by internal as well as external actions, as to know all its motives, even the smallest, and likewise all the external occasions that can influence them, we could calculate a man's conduct for the future with as great a certainty as a lunar or solar eclipse.[55]

The physical argument is much the same, except it appeals to mechanical determination by the properties of matter. The classic statement comes from mathematician Pierre Laplace:

> We may regard the present state of the universe as the effect of its past and the cause of its future. An intellect which at a certain moment would know all forces that set nature in motion, and all positions of all items of which nature is composed, if this intellect were also vast enough to submit these data to analysis, it would embrace in a single formula the movements of the greatest bodies of the universe and those of the tiniest atom; for such an intellect nothing would be uncertain and the future just like the past would be present before its eyes.[56]

Bergson claims that physical determinism reduces to a special case of psychological determinism, which is the fundamental form determinism must take. He says, "all determinism, even physical determinism, involves a psychological hypothesis," namely, the hypothesis, or rather fallacy, that consciousness behaves like a spatial system (TFW 142). For example, physical determinism argues that everything is necessitated by past conditions. If something takes place, then its antecedents were sufficient, so given the antecedent conditions the effect is necessary; reset the conditions and the same effect must follow—same cause, same effect. That is fine as far as it goes, but proves nothing against freedom because the antecedents of action are never the same twice. Not ever, not possibly. Whatever value the causal principle has (it has dropped out of fundamental physics), it implies nothing against personal freedom.[57]

One philosopher may speak for others when he writes, "Nothing ever was or ever will be caused merely by the passage of time."[58] This is not realistic. Passage makes us older and more experienced, it changes our memories, it evolves species, it divides the earth, "makes grow all that is hidden, and takes away all that has come to light" (Sophocles).[59] Mere duration changes consciousness qualitatively, as when we listen to the blare of an automobile alarm for ten seconds, thirty seconds, a minute. Bergson compares assembling a jigsaw puzzle to creating a work of art. Time does not matter to the puzzle because the end is given. We could retard or accelerate time arbitrarily without changing the form. But the time of creation cannot be manipulated. The duration of a work's genesis interpenetrates with the work itself. To contract or dilate the duration would make it a different work by a different artist (CE 340).

Bergson describes each moment of consciousness as "reenforced and swollen by the whole . . . past" (TFW 153). Not my past or yours, but the whole past, though these are not as different as the terms sound. What I call my past is my perspective on *the* past, a partial view of the whole past. I cannot stand on the earth without automatically acquiring a geometrical relation to every point on the globe, and I cannot endure a moment of time that is not conditioned, interpenetrated, reenforced, and swollen by the whole past. Every present is new and different. Reversibility is an artifact of mechanical analysis rather than a quality of natural systems. The atoms of Democritus remain the same until an external cause changes them, but consciousness does not require a cause to make it change. As an enduring temporal entity, it cannot *stop* changing.

It must be understood that Laplace's argument is a mathematical fantasy without a shred of support in modern science. Quantum physics makes a mockery of mechanical determinism.[60] Nature does not work that way. Even if mechanical determinism were true though, Laplace's calculator, who is not God but with us in space and time, could not predict the future. Even the best calculation can predict only the state of the calculator's environment at a specified future time *after* the arrival of the time in question. A delay is insurmountable when deriving information about an environment immanently, especially when the calculator has to take its own previous results into account. How can the calculation catch up with itself? As Bergson observed, "We never perceive anything but our own immediate past" (MM 195).

As we trace the antecedent conditions of a given event further into the past, we discover that factors significant for the effect increase without limit, these additional conditions differing qualitatively and introducing new contingencies. The measurements required to give Laplace's calculator information about the initial position and velocity of particles would require infinite energy. On quantum-physical grounds (Heisenberg's principle) the exact determination of initial conditions is physically impossible. It is impossible even on Newtonian grounds to know the positions and velocities of all the particles of an enclosed gas. To imagine such information about *the whole universe* is wanton fantasy.

Bergson contends that all versions of determinism come down to the idea that with adequate knowledge our actions are predictable to a certainty. It is not a coincidence that the common feature of the original Stoic determinism, later Christian theological determinism, and modern mechanical determinism is *prevision*.[61] If the future can be *known* (by a sage, or God, or a calculation), then personal freedom is compromised. With that, we arrive at the hypothesis on which all proofs of determinism turn, namely, that a calculator with adequate knowledge can foresee a given action from any point in the past. To support determinism, such a prediction must be to a certainty, like an eclipse. It is not deterministic prevision for you to "predict" a friend's response in some scenario, which is less a prediction than a statement about present character.

The question of determinism has to be whether, if Alice knows all the conditions under which Bob acts, she can predict his action to a certainty from any point in the past.

The prediction would require information about Bob's state of mind. Alice must know whether various desires are trifling or obsessive. It won't be enough to know that Bob's proposal of marriage was refused; she must know how that felt. Was he relieved, devastated, humiliated? Only with such insight could she duly factor these events in a prediction of future action. Unfortunately, the information is not available in advance. We must wait for action to know the quality of someone's anger, say, or desire. Alice will learn what value to assign past conditions only after the events she would predict have transpired. It is a mistake to think that something she knows after the fact (he was greatly relieved) could have been known all along if only her information were adequate. It is a mistake to think that passage is not effective or that time does not make a difference. These are assumptions of mechanical analysis, which is limited to abstract systems and proves nothing against the effectiveness of time in life. "Only after a deed is done can I know all of its causal premises."[62] That's not Bergson, it's Hermann Weyl.

Bergson describes duration as "invention, the creation of forms, the continual elaboration of the absolutely new" (CE 11). Time is an inexhaustible source of qualitative difference and thus newness in nature, this being the pure heterogeneity on which I have remarked. The novelty may be infinitesimal, but the wonder is that it exists at all. If every moment is qualitatively different, then the mechanical repetition of the same is as artful an idealization as a spherical star. Mechanical repetition is an abstraction suitable for artificially closed systems but does not actually, concretely, physically exist.

A determined determinist might reply that even if future action cannot be *predicted*, it is still *determined*, necessitated by natural law. The alternative is incomprehensible. Let's look into that. If action is determined, the only sufficient cause could be that changes in consciousness are either identical with or supervene on neurological change. There may be no law that determines which brain state goes with which mental state (so-called anomalous monism); or perhaps there is a law though we are unable to apprehend it (the mysterian thesis).[63] But the neurological antecedents of action are biochemical events, and if we assume that changes in consciousness either *are* or are *caused* by these neurological changes, which are physically determined, then our action is determined by physical antecedents and could not fail to occur when and as it does.

The argument presupposes a brain-consciousness correlation that is far from firm fact. Correlation means a one-to-one relation: one (token) mental state, and one (token) neurological state. But *one* conscious state is impossible. Every *one* is also many. The multiplicity of consciousness is qualitative, not quantitative, and condones no cardinality. Its duration is an original continuity without external parts or instantaneous boundaries. Consciousness lacks terminal points that would allow us to say when one "state" began or ended. It is impossible under such conditions to establish a correlation between consciousness and the biophysical parameters of a living neurology: "There is no feeling, no matter how simple, which does not virtually contain the past and present of the being which experiences it, which can be separated from it and constitute a 'state'" (CM 142).

Duration is endlessly heterogeneous and cannot endure a changeless interval however brief. Even the physically fundamental Planck time, 10^{-43} seconds, is a duration and contains a growing past. Stop a melody at an instant and it ceases to exist. Consciousness and, after Heisenberg, matter and energy are like that too. It is impossible to catch consciousness in a synchronic "state" and ask, *What caused that? What correlates with that?* The references are infinitely ambiguous.[64]

Determinism is dreadful because prevision seems incompatible with people having the power to make a difference in their lives. One philosopher says people have a natural interest in controlling their lives, "a control related to our being to some degree the ultimate creators or originators of our own purposes or ends and hence ultimate arbiters of our own wills. We cannot have that in a determined world."[65] So formulated, the problem appeals to a desire for personal ownership of acts. Robert Nozick, a political libertarian, defends metaphysical libertarianism too: "We want it to be true that in the very same situation we could have done (significantly) otherwise, so that our actions will have originative value."[66] J. S. Mill, another kind of liberal, says, "To be conscious of free will must mean, to be conscious before I have decided that I am able to decide either way."[67] My decision makes the final difference and makes the act mine, my property, mixed with my labor.

Bergson thinks it is a mistake to invest anything in this "could have done otherwise." Imagine coming to a junction in life, a decisive point where multiple courses lie before you. You hesitate, deliberate, decide, and act. You could have turned left, instead you go right. You could have joined the Resistance, instead you care for an elderly relative. The choice at such crossroads is free only if the hesitation is real. You really could have taken the other path and were not unconsciously pushed from behind. Bergson upends the melodrama of the crossroads, which is a *retrospective* representation of choice and a cliche of self-narration. We cannot stop as we might at a crossroad and survey the landscape of the future; alternatives are never equipollent; we are characteristically tending even as we think about what to do.

Bergson avoids saying much about freedom in his book. He says it would be counterproductive and is unnecessary for his argument, which refutes determinism, yet he does say something. Freedom can be social or metaphysical, and metaphysical freedom is individuality, because the greater one's individuality the less one is conditioned by anything external. Organisms can be considered from two perspectives. One is species-being: *Homo sapiens, Canis lupus,* and so on. The same organisms can be considered as individuals, each one different, struggling to survive. The simplest organisms express an individuality that is lost with the step to lifeless molecules and their parts. Electrons, for instance, are not individuals. Tests accurate to one part in 10^{34} find no difference between one electron and another.[68] They bear no scars, and have neither trajectory nor history, ideas that presuppose we can differentiate one from another and narrate its vicissitudes, which cannot be done. It is only when swarms of electrons organize into a greater system that we can begin to speak of individuality, which is a luxury of the complicated and comes at the price of mortality.

Personal freedom, or whatever freedom friends of determinism think they thwart, is another name for individuality. Your duration and my duration are as different as two events can be, and free action expresses this difference: "We are free when our acts spring from our whole personality, when they express it, when they have that indefinable resemblance to it which one sometimes finds between the artist and his works" (TFW 172). Only action that "springs from the self and from the self alone . . . [and] bears the mark of our personality, is truly free" (TFW 173). Freedom is not doing what you like; it is liking what you do, the consistency of action and character. Free acts are characteristic acts, expressive acts, phases of becoming who one is. This expression from Pindar—"become who you are"— recalls Nietzsche, who aptly says, "The freest act is that in which our own strongest, most finely practiced nature springs forth, and in such a way that at the same time our intellect shows its directing hand."[69]

Action expressing freedom is not an accident, not insincere, not conformist, or performed under duress; one deliberates, decides, and does the thing. Such freedom is necessarily relative and graduated because any tendency is beset by countervailing tendencies. Individuality is never absolute, nor is freedom normal—"we are rarely free"; "free acts are exceptional"; some people live and die "without having known true freedom" (TFW 167, 231, 166). We use common words in common ways to smooth over qualitative differences of experience, inducing faux-homogeneity and looking askance at tendencies to individuality, including our own (Bergson thinks this is why we laugh, at ourselves or others). The threat to freedom, that is, to the growth of individuality and its expression, is not determinism, not antecedent causes. It is conformism, domination by cliche, and docile compliance, a political not metaphysical problem, arising from the exclusionary values of what Bergson calls closed society (Chapter 4).

Bergson's arguments against determinism are three: The causal principle (same cause, same effect) is meaningless for consciousness; determinism requires the prediction of action to a certainty, which is impossible; and determinist arguments cannot be formulated except with a vicious spatialization of consciousness that overlooks characteristics such as interpenetration and heterogeneity. The idea of foreseeing or predicting action assumes that consciousness is composed of mutually external parts like bodies in space. The question, "Can future action be known with certainty in advance?" reduces to, "Is time really space?" If time is not space but rather duration, then the hypothesis of a mechanical, energetic, or psychological determination of future action is incoherent, and determinism "loses every shred of meaning" (TFW 239).

The Inside of Time

By the latter nineteenth century, European philosophers widely agreed that knowledge of the thing in itself is impossible, since on Kant's showing empirical knowledge is conditioned by the subjectivity of our cognitive powers. That was Schopenhauer's view and became Nietzsche's. It was Comte's view and was readily modified to take theories of evolution into account, as in Spencer, James, and Dewey. Bergson did not follow this path. From his perspective, pragmatism, utilitarianism, and instrumentalism are half-truths. Intuition is the missing element. This intuition is not what Kant called "intellectual intuition"; that is, it does not claim cognizance of things in themselves.[70] All that intuitive knowledge knows are the phenomena of duration, which are not things but rather movements.

From Francis Bacon and John Locke to Bertrand Russell and W. V. Quine, Anglophone philosophy favors continuity with natural science, but Bergson thinks there is a reality that scientific methods cannot apprehend though intuitive methods might. Science requires quantitative answers to quantitative questions and for a good reason, since only with such results can it produce the predictions that make its knowledge valuable. However, to think that resistance to those methods disqualifies a subject from reality is a utilitarian bias to which philosophy should not accede. Natural science is unavailing for understanding the phenomena of duration, which include growth, development, evolution, individuation, movement, continuity, melody, and consciousness. That is where metaphysics *à la* Bergson takes over. Natural science is a quantitative science of matter-energy, and metaphysics is an intuitive, qualitative knowledge of duration and its phenomena.

This argument raises several questions. Exactly what "reality" escapes quantitative methods? Can metaphysics attain knowledge of something unapproachable by natural science? And is intuition seriously a method of knowledge? To begin with the last question, Bergson suggests he is pioneering a new method that could be more widely applied to good effect in metaphysics.[71] After a century, nothing has come of his expectation, not in France or abroad. I agree with Leszek Kolakowski that Bergson "offered no applicable 'method' apart from his own results."[72] Nevertheless, his explanation of intuition is worth our notice, and helps to understand why Bergson valued it as he did.

Experience comes in two aspects. One takes the form of "facts side by side with other facts, which repeat themselves more or less, which can to a certain extent be measured." This experience "unfolds outwards" and "perceives things as external to one another." It is this experience that empiricism dignifies as the source of evidence and concepts, but there is more. The other aspect of experience takes the form of "reciprocal penetration, which is pure duration, refractory to law and measurement." This is our experience when consciousness "turns back within itself, takes possession of itself, and develops in depth"; for instance in recollection (CM 102). Philosophers tend to throttle inner experience, even the empiricists; however, as Maine de Biran urged against Condillac, reflection is a source of experience no less than the senses.[73] Bergson seizes this opening to define a more consistently empirical empiricism. "Existence can be given only in an experience. This experience will be called vision or contact, exterior perception in general, if it is a question of a material object; it will take the name of intuition when it has to do with the mind" (CM 36). Intuition is conscious auto-affection, a mind's experience of a mind.

There is more to experience than sense-perception, which is experience with bodies in space. Even odors are extensive, that is, spatial and embodied. We have a different experience of duration, which we do not perceive externally but apprehend internally. The fundamental meaning of intuition is "to think in duration"; intuition "has as its object the mobility of duration" (CM 155); "the intuition we refer to then bears above all upon internal duration. It grasps a succession which is not a juxtaposition" (CM 35). How else could we be aware of the phenomena of duration? We do not see or hear continuity or movement, only where they stop. What we experience of continuity is an intuition given by inner sense; for example, the intuition of personal continuity moment by moment or year by year, a feeling of change endured. When attention turns outward, we do not sense-perceive the phenomena of duration (movement, development, and the rest), instead, what we externally perceive is intuitively apprehended by sympathetic feeling.

Intuition is not an occult faculty. Sensory experience has its source in the senses and the source of intuitive experience is the body's instincts. Intuition begins as an instinctual feeling of relation. Because we are mortal, we must act on other bodies, for which we have instincts that track phenomena of duration like movement and season. These are instincts, presumably evolved, adaptive, and normally unconscious, though they can become conscious, and when they do we have the intuition of a relation, the feeling of a connection. Feeling is also the word William James used in his account of the cognition of relations.[74] Feeling paints many with one affective brush. We think A and B are related when we feel a connection. When the relations are phenomena of duration, sense perception shows us movement's spatial boundaries, but we experience the moving, the passage, by sympathetic self-feeling.

Bergson systematically differentiates intellect, instinct, and intuition. To begin with instinct, it is unconsciously enacted; we do it, but do not understand why. By contrast, intellectual knowledge is thought-out, consciously understood, and deliberately applied. The principal use of intellect is to illuminate choice, while with instinct choice is diminished and preference becomes conscious only when instinct is thwarted. A second difference is that intellectual knowledge is primarily knowledge of form. Intellect habitually adopts a hypothetical orientation—"what would happen if...?"—unlike instinct, which is categorical, its extension difficult to enlarge beyond the object for which it is specifically adapted. Intellect is limited in a different way, not in extension but in the quality of its attention. The objects of intellectual knowledge are potentially unlimited, but only with effort do we overcome the pragmatic bias of practice.

Invention is the principal good of intellect, which, combined with hands enables the unlimited efficacy of tools and techniques. By contrast, there is little that is inventive about instincts. An example from Bergson illuminates the difference (CE 171–75). There are several species of wasp whose females have the adaptation of paralyzing prey and leaving a living meal for freshly hatched eggs laid before departing. One of these (genus *Ammophila*) flawlessly wounds its prey in three surgically precise positions on its nervous system, inducing paralysis without death. Such behavior seems to combine entomological expertise with the art of the surgeon, though of course the wasp's knowledge is in no way intelligent, expressing no art or *techne*.[75] Unlike a surgeon with a scalpel, these insects do not have a free-floating finesse with their stinger. The wasps' instinct differs from technical knowledge because it works on one body only, a fixed form of prey, and does one thing only. The knowledge is mechanized, locked in place, and cannot be extended to new situations or needs.

We must not confuse instinct's lack of hesitation with the certainty of hesitation overcome, which is characteristic of invention. Instinct is lived rather than chosen. Asking how the wasp does it is like asking how you breathe. We can call instinct knowledge because it is adaptive behavior.[76] But the instinct or its knowledge does not have to be used that way. Not to do so is difficult, it goes against the grain of all that makes us a successful species, but it is possible. We can suspend pragmatic prejudice, concentrate on experience in advance of a practical response, and perceive changes for what they are, not what we can do with them. That is the goal of intuition and its method: "By intuition I mean instinct that has become disinterested, self-conscious, capable of reflecting upon its object and of enlarging it indefinitely" (CE 176).

Such attention is not natural, easy, or spontaneous. The point is, it can be done, or so Bergson says. He calls it "thinking backwards" (MM 122).[77] To make intuition cognitive requires that we "reverse the normal direction of the workings of thought" (CM 160). The normal direction is perception for action, concepts for application, analysis for efficiency and advantage. To reverse this requires attention to experience at a point in advance of "that decisive *turn* where, taking a bias in the direction of our utility, it becomes properly *human* experience" (MM 241). That is, the practical, utilitarian, experience of common sense. To direct attention past these horizons turns thought against its own habits, which is Bergson's design: "By unmaking that which [our] needs have made, we may restore to intuition its original purity and so recover contact with the real" (MM 241). In this case, "the real" are the phenomena of duration, such as endurance, movement, and generation. We feel these qualities intuitively, know them intuitively, a qualitative knowledge of relations that resists development as a science.[78]

Something Bergson says about instinct and intuition complicates my account. Despite having written that "by intuition I mean instinct that has become disinterested" (CE 176), elsewhere he says, "We will say nothing of those who would think that our 'intuition' is instinct or feeling. Not one line of what I have written could lend itself to such an interpretation" (CM 69). I suggest he is thinking of instinct as conceptualized in ethology, where it is an involuntary reaction to a sensed elicitor.[79] That, indeed, is not what he calls intuition, which is instead a pathos or auto-affection apprehending duration. Such cognition is not instinct *sensu* ethology, not an involuntary behavioral response to external stimuli, though it *is* that instinct detached, sublimated, and transposed into conscious self-feeling.

Bergson says "philosophy should be an effort to go beyond the human state" (CM 163). He means an effort to think beyond fixation on the present, on utility, bodies, and spatial representation. He calls on philosophers to disengage from the compulsive certainty of common sense: "The philosopher's sole aim should be to start up a certain effort which the utilitarian efforts of mind of everyday life tend in most men to discourage" (CM 139). Sympathy is an external expression of consciousness enlarged beyond attention to life. We feel our own duration respond sympathetically to another's movements, including movements of speech. Any attentive perception of movement evokes this sympathetic intuition. "I attribute to what is moving an interior and, as it were, psychic states . . . [and] I sympathize with the states, and I insert myself in them by an effort of imagination" (CM 159).

For instance, you watch, let us say, a snake stalking a mouse through seagrass on a beach. You may feel as though you see its purpose, you may feel you know what it is doing. That is what Bergson describes as attributing an interior to the movements and inserting oneself in them. Attributing an interior does not mean attributing conscious mentality. Bergson only said they are psychical states "as it were." He attributes to perceived movement something *analogous* to mental states, *analogous* to consciousness, which, as phenomena of duration, are interpenetrating or temporally continuous. It is because of these similarities that an intuition of our duration (a feeling of relation) can be externalized as sympathetic cognition of duration and its phenomena. Deleuze sums up the point: "Intuition is not duration itself. Intuition is rather the movement by which we emerge from our own duration, by which we make use of our own duration to affirm and immediately to recognize the existence of other durations."[80]

Science is for enlarging our action on matter and is not a philosophy of nature or a metaphysical theory of reality. The point of science "is not to show us the essence of things, but to furnish us with the best means of acting on them" (CE 93). That is why it makes no difference to the value of science that its knowledge is relative—to an observer, a system of measurement, a theory, culture, or species. The point is, it works. But that same utilitarian standard guarantees the incapacity of science to incorporate phenomena of duration in its understanding. Bergson therefore delegates the task to metaphysics in a new key, relieved of rationalism and its antitemporal assumptions.

A Bergson-model metaphysics would be about the inside of time, as intuited in the phenomena of duration, and because experience, albeit inner, is the data, this metaphysics qualifies as a radical empiricism: "A true empiricism is the one which proposes to keep as close to the original itself as possible, to probe more deeply into its life, and by a kind of spiritual *auscultation*, to feel its soul palpable; and this true empiricism is the real metaphysics" (CM 147). The medical allusion recalls ancient medical empiricism, which insisted on the individual, distrusting generalizations and hypotheses.[81] Like those ancient physicians, Bergson eschews schematic concepts and seeks individual variation: "One recognizes the real, the actual, the concrete, by the fact that it is variability itself" (CM 152). A power to find the individual amid the cliches and pragmatic compromises that pervade everyday life is something Bergson admires in the fine arts (Chapter 4).

Philosophy would be impossible if we had to choose between intellect and intuition, or if these faculties could not collaborate. That defines Bergson's aspiration for philosophy: to be neither intuitive nor analytical, but rather to enlarge each through the experience of the other, making intelligence more intuitive and intuition more intelligent. Nothing is wrong with sense perception or its experience. The point is not to correct the senses, as Plato expected dialectic to do, but rather to extend and enlarge experience. Intuition is not offered as an alternative to intellectual knowledge but as an enhancement that rationalism with its hatred of time has withheld.

Bergson anticipated collaborative research to develop methods for thinking qualitatively and nonspatially about the phenomena of duration. The results would not be continuous with natural science but complementary, a metaphysical supplement that closes a gap as old as philosophy itself. The word "science" in Bergson generally means mathematized knowledge supporting quantitative prediction. Descartes taught Europeans to count the possession of such knowledge as mastery. Biology and the human sciences were disturbing this Cartesian legacy in Bergson's time and under his eyes, and he wanted to stimulate a response in philosophy:

> We need to break out of mathematical frameworks, to take account of the biological, psychological, and sociological sciences, and on this broader base construct a metaphysics that can go higher and higher through the continual, progressive, and organized effort of all philosophers, in the same respect for experience.[82]

Bergson's expectations for this collaboration came to nothing, and the idea was swept away with the rest when attention to Bergson's work collapsed after the First World War.

The Duration of the *Dao*

Thinking in duration is a theme of traditional Chinese thought, though Bergson assuredly knew nothing about it. The Daoist classic *Zhuangzi* introduces a distinction between small or petty knowledge and knowledge big or great.[83] Both are knowledge but only one is sagacious. Small knowledge is seeing and hearing, understanding linguistic distinctions, respecting common sense and a scholar's so-called facts. Small knowledge is nevertheless knowledge because what it lacks is not truth or justification but sagacity. Such knowledge thrives in scholarship. Any dispute, any contention, about what is called what or how to use words is ipso facto little knowledge.

To describe what is great about great knowledge *Zhuangzi* describes artisans. The impressive quality of skilled action is responsiveness to change. The technician's perception is unencumbered by conventional thinking or scholarly baggage, responding with the spontaneity of practiced habit to the opportunities of the material. Great knowledge releases this virtuosity from the constraint of labor, so that it may contribute to an ethical art of life. Beside the many arts, each with special tools, materials, and methods, there is an unspecialized surplus, an art of response or resonance, a *dao*-art of viably changing with changes.

To transition from small to great knowledge requires experience in seeing through boundaries, evading perspectives, and forgetting names. We are to begin thinking in time, as Bergson said of intuition. Practice emptying consciousness of quasi-spatial boundaries, thinking in terms of movement rather than stops: "Intuition starts from movement, posits it, or rather perceives it as reality itself, and sees in immobility only an abstract moment, a snapshot taken by our mind, of mobility" (CM 22). To think in terms of distinct forms—this, not that, here, not there—is to be condemned to small knowledge. Relief requires one practice what *Zhuangzi* calls settling into the pivot of the *dao*: "The place where neither *this* nor *that* finds its counterpart is called the pivot of the *dao*. Once the pivot finds its socket it can respond endlessly."[84]

We settle into this pivot when we settle into duration, which is intuition. To settle yourself in duration is to forget about the discontinuities that obsess prosaic minds. Bergson had no idea how close he is to the Daoist classic. What he says of philosophical schools and their disputes is like a paraphrase of *Zhuangzi* on little knowledge:

> There is scarcely any concrete reality upon which one cannot take two opposing views at the same time, and which is consequently not subsumed upon the two antagonistic concepts. Hence a thesis and an antithesis that it would be vain for us to try logically to reconcile, for the simple reason that never, with concepts or points of view, will you make a thing. (CM 148–49)

To be trapped by such exchanges, committed to something being right, something wrong, is the little knowledge of *Zhuangzi*'s famous *Qiwulun* chapter.

> That comes from this, and this follows from that. Such is the doctrine of the parallel birth of "this" and "that." Even so, born together they die together. . . . If they are both okay, then they are both not okay. If they are both not okay, they are both okay. If they are right in a way, they are wrong in a way. If they are wrong in a way, they are right in a way.[85]

Everyday life is this Hell of small knowledge. Daoists aspire to get past these obstacles, to stop being stopped by them, cultivating an art of the unencumbered path. It takes practice. Zhuangzi whimsically imagines a dialogue between Confucius and his favorite disciple, Yan Hui. Yan breaks in on the Master, "I'm improving!" How? He has forgotten about benevolence and righteousness, the principal Confucian virtues. The next day brings more improvement.

He has forgotten about rites and music, the chief Confucian performances. On the third day, however, there is nothing to report. Now, he says, "I just sit and forget" (*zuowang*). Confucius asks for an explanation. How does one do that, just sit and forget? "I cast off my limbs, dismiss my hearing and sight, leave my form, abandon knowledge, and unify them in the great comprehension." Gobsmacked, Confucius asks to become Yan's disciple![86]

Deletion is only one model of forgetting and an obviously mechanical one. Forgetting can also be the effect of enhanced continuity. One becomes oblivious to boundaries that others cannot avoid and which are for them obstacles and halting places. Such forgetting requires getting past the glaring discontinuity of ordinary life and its reinforcement by ordinary language. To become oblivious to all that would be a cognitive breakthrough. To think in duration is to think in movement and forget about halting. Movement only halts before an obstacle, while to think in duration is to evade and finally forget about obstacles, mastering the art of the unobstructed path.

This forgetting is not deleting experience but sublimating it, removing what makes it limited, which is spatialization and the compulsion to think in terms of static forms and halted motion rather than continuity and development. Very little is proprietary in Chinese thought. The Confucian name for thinking in duration is "extending knowledge" (*zhi zhi*), which is thinking not "thing" or "form," but rather continuity and interpenetration, milieu and ecology.[87] Sagacious analogy extends knowledge past the mere form merely present to the becoming it expresses and the change it foretells.

* * *

Bergson is without doubt the most profound thinker about time since antiquity. In referring to time we refer to duration, which is always an interval, never instantaneous, and therefore always marked by differences of past and present. This time, this duration, is real, that is, not imaginary or subjective, and it is effective, a power for change, as we see in geology, the evolution of life, and other phenomena of duration.

The study of mental intensity led Bergson to the problem of our tendency to spatialize consciousness, for instance when we treat consciousness as a series of states, like a machine. That is a mistake because mechanical systems can be measured or quantified, something impossible for consciousness due to the quality, several times noticed, of pure heterogeneity or original multiplicity. Moments of consciousness are not "states," which connote instantaneous boundaries demarcating a homogeneous interval. To describe consciousness as pure heterogeneity means that it is never the same on two occasions. Cut the interval as closely as you like, there is always a difference between the present and the whole past. There is no element, no unit, no primitive identity of which this multiplicity is a combination—not for consciousness and not for time. We rediscover the heterogeneity of consciousness in all the phenomena of duration, which include endurance, movement, melody, development, individuality, consciousness, and evolution. All resist reduction to the mechanical repetition of a homogeneous unit.

There is more to Bergson's philosophy of time than can be gleaned from *Time and Free Will*. If we don't consider later work, we will think that he is a space-time dualist: space is exterior and timeless, time is interior and immaterial. It is only as we read on, especially in *Creative Evolution*, that we see this dualism shaken off and a more original theory emerge. The little fact that Bergson found full of meaning—he has to wait for the sugar in his drink to melt—implies that the future does not exist and has to develop, which takes time. Nothing happens instantaneously; the universe has its own duration, enveloping not just life and consciousness but matter in a single qualitatively multiple, densely interpenetrating passage, open and unfinished.

Time without memory is time that has no effect, a merely virtual time whose actuality is confined to a present that is always starting over. Time becomes effective when the past becomes effective, which is memory and implies consciousness. The theory of Relativity does not eliminate the difference between space and time; instead, it eliminates their isolation, which is Bergson's argument too. All the classical proofs of determinism apply spatial thought to consciousness, which they treat as a theater of quasi-mechanical causation. Once we take time seriously, which is to acknowledge its reality as duration and it effectiveness as memory, then the proofs of determinism become insupportable. Bergson's idea of intuition and an intuitive method in philosophy are developments of his thinking about time and consciousness. Temporal continuity cannot be discerned by the external senses; we see and hear only where events stop or start, not the interpenetration of movement, which calls on intuition.

2
Making Memory Matter

In *Matter and Memory*, Bergson introduces theories on perception and memory that feature his concept of the virtual. Perception is virtual action, and memory is virtual experience. Virtual existence gets a lot of attention in this chapter because I think it is a valuable concept for philosophy and want to explain why. Bergson's ideas about memory are at odds with practically everything said on this topic since Aristotle. Memory is the effectiveness of the past in the present, an effectiveness carried by the virtual action of tendencies. We'll see Bergson's argument lead to a new variation on the old theme of panpsychism. Bergson's thought on matter and body interestingly meshes with ideas from physics on entropy and quantum entanglement. His deflation of a classical question of metaphysics—*Why is there something, not nothing at all?*—is a bridge to the evolutionary argument in Chapter 3.

An Image of Matter

Near the beginning of *Matter and Memory*, Bergson says, "I call *matter* the aggregate of images, and *perception of matter* these same images referred to the eventual action of one particular image, my body" (MM 8). He is saying that matter—all bodies, the physical universe—is an aggregate of *images*. Of course, everything depends on what "image" means.

Comparison with photographs is helpful though imperfect. The photographic apparatus slices off the surface of things, severing them from their environment and from their own continuity.

Bergson's images are like that. An image is a portion, cut out, discontinuous against a background. However, unlike photographs Bergson's images are volumetric tableaux, solid surfaces we see and touch, as well as the acoustic images (melodic and rhythmic) of audition. He describes these images as pictorial, which means they have the qualities they are perceived to have. In a picture of a man wearing red trousers the picture itself is red, the color really on its surface. Bergson's images are pictorial like that, having the qualities they express. All we perceive are such images, ever changing, like a rotating kaleidoscope. These images are the bodies among which we move, affording perceptual stability for senses adapted to perceive them.

Another difference from photographs is that Bergson's images do not copy anything; they are poetic rather than mimetic, and artifacts of contingently evolved perceptual categories. Bergson's images do not appear camera-like with the snap of a shutter. They are instead results of perceptual sampling for invariants and synchronies. Body presupposes discontinuity, standing out from a background. Such discontinuity is not in nature, which is easily proved since we need only change scale and it disappears. The discontinuity that defines a body comes from perception and correlates with an organism's species-specific competence for interaction.

Why equate matter with images, what does Bergson win from this unwonted usage? A short answer is to take Darwin seriously. Bergson was not a Darwinist, that is true (Chapter 3), but he took on a lot from Darwin, including an understanding of sense perception as an adaptation formed under natural selection. Like Nietzsche (and C. S. Pierce), Bergson unfolds the implications of evolution for the objects of perception and the values of knowledge and truth. These were new problems for European philosophy in 1896, when Bergson brought *Matter and Memory* to the public, and his theory of images responds to them. But his argument goes further, responding also to an ancient question about being and becoming.

European ontology has mostly followed Plato, who was embellishing Parmenides. Being comes first, then becoming and difference. *Being is* (Parmenides), and *is what it is*, itself by itself (*auto kath auto*) (Plato). Becoming is an accident that happens when copies of self-identical beings fall into time and suffer change. These are the axioms Bergson reverses. Becoming is the original condition and time the only given. What count as "beings" are more or less stable phases sampled from the flux of local becoming by an evolved, adaptive neurology, human or some other. Beings, then, entities and forms, are images. Everything substantial, any enduring body, is an image in this specific sense, namely, a punctuated, artificially discontinuous, species-specific, perceptible stability. To follow Plato and place being first consigns phenomena of duration such as movement, growth, and continuity to accidents of an ideal Being untouched by time. Taking time seriously, however, makes duration and becoming time's primary reality and not accidents befalling timeless being.

It is being, not becoming, that is the accident, an artifact of fortuitous synchronies in local becoming and relative to scale of life and perceptual modality. If there were no organisms, there would be no perceptual centers to synchronize fluxes of local becoming, hence no images, no bodies, no discontinuity. Nature as we know it (*natura naturata*) would not exist. Nothing human makes this difference; it is life and perception. The temporal synthesis of bodies from continuous extensity presupposes a vital response. Material extensity is a flux without individuation; apart from perception, "bodies and corpuscles tend to dissolve into a universal interaction" (CE 188). A *thing* "results from a solidification performed by our understanding" (CE 249); "things and states are only views, taken by our mind, of becoming. There are no things, there are only actions" (CE 248).

The images people see are not those seen by an octopus, despite the similarity of the optical organ. Our two organisms respond differently to different energetic invariants whose values depend on different capacities for movement in profoundly different environments. Octopus ontology must be unfathomable, but their images are, like those of human perception, material bodies in their environment.[1] That is because bodies are relative stabilities, relative to a form and scale of life. The scale is not found in nature, which is all continuity, no boundaries, no forms or species. What pervades the unperceived totality of concrete extensity are "*modifications, perturbations*, changes of *tension* or of *energy*, and nothing else" (MM 266). Form and discontinuity are diagrams of action, instrumentally valuable but misleading if taken for insight into nature.

Perception and Virtual Action

If matter is the aggregate of images, perception perceives those same images, though conditioned by the perceiver's potential action. In vision, we see an image numerically one with an image (tableau) physically present in the environment, albeit reformatted to our species-specific capacity to respond. We perceive images, pictorial tableaux in all directions, but the way we see them, the perspective, the salience, what figures against what ground, make the image perceived near to a caricature. It is the original material image simplified, reduced, reformatted to our potential interaction.

An image is a physical body connected at every point to every part of its environment and ultimately the universe, to which it transmits the whole of what motion it receives: "To reply, to an action received, by an immediate reaction which adopts the rhythm of the first and continues it in the same duration, to be in the present and in a present which is always beginning again,—this is the fundamental law of matter" (MM 279). These endlessly related and mutually reactive images become perceptual, perceived images by stimulating the selective sensitivities of an organism, which analyzes image qualities according to species-specific capacities for interaction. This image of diminished action is not the body (or tableau) in its present fullness, though it is a representative cross-section. Perception cuts into the image, takes a representative sample, sampling information useful to the organism in an adaptive response.

Sense organs do not passively await affection; they instigate it almost with a mind of their own. Perception samples an environment according to the adaptive needs of an evolved form of life. What we see is a body, though how we see it and what of it we see—what is salient, what indifferent, what continuous, what discontinuous, what figure, what ground—are conditioned by our species-specific potential for interaction, which is why Bergson refers to the perceived image as a representation. The discontinuity perception introduces is undermined at every closer look. Edges, surfaces, isolated bodies, and impermeable membranes do not exist per se. They are artifacts of scale; change magnitudes and they melt away. Perception therefore does not *add* to the image, as it was supposed to add secondary qualities. It *reduces, simplifies, translates, and eliminates* qualities, cognitively reformatting their energies according to a species-specific capacity to respond and ignoring the rest.

Awareness of images is not the *telos* of perception, not the climax where the process finally comes to an end, because the function and tendency of perception is to prepare action: "Perception as a whole has its true and final explanation in the tendency of the body to movement" (MM 41). That requires more than sensory-surface stimulation: "In the visual perception of an object, the brain, nerves, retina, *and the object itself* form a connected whole, a continuous process in which the image on the retina is only an episode. By what right, then, do we isolate this image to sum up in it the whole of perception?" (MM 285–86). The retinal image is overrated. It is not what we see, nor is perception the cerebral synthesis of an image. To perceive an environment is to analyze it for interaction.[2]

It is in this context—explaining a theory of perception—that Bergson unceremoniously begins to use the idea of virtual existence, which he will use more widely as his arguments unfold.[3]

Perception is not an *impression* of a body, which would just be a second body, now "inside." The office of perception is to prepare action—not to *do* but to ready, which Bergson calls *virtual action*. Perceptions "foreshadow at each successive moment [the body's] virtual acts" (MM 10); perception "never expresses anything but a *virtual* action" (MM 58); perception "exactly measures our virtual action on things" (MM 233).

Looking around, we perceive a panoramic image-tableau. The forms we see, the shapes, the figures, the edges of discontinuity, indicate the stability and change we implicitly expect and for which perception prepares us. Merely prepares. What we feel is not necessarily what we do, but it is what we tend to do, a tending that is felt, an intuition. William James noticed this too, writing that tendencies "are not only descriptions from without, but they are among the objects of the stream [of consciousness], which is thus aware of them from within." He thought consciousness "must be described as in very large measure constituted of feelings of tendency."[4] For Bergson that includes perception, which is a motor power, a felt tendency to respond to a stimulus, and a virtual response, not actually performed but tending.

A camera is a wretched model for vision. Unlike a camera, which has to be motionless, vision functions by the detection of invariants under self-induced changes of illumination and position, which are normal effects of exploratory movement. The immobility that makes the camera's image perfect would leave an animal sightless. Vision discerns the visibly invariant, which presupposes movement and change. The mode of presence, how this invariance becomes present for us, is what psychologist of perception J. J. Gibson calls *affordance*.[5] The principle by which the visual system, for instance, analyzes its stimulus is to search for invariants—synchronies and rhythms—that afford action. To see a thing is to see how to approach it and what changes to expect.

Perceptual affordances are not interpretations. Vision, for instance, is not seeing something *as* affording, say, a pincher grip. Interpretation implies a text, so if affordances were interpretations, they could not be what they are, which is how the given is given. It is not given in a moment of presence, it is not a simple sensation, vivacious impression, or computational representation. The given, for evolved perception, are the affordances of virtual action. The stimulus information of vision are affordances—for manipulation, locomotion, nutrition, social interaction, even epistemic affordances, perceptible qualities that afford operations like classifying, reidentifying, segmenting, and matching.[6]

With matter as an aggregate of images, surfaces are fundamental, not the volumes we imagine behind them. There are not two items—bulky things, and images on their surface; there are only surface events revealing information about other surface events. The point is not that unseen depths do not exist, but to make them matter we must make them surfaces. The depth inside an image is a virtual surface. If I cut into it, I get more images, but they were not already inside, because an image has no inside. The inside of an image is a new image on the outside.

Virtual Existence

Bergson thinks memory shows better than anything what only consciousness can do. To follow his argument requires obedience to a few distinctions. Let us say that a *perception* is an image (visual, auditory, olfactory, etc.) selectively simplified according to a perceiver's species-specific potential action; a *recollection* is an actual image, not perceived (as present) but recollected as past, for instance, you now recollecting Barack Obama's face; finally, *memory* (your memory of childhood, say, or of your kitchen), which is not an image or a collection of images, but instead a nonsurveyable field of potential recollection, like all the images of childhood that you *could* recall once you start reminiscing.[7]

Recollection combines past images with present perceptions and supplements them, or at least it can do so when we are experienced and paying attention. But memory itself is all virtual. The virtual images of memory are formerly present perceptions that have passed into the past and are qualitatively different from any actual image, whether of perception or recollection. To use a nice expression from Deleuze, virtual images are obscure and distinct—distinctly, qualitatively different, but obscure, that is, greatly undetermined.[8] Virtual Adam is distinct from virtual Eve but obscure in himself, a virtual sinner virtually without sin.

Present images do not fall into oblivion with the arrival of a new present; instead, they abide, endure, surviving passage into the past. Of course, past images do not actually exist, since actual existence means present existence. However, there are modes of existence other than actual and present, and the past is one of them.[9] The past is real, really exists, is not fictional, imaginary, or nonentity, though it is not actual and never present; its existence is virtual. Present images no more vanish into nonbeing with passage into the past than furniture vanishes when we leave our rooms. Past images become *unconscious*, not unreal. They are no longer *actual*, that is, present. They are virtual, that is, past.

In optics, a virtual image is one that does not form at the place where we see it, for example a mirror image, which we see as if located behind the mirror, even though that is not the actual location where the image forms (it forms in our eyes). By contrast an optically real image is one that forms where we see it, like an image projected on a screen. In these cases, it is location that qualifies as real or virtual. With computer simulation, causation can become virtual, for example simulating the causality of an aircraft's control surfaces. The actual forces that users introduce (behind the interface) have completely different values and effects from those of a pilot in flight. These are examples of virtual location and virtual causation, but neither is what Bergson wants. His idea is virtual *existence*, where a thing's very being is qualified as virtual.

In a paper of 1908 on the phenomenon of *déjà vu*, Bergson explains virtual images with the example of a mirror. Memory is to perception as a mirror image is to the reflected object: "The object can be touched as well as seen; acts on us as well as we on it; is pregnant with possible actions; it is *actual*. The image is *virtual*, and though it resembles the object, it is incapable of doing what the object does. Our actual experience, then, whilst it is unrolled in time, duplicates itself all along with a virtual existence, a mirror-image" (ME 165). A mirror-image is an imperfect metaphor for the virtual image because a mirror image is an actual image. What is virtual about the images seen in mirrors is not *the image*, as Bergson implies, but its location. That a mirror image is actual is proved by the fact that one can photograph it. Were the image not actual that would be photographing fairies.

A concept of virtual closer to Bergson is the virtual particle of quantum physics. Suppose we could empty space, creating the void of Democritus. According to Heisenberg's indeterminacy principle it is not possible for both the state of a field and its rate of change to be fully determined. If a field has a definite value at a moment, *even zero*, then its rate of change becomes random. The void of Democritus wouldn't last long enough for experiment to confirm that it was ever there at all. It is impossible for any point in space to have zero energy for more than a vanishingly small interval; even a void teems with virtual quantum activity. Random fluctuations of that void create particle pairs, which take a moment to find each other and annihilate. For the interval, among the briefest events measured in nature, they are so-called virtual particles, also known as quantum fluctuations.

Let's review their genesis. We begin with empty space, no fields, no particles, then unpredictably and extremely briefly, a pair of particles appear, *created from nothing* (nothing actual or present). They interact, then annihilate. The conservation of energy is an average, not an absolute. Violations are possible provided they are sufficiently brief, and that is what virtual particles are. Their occurrence (they have been experimentally detected) manifests a tendency that must exist in the vacuum, and this existence must be virtual because in a vacuum nothing is actually there. Actually empty, this vacuum is full of tendency, the tendency of particle-antiparticle pairs spontaneously to emerge when there is nothing to oppose their action; and these *tendencies* (not the particles) are virtual in Bergson's sense. As emergent, the particles are actual, but the *tendency* that the fluctuation materializes is virtual. Before their actualization, the particles exist obscurely (unpredictably) and distinctly (electron or positron). That is Bergson's virtual. What is metaphysically virtual about virtual particles is the obscure yet distinct existence *of their tendency* in a quantum void.

A virtual entity is real, that is, effective, a power, not actual or present but tending.[10] What is tending about virtual existence is the aspiration to act, and what is virtual about tendency is the interpenetration of presence and nonpresence. Tendencies are not actual but tending, inclining, and encountering resistance. Every tendency tends to become actual, but never unopposed and usually unconsummated. Tendency is tending toward a limit, furthered or frustrated by other tendencies, virtually verging on a culmination, when a body finally becomes all that it can be. This limit is a final cause, and tendency is an immanent teleological finality. Bergson explains it like this: "A tendency is the forward thrust of an indistinct multiplicity, which is, moreover, indistinct, and multiplicity, only if we consider it in retrospect, when the multitudinous views taken of its past undivided character allow us to see it composed of elements which were actually created by its development" (TS 294).

Tendencies exist because duration exists though the future does not. Since the future does not exist, something must be tending, processual, underway, and it cannot be present or actual, which would make it finished, not futural. Different tendencies are as distinct as *trot–run–gallop* or *zygote–blastula–gastrula*. Each element of the series is qualitatively distinct from the others, though when, for instance, trotting ceases and running commences remains obscure. These obscure differences are virtual series, and despite their palpable reality they cannot be identified with anything actual. Tendencies are their own causal basis and tend to become all they can be, with nothing repressed or reserved, restrained solely by the tending of every other tendency. Nothing actual manifests all that it is capable of all at once; a readiness potential exists even when the manifestation conditions do not and may never exist.[11]

Aristotelian potential (*dunamus*) lacks this puissance. Everything in Aristotle's theory turns on the actuality of accomplished form: "Actuality is the end, and it is for the sake of this that the potency is acquired."[12] This potential is impotent, having no impetus to act. Matter, the matrix of Aristotelian potential, engenders nothing that did not already exist as form. Aristotelian actualization is not creation because what materializes, a sense-perceptible expression of a timeless essence, is nothing new.

Leibniz distinguishes simple passive capacity from tendency, which is not yet the act, but something followed by the act if obstacles that hinder it are removed. He explains that "active force differs from the mere power familiar to the Schools," that is, Aristotelian potential:

> The active power or faculty of the Scholastics is nothing but a close (*propinqua*) possibility of acting, which needs an external excitation or a stimulus, as it were, to be transformed into action. Active force, in contrast, contains a certain act or entelechy and is thus midway between the faculty of acting and the act itself and involves a conatus. It is thus carried into action by itself and needs no help but only the removal of an impediment.[13]

Leibniz makes this point against Descartes's idea of movement. Unconsciously following the nominalism introduced by William Ockham and Jean Buridan, Descartes reduces movement to a series of positions. The location of A is the set of objects with which A is contiguous, and motion is a difference of location. When A moves, it goes from being contiguous with B to being contiguous with C, D, and so on. Motion is "that by which bodies pass from one place to another and successively occupy all the spaces in between."[14] Notably on this account, motion is indistinguishable from stasis; however much a thing moves it is always stationary, never *in* motion.

Leibniz wants to dynamize the series with a conative nisus that makes natural bodies continuous and striving, expressing their tendency to exist. His effort inspired a tradition in logic of explaining causation in terms of tendencies that can be counteracted; for instance, J. S. Mill: "All laws of causation, in consequence of their liability to be counteracted, require to be stated in words affirmative of tendencies only, and not actual results."[15] Nelson Goodman explains that "besides the observable properties it exhibits and the actual processes it undergoes, a thing is full of threats and promises. The dispositions or capacities of a thing—its flexibility, its inflammability, its solubility—are no less important to us than its overt behavior," and are, he claims, irreducible to categorial terms.[16] Against this idea, W. V. Quine takes the Cartesian line that dispositions must reduce to categorial microphysical properties, rendering the use of dispositional predicates in scientific language provisional, merely registering current ignorance of microstructure.[17] To do what Quine expects and be the actual, categorial reality of disposition or tendency, "microstructure" would have to be completely free of dispositional qualities, simply being what it is, fully actual, identical with itself, but those are precisely the qualities physical theory excludes at the microlevel. "The quantum world cannot be conceived of as inhabited by entities whose identity is given by intrinsically possessed properties," that is, properties having definite values in advance of measurement. "The relational aspect of such entities is much more important for understanding what they really are."[18]

The scientific credibility of capacities, a subclass of tendencies, namely, tendencies to make things happen, is a thesis of philosopher of science Nancy Cartwright, who observes that "the assumption and use of powers and their influence on effects is endemic in scientific practice."[19] Her ontology is the opposite of Quine's Cartesian actualism and makes better sense of physics. Capacities belong to the phenomena natural science investigates as much as do occurrent properties and measurable quantities: "Nature selects the capacities that different factors shall have, and sets bounds on how they can interplay. Whatever associations occur in nature arise as a consequence of the actions of these more fundamental capacities."[20] Once set tending, tendencies press to actuality unless interfered with, as they normally are. That is why the right sort of interference by us can bring otherwise indiscernible tendencies to light, which experimentation exploits. The reasoning that uses what happens in ideal cases like frictionless planes to explain what happens in real cases is a logic of tendencies. When nothing else is going on (the experimentally contrived idealization), you can see what tendency a factor has by looking at what it does.[21]

Capacities and tendencies are real and exist regardless of manifestation. Mere logical analysis cannot determine their conditions of expression: "What marks out all capacities as capacities is not primarily that they enable systems to do things, but rather that they can be stopped—they can be interfered with." The life of a given tendency "is spent mostly in the presence of other dispositional states whose manifestation is the prevention of those former states from having their manifestation."[22] Nevertheless tendency is not a mere potential that requires an actualizing act; it has its own spring of activity, an immanent finality tending to act. A tendency tends to a limit—an end, a finality; it leans, inclines, verges. Its "to be" is this pressing passage, it *is* (actually) nothing at all. Where Aristotelian potential is static, the tendency of virtual existence is potent, dynamic, even vital.

Memory in Mind

Memories are tendencies, past images tending to become present again, whether to enhance perception with their experience or stun consciousness with their trauma. Perception is virtual action, and memory is virtual experience, tending to become actual experience as a supplement to perception. We have no experience in advance of memory and no perception without it. Experience is not mere perception or sense awareness; it is perception remembered, infused by memory, a mnemic synthesis. We should retire the expression "my present experience," used for current sensory awareness. Instead of describing present perception as "experience," it would be better to say that present perception owes its wealth of information to the experience one *has had*. When we are experienced, not seeing things for the first time, we reap the reward of the past with perception enhanced by memory. We do not *have* experience, rather we *become* experienced, as perception passes into the past and changes what we tend to do.[23]

Perception and memory are discontinuous and different, although it is practically a tradition in philosophical psychology to conflate them and construe memory as a diminished perception. One would think the difference is impossible to miss. Perception almost instantly elicits a whole-body response, while memory is pure idea, impassable, without efficacy. It prepares nothing, initiates nothing, has no actual power. Contemplating a memory of something past we find that no action changes it. Unless keyed to current perception, such memories are no more than dreams. Changing nothing, they have no application, not until matched with a perception that can be enhanced by interaction with memory. However, memory does not merely enhance perception, because perception itself depends on memory. Perception entails discerning invariance and how could an organism discern invariance without memory? Perception cannot always be starting over again.

Sensation is intelligent only when melded with memory, for only then does an organism learn from experience. Pure sensation innocent of memory is useless; blind mechanism would be better. Memory is so vital to perception that Bergson says "perception ends up being merely an occasion for remembering" (MM 71). New memories and new perceptions arise simultaneously: "Step by step, as perception is created, the memory of it is projected beside it, as the shadow falls beside the body" (ME 157). Any perception however fleeting endures a duration and calls on memory: "Every moment of our life presents two aspects, it is actual and virtual, perception on the one side and memory on the other" (ME 165). That applies to every organism capable of perception, which is, in effect, every organism. Memory has a force of interpenetration, prolonging one moment into another as with tolling bells or music. Recollection pours over perception and contracts the past, drawing it into the present with recognition. Bergson said memory would show what only consciousness can do, and here it is. Memory, this power of contracting past and present, stitching them, making them interpenetrate, is the source of quality, including qualitative differences in perception. Color, for instance, whose perception is a perceived continuity sustained by memory, as an example will explain.

The minimum exposure required for human sight to perceive a flash of light is between two and four milliseconds; anything quicker is not seen.[24] Suppose we set a flash to last four milliseconds to be sure it is just noticed, and let's make the color of the light red. Red light is electromagnetic radiation at around 400 THz, or 4×10^{13} cycles per second. In the barely noticeable interval of four milliseconds, that comes to forty million electromagnetic events, as discrete and mutually external as such events can be. The visual perception of color is a mnemic contraction of these physical changes into one continuous qualitative flash, illustrating Bergson's thesis that "every concrete perception, however short we suppose it, is already a synthesis, made by memory, of an infinity of 'pure perceptions' which succeed each other" (MM 238). Comparison with a tolling bell is helpful. The bell's first noon-time toll is no longer actual when the seventh or ninth sounds. Yet to a listener the first survives in the last as the beginning of a rhythm just ended. We can replace a tolling bell with photons exchanged between our eyes and a luminous source. Apart from the incomparable intervals, seeing red is like hearing a melody. Both are mnemic syntheses, executed in time by memory, syntheses of qualities from quantities.

Memory is the Philosopher's Stone of metaphysics, possessing the hermetic power to transmute quantities into qualities. The perception of qualities is a mnemic synthesis; quality is a memory of quantity. Memory supplies the tension, the *tonos*, or tensed contraction that makes the elements synthetically interpenetrate: "Thus, by the idea of *tension* we have overcome the opposition between quality and quantity, as by the idea of *extensity* [we overcome] that between unextended and extended" (MM 330). Memory does not actually transmute bare quantities into sensible qualities. Instead, those "bare quantities" are an abstraction without physical reality. There is no pure quantity or qualitatively undetermined motion: "Quantity is always nascent quality: it is, one might say, its limiting case" (CM 161). A pure quantity in a mathematical formula is physically meaningless apart from stipulations on how to measure it, which would be impossible in a purely quantitative world. A simple measurement of length requires an observable difference between endpoints. Empirical science presupposes that matter is more than mere quantity; some qualitative factor must make quantity discernable: "Quantity is imbued with quality; quality exists only in a quantitative pattern."[25]

Perceiving a color like red "analyzes itself into repeated and successive vibrations bound together by an inner continuity" (MM 269). Memory is the binding agent, making the series continuous and sensibly qualitative. Memory introduces interpenetration, when each of those millions of events become moments in the past of others for the duration of a perception. Bergson likens a quality to a chrysalis. Its monotonous simplicity arises from an unseen immensity of movement: "Motionless on the surface, in its very depth it lives and vibrates" (MM 270). Objectively, a quality is electromagnetic radiation, and its perception is a synchrony of motions, a correlated series, like a handshake across trains moving at the same rate, "a certain regulating of mobility on mobility which produces the effect of immobility" (CM 131). Suppress the memory that establishes coordination, "and sensible qualities, without vanishing, are spread and diluted in an incomparably more divided duration. Matter thus resolves itself into numberless vibrations, all linked together in uninterrupted continuity, all bound up with each other, and traveling in every direction like shivers through an immense body" (MM 276).

Leading *Matter and Memory* to its conclusion, Bergson raises "the problem toward which all our inquiries converge," which turns out to be "the union of body and soul" (MM 293). He means their continuity, how they belong together and are not isolated by abyssal dichotomy. Body and soul seem irreconcilable because bodies, being material, are extended in space, while souls, being conscious, are immaterial. How could they meet? We associate this problem with Descartes, though he did not think it was a problem.[26] He had two ideas about matter. According to one, matter is inert, dead stuff, moving only by contact. This is an old idea, going back to the beginning of materialism with Democritus. Descartes's other idea identifies the essential property of matter as geometrical extension, which draws geometry deep into nature. Cartesian coordinates are not just our diagram; they express nature's own principle, which equates body and extension.

This was an innovation and a necessary one for Descartes's dream of mechanical physics, though he declined to add materialism to his already tenuous theological exposure, instigating our mind-body problem instead. With Bergson, matter and consciousness resume the continuity they have always enjoyed in practice. Like bodies, perceptions are extensive and voluminous, and like perceptions, bodies (especially organisms) have duration and endure. So, there is "no impassible barrier, no essential difference, no real distinction even, between perception and the thing perceived" (MM 291). Body and soul, spirit and matter, are not different in kind. They are like time and space or quality and quantity—endpoints of continua: "We pass insensibly from one to the other" (MM 297); for instance, when we pass insensibly from a quantity of photons to a flash of red.

Panpsychism

Anglophone philosophy of mind in the latter twentieth century did not encourage alternatives to materialism. But a conspicuous lack of movement on a materialist explanation of mind (especially the seemingly intractable problem of consciousness), combined with new enthusiasm among new-millennium philosophers for speculation, opened a door one might have thought was closed for good. I mean panpsychism, which has undergone a renaissance in analytic philosophy.[27] The roll of history's panpsychists is distinguished, including Spinoza, Leibniz, Diderot, Schopenhauer, and nineteenth-century scientific thinkers like Ernst Mach and William Clifford.[28] The new panpsychism of the twenty-first century advances over the failure of every other credible metaphysics of mind. Materialism cannot account for consciousness. Dualism cannot explain interaction and has only inspired more desperate systems like occasionalism and preestablished harmony. And idealism is inadequately deferential to natural science, as if metaphysicians knew something about matter that science cannot know.

By this point it no longer seems mad to wonder whether consciousness might be an intrinsic property of matter like mass or energy, especially when we bear in mind that no strictly scientific theory of matter precludes this hypothesis.[29] From Democritus to Descartes, matter was conceived as a single kind of stuff, all parts alike except for location, all undergoing a single kind of change, local displacement. Quantum physics exploded the physical basis of this world-image. Physical reality in physics is fields that exist in a high-dimensional space beyond experience, where excitations appear as particle-like apparitions in the experimental apparatus.

Most of what physics has to say concerning "what matter is" are facts about such fields, with no claim to closure or having all the facts, leaving the door open for the panpsychic hypothesis. With speculative verve, analytic metaphysicians have proliferated theories and distinctions, including several variations on older ideas. There is a cosmological panpsychism, with the universe as a whole as the ultimate locus of mind. Constitutive panpsychism holds that human or animal consciousness is not fundamental but realized by more fundamental forms of consciousness, a thesis defended in two forms. Constitutive micropsychism places fundamental consciousness at the microphysical level, while constitutive cosmopsychism finds fundamental consciousness in cosmic-level facts.

Natural science says nothing of matter's intrinsic properties. Experimental science is about relations, not intrinsic properties. Physical theory yields a relational structure operationally linked to observables, but must there not be more? To restrict natural science to pure structure (as Rudolf Carnap proposed)[30] would mean that it has nothing to say about nature. No purely relational theory can be a physical theory of nature because a structural description can be realized by any items whatever (dominos, marshmallows), provided we have enough of them, with no way to tell whether a theory in physics is about electrons or marshmallows.[31] Something has to distinguish a structure as natural or physical, and whatever that is, its identity and quality must be inherent, intrinsic, nonrelational. But that's consciousness!

Natural science leaves unanswered the question of reality's intrinsic nature. The only intrinsic nature we know is our own consciousness, and the way to explain the intrinsic quality of physical reality is by analogy with consciousness. This was already Schopenhauer's argument in 1818: "If the corporeal world is to be anything more than merely a presentation to us, then we have to say that, beyond presentation, thus in itself and in its innermost essence, it is that which we find immediately in ourselves as will."[32] There seems unanimity among the new panpsychists that consciousness implies a qualitative "what it is like"—a colloquialism they have turned into a technical expression.[33] A being is conscious just in case there is something that it is like to be that being. This "what it is like" is self-presence, and consciousness is subjective, owned presence.[34] In their nuanced ways, the new panpsychists say that subjective self-presence is coextensive with physical reality, indeed that this subjectivity gives physical reality its substance, making it more than a relational structure.

Bergson is not counted among history's panpsychists, though if we recall the arc of argument in *Matter and Memory*, he eliminates the dichotomy of space and time and introduces duration into extensity, which makes consciousness and matter interpenetrating and temporally continuous. That overcomes the mind-body problem, while implying a panpsychism that Bergson unfolds on two lines: one arguing for consciousness as ubiquitous in life, the other for the continuity of consciousness and matter.

Consciousness and Life. He says consciousness means as much as "life . . . launched into matter" (CE 181), and that "consciousness in general . . . must be coextensive with universal life" (CE 186). This consciousness remembers the past, anticipates a future, and makes choices. That is what consciousness is for, choice: "The chief office of consciousness is to preside over action and to enlighten choice" (MM 182). A consciousness proportionate to a living being's power of choice "lights up the zone of potentialities" that surround its action (CE 179). Choice is a product of the freedom that comes with neurology, however primitive: "The humblest organism is conscious in proportion to its power to move freely" (CE 111). To be an asset, a power of choice requires perception, and perception is of no account without learning and habit, which call on memory.

Bergson struggles with plant consciousness. If he sticks to the criterion of choice, then because it cannot move, "the plant is therefore unconscious" (CE 111): "The vegetable renounced consciousness in wrapping itself in a cellulose membrane" (CE 131). But perhaps plants have more movement than he knew. Conscious and unconscious are for Bergson differences of degree, not kind. "In the plant, the consciousness and mobility of the animal, which lie dormant, can be awakened," while "the animal lives under the constant menace of being drawn aside to the vegetable life," reduced to a sessile accumulator like a barnacle (CE 135).

Bergson's hesitation was sound, as research has brought to light evidence of plant neurobiology. "Every plant continuously registers a great number of environmental parameters . . . and, on the basis of those data, has to make decisions regarding food, competition, defense, relations with other plants and animals."[35] Plants roots do not operate under an automatic direction like "seek moisture" or "follow gravity." They are instead coated with sensitive tips that register environmental variables and inform root behavior "on the basis of a real calculus that takes into account the plant organism's different local and global needs."[36] So we have another theater of consciousness, vegetable consciousness, qualitatively distinct from animal consciousness though still consciousness understood with Bergson as a power for choice.

Bergson says something else about consciousness and life when he describes consciousness as "the motive principle of evolution (*le principe moteur de l'évolution*)" (CE 182). I understand this to say that the evolution of life is the same dynamic or tendentious process as we know from consciousness, which is why he also says that the essential causes operating in evolution are "of psychological nature" (CE 54). The causes are psychological in being *like* the causes of conscious states, analogous to conscious psychology, the analogy being that both owe their existence to duration and their continuity to temporal interpenetration. Hence, "organic evolution resembles the evolution of a consciousness, in which the past presses against the present and causes the upspringing of a new form of consciousness, incommensurable with its antecedents" (CE 27). The consciousness of life is perceptual, involving sensation and memory. The consciousness extended by analogy to evolution is *like* the consciousness of organisms, not qualitatively ("what it is like"), but in sharing memory's interpenetrating mode of temporal continuity.

Consciousness and Matter. Natural systems require more than relational properties; they require qualities. The new panpsychists endow matter with qualitative consciousness, while Bergson works with mnemic consciousness. There is a reason for the difference. What makes relations concrete and detectable, giving them a natural reality, is time, the mother of qualities, which are vibrations. It is time that incorporates structure, making it qualitative, concrete, and conscious. Bergson says that "concrete movement," meaning local movement, is "capable like consciousness of prolonging its past into its present, capable by repeating itself of engendering sensible qualities," and therefore "already possesses something of consciousness." (MM 246–47) The succession of material events is never instantaneous and always involves the interpenetration characteristic of psychological duration. To actually exist, a structure has to endure, however fleeting the interval, and that presupposes not a qualitative but a mnemic consciousness. Thus, Bergson's panpsychic thesis: "The material universe itself, defined as the totality of images, is a kind of consciousness" (MM 313).

One of our new panpsychists might wonder what happened to phenomenal qualia and "what it is like." I think Bergson would question the notion that consciousness is helpfully defined in these terms. Thomas Nagel's original statement has never been improved: "An organism has conscious mental states if and only if there is something that it is like to *be* that organism—something it is like *for* the organism."[37] This conception of consciousness presupposes a subject possessing an intrinsic quality absolutely, that is, nonrelationally. However, intrinsic qualities are not as simple as they seem. Bergson likened them to a chrysalis, a still and uniform surface beneath which is an immensity of internal movement.

Bergson's argument overcomes the gap that is supposed to isolate consciousness from physical explanation, another prominent assumption tracing back to Nagel: "It is difficult to imagine how a chain of explanatory inference could ever get from the mental states of whole animals back to the proto-mental properties of dead matter. It is a kind of breakdown we cannot envision, perhaps it is unintelligible."[38] The implication is discontinuity, an incommensurability of qualitative and quantitative. Bergson might argue that phenomenal qualities and material properties are not so incommensurable, as they share the temporality of duration. A phenomenal quality is a duration, a process rather than a state, and so too is fundamental matter, when force and matter become interchangeable according to Einstein's formula (MM 264–65). Bergson might also press the new panpsychists to acknowledge that phenomenal presence ("what it is like") is not primitive; it arises from temporal differences concealed in simple qualities and contracted by consciousness in a qualitative, mnemic synthesis. The gap between physical vibration and conscious qualia is bridged by memory. It is "the primal function of perception" to "grasp a series of elementary changes under the form of a quality or of a simple state by a work of condensation," that is, mnemic synthesis (CE 301).

In remarks spanning fifteen years Bergson reiterates the equation of consciousness with memory:

Matter and Memory (1896): "The subjectivity of our perception consists, above all, in the share taken by memory." (MM 75)

Collége lectures (1903–04): "Memory is the general form of consciousness. There is no conscious state without memory, that is to say, without the impression of what precedes and what follows."[39]

"Life and Consciousness" (1911): "[To] characterize consciousness by its most obvious feature: it means, before everything else, memory." (ME 7)

There is no qualitative, phenomenal "what it is like" except for a memory-consciousness that endures, presupposing the duration Bergson identifies with time itself. The panpsychic ubiquity of consciousness is the ubiquity of duration, or the fact that, like consciousness, the universe endures: "We place consciousness at the heart of things for the very reason that we credit them with a time that endures" (DS 49).

Virtually everything alive is conscious, expressing perception and memory. As this implies, there are two ways for something to be "like consciousness," two directions in which to develop an analogy: to be like perception or to be like memory. The new panpsychists pursue the analogy of perception and Bergson the analogy of memory. The first quality of memory is a distinctive mode of temporal continuity—interpenetration. Phenomena that share such continuity share what is conscious about memory. Life and matter are such phenomena. They are like consciousness in sharing its interpenetrating mode of temporal continuity.

The qualitative, phenomenal dimension of consciousness ("what it is like") depends greatly on the physiology of the body affected and does not support a robust analogy beyond our skin: "Our present is the very materiality of our existence, that is to say, a system of sensations and movements, and nothing else" (MM 178). We cannot imagine what it is like to be a bat because we cannot perform the movements that express bat consciousness. However, sense qualities are not a good foundation for a theory of consciousness because "sensible qualities [are] contractions effected by our memory" (MM 36). Among the presuppositions of consciousness, therefore, memory has priority over phenomenal qualities. "What it is like" is inadequate as a definition or even a criterion of consciousness: "The subjectivity of our perception consists, above all, in the share taken by memory" (MM 75).

Spirit

Spirit was an important concept in early modern science. Newton was persuaded that mechanism is a dead-end and some form of spiritual life is the basis of the system of nature.[40] Comparable ideas are found in William Harvey, Robert Boyle, Leibniz of course, and even Galileo.[41] They offer variations on a pneumatic, spiritual principle to explain phenomena that mechanism can only ignore. "Pneumatic" refers to pneuma, the medium by which the Stoics' first principle energizes matter, introducing a tension or contraction that makes all things interpenetrate.[42] Hegel in *The Phenomenology of Spirit* is drawn to the concept of spirit for the same reason Newton was, and for which the Stoics introduced pneuma, namely, to endow forms with the continuity and dynamism of life.

We also find this theme in Bergson.[43] Spirit is another word for memory, more precisely for memory's power of temporal contraction and the synthesis of multiple durations: "With memory we are in very truth in the domain of spirit (*le domaine de l'esprit*)" (MM 320). Spirit is a word for the tendentious power that interpenetrates and contracts duration: "The humblest function of spirit (*l'esprit*) is to bind together the successive moments of the duration of things" (MM 295). It creates "a synthesis of past and present with a view to the future" (MM 294). He finds spirit, less humble but no less effective, wherever there is "progress to ever new creations, to conclusions incommensurable with the premises and indeterminable by relation to them" (CE 212).

Contracting and tensing are images for spirit's power to temporalize unity, to draw unity into time, binding many together in a form that endures, whether for nanoseconds or eons. The elementary work of spirit is to make successive phases of duration interpenetrate and define a continuous, enduring form, a "being," despite transient material fluctuations, and this it does by the simple expedient of memory, which is another word for consciousness. With spirit in matter, that is, with duration and memory, the past becomes effective and as Bergson said, bites into things. He describes this power as spirit for the same reason Newton did, to imply a difference between its action and mechanical causation. Spirit is a power but not a mechanical cause like inertia, gravity, or electricity, being instead a power of tendency, or what is tendentious about tendencies, what makes tendency *tend*, *tense*, *lean* into the future, contributing finality to the changes that draw it into existence.

A Strange Hypothesis

If Bergson's right, then it is a mistake to think our brain generates the images we perceive. Brain, blood, nerves, eyes—these are *images*. Images cannot generate images; all they do is change in response to other images. Brains do not produce images, they are part of them, part of matter, the aggregate of images. A related mistake is to think that memories are archived in the brain, even though practically every theory of memory in our scientific tradition is some version of this "trace" model.[44] Venerable as it may be, Bergson finds the hypothesis of trace and archive "strange," and it is easy to see why (MM 104). A brain is an image and so is a recollection. Can one image archive another image? If you photograph a photograph, the former photo does not remain one. Instead, one image (the first photo) changes into another (the second photo). Try to archive an image in an image and all you get is a new image, not the preservation of a past one.

The psychology of the trace explains recognition as follows. I perceive something X; at a later time, I perceive something Y, and am caused (by laws of association) to perceive (albeit less vivaciously) a trace-image of the earlier perception X. I recognize what I perceive when I perceive the resemblance between present perception, Y, and Z, the present trace drawn, from memory's archive, of the past X. However, since any two ideas are somewhat resembling, resemblance cannot explain the association between, in this case, present perception, Y, and the recollection image, Z, nor can Z's mere faintness account for memory's pastness. Recollection must *refer* to the past, which requires intentionality, not resemblance, nor can faintness make an image refer to the past and not instead mark it as a dream or enervated sensation.

Perception is incapable of evoking the memory that resembles it because to do so the perception must already have its complete form, which no perception attains without the supplement of memory. Perception "only becomes complete and acquires a distinct form through that very memory, which slips into it and supplies most of its content" (ME 207). So memory is required for perception and cannot be a secondary effect of it, as trace theories assume. The objection to this venerable psychology is to its conceiving memory as a kind of perception and perception as a kind of knowing. Bergson thinks perceptual recognition is a kind of movement, a motor behavior, namely, fluent action with apprehended affordances. Such action expresses the adaptive alliance of memory and perception, in other words, experience.

The brain is not an archive and the past requires no storage. On Bergson's account, neurology is a channel and filter, selectively initiating attention to virtual images of the past. The brain and entire nervous system afford past images a conduit by which to communicate their experience to present choice. The need for a response to sensed change is a lure to draw relevant, "resembling" memories from the past, contributing their experience to perception. Perceived images resemble memory images not merely by some common quality, but by eliciting a resembling response, sketching the same attitude, beginning the same movements: "It is the identity of reactions to different actions which . . . gives them resemblance or brings it out" (CM 40). Resembling perceptions are alike not in their qualities or appearance but in the action they tend to initiate.

Beginning with the first neurons, evolution has predisposed nervous systems adaptively to modulate life's interface with the past, making memory functional for survival. Not just *anything* you might recollect is going to promote adaptive action. If you are attacked in the dark and find yourself flooded with recollections of a recent party (this happens), it's no advantage. Memory is adaptive only when something controls the gates of the past, which is the function of neurology. It limits memory to recollections that are useful and adaptive and lets the rest lapse in unconsciousness. Bergson says that "the brain's part in the work of memory" is not to *preserve* the past, "but primarily to mask it, then to allow only what is practically useful to emerge through the mask" (ME 71). The whole past is constantly pressing "from the depth of the unconscious," while "consciousness, attentive to life, only admits, legally, those which can offer their assistance to the present action" (ME 177).

Since memories are not stored in the brain, no lesion to the brain can affect memory. Lesion, or brain damage, can impair movement, including speech, but it cannot impair memory because nothing of memory was ever in the brain at all. Memories are in the past. The brain is a medium by which past images become effective again, and that is what lesion can impair. For instance, should lesion damage the fine motor control required to produce speech, it would look to the world as if a person forgot how to talk. This can happen in different ways, which medicine knows collectively as the aphasias. Bergson thinks these disorders are wrongly regarded as pathologies of memory (as they were in his time) and are better understood as pathologies of the sensorimotor system (as they now are).[45] Neurological lesion damages not memory-traces, but rather the channels through which the past is effective. "Memories need, for their activation, a motor ally" (MM 152), and the brain "is a storehouse of motor habits [i.e., allies] but not of memories" (ME 35). The supposed destruction of memories is a disruption of these motor habits. French neurology eventually warmed to these arguments and to Bergson's alternative, which is to regard aphasias as sensorimotor impairments rather than diseases of memory.

Neurons in Action

Even the most primitive organism is irritable and selectively responsive to stimuli. The same stimulus by which an organism becomes aware of change initiates a typically adaptive response. So perception is not a "state." It is a process, a movement, an ensemble of reciprocally activating tendencies to action and associated physiological changes. In higher organisms, peripheral excitation is made to pass through the brain before descending back down the spinal cord to muscles and eventually whole-body action, which amplifies the indeterminacy, hence flexibility, of response.

Bergson did not live to experience electronic computers. He takes his metaphor for the brain from an older technology, the telephone exchange or switchboard (MM 19). This was a wall-size assemblage of cables and switches connecting incoming and outgoing telephone lines, the machine the first telephone "operators" operated, and it is Bergson's brain in a nutshell. Incoming lines are the afferent, sensory nerves, outgoing lines the efferent nerves activating muscles, with the brain routing, rerouting, allowing, and delaying contact, creating a buffered zone of indeterminacy that begins with hesitation and ends with choice. Such a brain is "an instrument of analysis in regard to the movement received, and an instrument of selection in regard to the movement executed" (MM 20).

This instrument has a power new in life's evolution, a power to reconnect itself, thus evading fixity. Bergson returns to the brain-as-switchboard in *Creative Evolution,* where the image has mutated into a machine that behaves "as if it were made of india-rubber and could, at any moment, change the shape of all its parts" (CE 252). Material systems have never been so non-mechanical as the human neurology. Our body is a machine as any body is a machine, yet its evolution found a path through mechanical determination to a point where it overcomes it. Life has contrived "to create with matter, which is necessity itself, an instrument of freedom, to make a machine which should triumph over mechanism, and to use the determinism of nature to pass through the meshes of the net which this very determinism had spread" (CE 264).

Neurology introduces an indeterminacy that did not exist before the evolution of metazoan life and the first neurons. Animals adapted to this uncertainty need to be good at selecting and preferring, choosing in adaptive rather than suicidal ways. As instinct recedes, the need becomes urgent for clever, cunning, above all adaptive choice. Before choice becomes adaptive, an organism must be capable of changing its environment in novel ways by organ-instruments (e.g., limbs). With that, a zone of uncertainty surrounds every perception and affords a diagram of potential interaction. We see where we can grasp things, where we can introduce pauses, make them stop, link or divert their changes. It is appropriate for Bergson to regard hesitation as the primary expression of consciousness (CE 144). That's what memory does to us; we pause, consult experience, then choose. The more experience the more alert the consciousness. He had written in *Matter and Memory* that "the chief office of consciousness is to preside over action and to enlighten choice" (MM 182). Five years later, he tells readers to "think whatever you like about matter 'in itself' or mind 'in itself'; at the point at which true, precise consciousness appears, I can show you something absolutely novel, a certain indeterminacy or contingency, a *capacity to choose*."[46]

The Reality of the Past

Belief in things continuing to exist unseen is common sense, so why not continuing to exist in the past? We take for granted that the bed we left this morning remains where it was, but we suppose that the events of the past are gone. The reason is that bodies in space obey a strictly determined order. Lines link any point to every other. The points they pass through are independent of perception and constrain the order of our sensations. To draw a two-dimensional analogy:

A———————B———————C

You cannot depart from A and arrive at C but not pass though B. Ghosts do that and you can do it in a dream, but bodies in space never behave that way. It is this geometry, not experience, that convinces us things do not change merely by withdrawing perception. Bodies are held in the embrace of spatial order and do not move unless displaced by another's motion. Withdrawing perception cannot alter a body's location, instead it merely falls out of view.

The past is different from that, it is not geometrical; memories are not laid out like stations on a line. We remember in any sequence and do not have to pass through more recent memories to reach a deeper past. A present image passing into the past is no different from an image withdrawn from perception by someone's exiting a room. Unperceived, the room and its contents are unconscious images, and so is the past. Images survive the passage of time as they do the withdrawal of perception. Passing into the past is passing into virtual existence. Virtual existence in the past is as real as unseen existence in vacated rooms.

Augustine in *Confessions* says, "Neither the past nor future but only the present truly is."[47] He may be remembering a Stoic teaching, "Past time and future time do not exist but subsist; only present time exists."[48] For Bergson this idea is entirely without merit: "If the past were annihilated from moment to moment, thought would be annihilated with it. The 'pure present' is unawareness (*présent pur, c'est l'inconscience*)."[49] What is lost with the passing of the present is attention, because attention fixes the here and now of "the present." Withdraw attention and a present passes and becomes ineffectual, which prejudices us against its reality when the truth is we merely cannot act on the past. Since we can act only on the present, pragmatic prepossession equates presence with reality.

We cannot search the past or memory as we might search a drawer. We can act on a drawer, empty it, take it apart, but we cannot act on the past or search it methodically, like sweeping out a galaxy with telescopes. We can only make ourselves receptive (that was the point of Freud's couch and the analyst out of sight). Memory "does not consist in a regression from the present to the past, but, on the contrary, in a progress from the past to the present" (MM 319). It comes back to us; we don't go looking for it: "Little by little it comes into view, like a condensing cloud; from the virtual state it passes into the actual; and as its outlines become more distinct and its surface takes on color, it tends to imitate perception" (MM 171).

The past and its experience come to bear on the present due to need for a response to local change. Perception, even incompletely recognized, will have initiated movements in anticipation of interaction. It is the feeling of incipient movement that opens a channel to virtual past images, which enjoy renewed actuality as a supplement to perception. If we are experienced, then we have prepared this action before, the body has felt this way before. Memories of past action recollect the whole bodily disposition, preparing for and enduring the change. Memory remembers skin conduction, pupil dilation, and sweat, an entire record of past interaction.[50] Such feelings open the present to memories of their felt quality, which contract with the present, interpenetrate, and enhance perception with their experience: "Any memory-image that is capable of interpreting our actual perception inserts itself so thoroughly into it that we are no longer able to discern what is perception and what is memory" (MM 125).

We open ourselves to the virtual past, attentive to felt resemblance, under the prompting of preparatory movements that sensation initiates in response to change. We *feel* a memory's relevance before we attend to it; "we perceive the resemblance before we perceive the individuals which resemble each other" (MM 214). Indeed, it is because of the feeling that we *do* attend to it, felt resemblance being the lure. We apprehend the resemblance of the past not by recognizing a good, sharp outline. Memories, images existing virtually in the past, have no form. "Form" is a metaphysical synonym of "actual" and "fully present," which makes it an inappropriate designation for past existence. We recognize the past image by recognizing the feeling with which we formerly responded, feeling its consistency with current feeling, which opens the way for past images to enhance present perception with their experience.

Absolute and Relative

Whether a body moves or not depends entirely on perspective. Geometry cannot distinguish between the rotation of a body and the rotation of its grid, or between things that grow and rulers that shrink. This relativity does not arise for the phenomena of duration. Suppose a body moves. Its boundaries and qualities are relative—to the organism, to the mode of perception, and to perspective; but the *moving*, the *passage*, is not relative at all. It is actual and absolutely so. Given a motion, the choice of coordinates is arbitrary, but that does not make the motion or its duration arbitrary. Movement and duration are independent of geometrical measurement. Body is relative; duration is absolute.[51]

"When I speak of an absolute movement, I mean that I attribute to what is moving an interior and, as it were, psychic states" (CM 159). A motion is like a moment of consciousness in being a phenomenon of duration, interpenetrating and temporally continuous. Bergson sets aside the nominalist analysis of movement, which equates it with a series of positions. I mentioned this nominalist legacy, which, passing through Descartes has dominated modern thought; for example, Bertrand Russell: "Motion consists in the fact that, by the occupation of a place at a time [i.e., an instant], a correlation is established between places and times; when different times, throughout any period however short, are correlated with different places, there is motion." At any interval we always have an instantaneous body at a point: "Motion consists *merely* in the occupation of the different places at different times . . . there is no transition from place to place."⁵²

By this means, the passage of time is eliminated in favor of spatial displacement, a difference of places, which allows quantitative measure but eliminates temporality, treating movement not as a duration but as a spatial series. Ockham says all that is needed for motion "is that the body was first in one place and afterwards in another place, and so on continuously, so that never in the entire time does it rest in any place. And it is clear that outside of all these, nothing different from permanent things is assumed." Motion (*motus*) "is not something else in addition to enduring things."⁵³ In other words, it is nothing in itself, which is Zeno's conclusion again. Bergson reverses Ockham's axiom. Instead of motion being nothing in addition to enduring things, enduring things (bodies, images) are nothing in addition to motions. A body is an image; suppress action and discontinuous form melts into universal interaction. "There do not exist things made, but only things in the making, not states that remain fixed, but only states in process of change. Rest is never anything but apparent, or rather, relative.... All reality is, therefore, tendency (*tendance*), if we agree to call tendency a nascent change of direction" (CM 158–59).

In Plato's *Timaeus*, the eternal model of the Ideas imposes regularity on the directionless motility of elements. On Bergson's account, a cosmos arises with the introduction of duration into extensity, contracting past and present, seeking repetitions, and creating forms (i.e., images). This is the work of life, which introduces enduring bodies (organisms) to formless extensity.

Despite the continuous nature of stimuli, whether light, sound, or other media, organisms reliably divide the signal into discrete categories, introducing discontinuity. Discontinuous, categorical perception may be the most basic phenomenon of cognition and is ubiquitous in life.[54] Perception, Bergson says, "marks out divisions in the continuity of the extended, simply following the suggestions of our requirement and the needs of practical life" (MM 278). Needs are "so many search-lights which, directed upon the continuity of sensible qualities, single out in it distinct bodies" (MM 262).

We punctuate the material continuum wherever perceived invariants, synchronies, and rhythms afford opportunities to interact. Discontinuous bodies are artifacts of the form of life that perceives them. The objects of perception, by any sense on any scale, are centers of potential action and initiate a response, calling forth a virtual action that tends to actuality. We do not perceive *what things are*. We perceive tendencies, affordances, and "in our eyes, form is always the outline of a movement" (L 20). This is Bergson's point that the expression of perception is more muscular than propositional knowing-that.

The physical bodies of physical nature are physical images. Our perception of them is adjusted to species-specific adaptive interaction. Categorical perception induces discontinuity and that implies a substrate, which Bergson calls extensive becoming (*le devenir extensif*). Matter considered as a whole—the physical universe—is not a simultaneously present substance. It is a duration as yet unclosed, an unfinished movement and tending to a finality Bergson will name only in the last sentence of his last book, where he refers to the universe as "a machine for the making of gods" (TS 317).

Physical Matters

Writing of physics in 1907, Bergson says, "the scientists who are pushing the study of their science furthest incline to believe... that neither creation nor annihilation, for instance, is inadmissible when we are concerned with the constituent corpuscles of the atom. Thereby they tend to place themselves in concrete duration, in which alone there is true generation and not only a composition of parts" (CE 368–69). To think of matter as Max Planck and especially Niels Bohr began to enacts a profound break with classical atomism. The constituents of atoms (we say electron, proton, and neutron, though this is later physics) do not behave like Epicurean ultimate particles. Their movement is discontinuous and they undergo creation and annihilation, flouting everything that had made atoms an enticing speculation.

Erwin Schrödinger thought that "we are forced by observed facts to deny the ultimate constituents of matter . . . the dignity of being an absolutely identifiable individual."[55] The persistence of a photon, for instance, is not that of a corpuscle on a trajectory, but more like a melody, a resonant series of events momentarily coordinating emission and absorption. Schrödinger again: "A piece of matter is the name we give to a continuous string of events that succeed each other in time, immediately successive ones being as a rule closely similar."[56] Formed matter, bodies, have no instantaneous existence, resolving instead, as Bergson says, "into elementary vibrations, the shortest of which are of very slight duration, almost vanishing, but not nothing" (CE 201). These vibrations—quantized fields—endure and have duration (whatever the scale), which implies memory and panpsychic consciousness.

To conceive of matter as endowed with memory does not require one "to take one's own memory and transport it," for instance, into a rock. Bergson has a better help to the imagination. Imagine "a moment in the unfolding of the universe, that is, a snapshot that exists independently of any consciousness"; then imagine a second snapshot from as close as possible to the first. Do we not now have an interval, a duration, without involving memory? No. "Without an elementary memory that connects the two moments there will be only one or the other, consequently a single instant, no before and no after, no succession, no time" (DS 48). Material extensity is not timeless, but its past does not grow, the temporality reduced to a present that is always starting over. The advent of life comes not with the entry of memory or duration into matter, which were always virtually there. With life comes perception, which is the *actual use of memory* as an adaptation.

Human senses depend on chemical action with an energy of about one electron-volt.[57] Having evolved to interpret change on this scale, our senses obviously cannot detect movement among the molecules. A pion is a particle that typically decays (into gamma rays) after a lifetime of 10^{-16} seconds. Physicists call it stable, but its timescale is not one we can interact with except, of course, in a laboratory, where we supplement our senses with high-energy probes. Laboratories facilitate an experimental departure from the conditions of adapted perception, relieving perception of a compulsion to be practical and providing an opportunity to cultivate arts of disinterested observation.

With the instruments of experimental research, we can probe tendencies of formed matter at their scale, not limited by the scale of life beyond the lab. Objects of specialized and searching observation begin to resemble organisms; they have their own organization and do not merely reflect our virtual action. To entice a Higgs boson to allow us to measure it is more like convening a diplomatic interaction with an alien form of life than making an adaptive response to a changing environment. Yet even in the laboratory, perception does as it always does, seeking invariants and synthesizing discontinuity. That is how we count and measure. But the discontinuity pursued in the laboratory arises not from where *we* stop, having arrived at a convenient platform for action, but where the movement that we're following stops or at least changes rhythm. The fundamental temporal unities in nature, such as the electron mass, the velocity of light, and Planck's constant, are on a scale as far removed from human practice as can be imagined.

Bergson's concrete extensity, the matter bodies embody, is probably not the perfect continuity Bergson expected when in 1896 he foresees future physics dissolving "the solidity and the inertia of the atom," and reinstating "universal continuity" (MM 265). He expected that "the nearer we draw to the ultimate elements of matter" the more we will observe "the vanishing of that discontinuity which our senses perceived on the surface." This discontinuity "is relative to our needs" and "every philosophy of nature ends by finding it incomparable with the general properties of matter" (MM 266). The discontinuity of the senses disappears on a microscopically closer scale, but if Bergson expected that discontinuity would ultimately vanish into pure continuity, he was probably wrong. Instead, the molar discontinuities of lifeworld experience are replaced by the unexpected discontinuities of quantum physics. Yet this physical theory did more than introduce discontinuity deep into nature. It also discovered new and unexpected continuity, foremostly the phenomenon of quantum entanglement.

Schrödinger observed that entanglement (a word he introduced for the phenomenon) "is not *one* but rather *the* characteristic trait of quantum mechanics."[58] When we try to put two fundamental particles with a history of interaction in two different places, we find it cannot be done. The particles have become so "entangled" that operations performed on one cannot be distinguished from operations performed on the other, regardless of the distance that separates them. Einstein thought this implication of the quantum theory was absurd, confirming his suspicion that the theory was incomplete. It is impossible for something *here* to affect something *there* except by an exchange of energy, which cannot exceed the limit velocity of light.

But such an exchange, a so-called a transluminal signal, is exactly what happens, as many experiments have confirmed. Nature does not respect locality, meaning that things can change in ways that cannot be explained mechanically in terms of local spatial changes. Einstein called nonlocal change "spooky action at a distance," but the intuitive locality he expected to refute the quantum theory instead inspired experiments that confirmed nonlocality. Entanglement has been observed in pairs of photons separated by more than a hundred kilometers.[59] Once fundamental particles have interacted, we apparently cannot separate the properties of one from the properties of the others, no matter their distance. The temporal continuity of an entangled past compensates for spatial discontinuity. No matter where they are, the most fundamental particles of matter cannot forget their past. As temporally interpenetrating, they do not need to be juxtaposed spatially to experience the same changes.

If, as Relativity concludes, there is no purely spatial distance, then while entangled bodies may be spatially discontinuous, they remain temporally contiguous and interpenetrating from their entangled past. On a molar scale these continuities are swamped, with results that confirm Einstein's intuition of locality, but on their own quantum scale the entangled entities are one melody unaffected by spatial difference. For geometry this may be a new face of continuity, nonlocal continuity, but that is what temporal continuity has always been. The granularity quantum physics finds at the bottom of nature, at the Planck scale of space, time, and energy, does not subvert continuity. It subverts a substantialist *idea* of continuity, the continuity of the homogeneous, which it replaces with unexpected modes of continuity (like quantum entanglement) that flout humanity's evolved, macroscopic expectations.

Time is distinguished from space by a kind of asymmetry called anisotropy. Isotropic space has no intrinsic orientation, like Cartesian space, with no up or down, left or right. Time, however, is anisotropic, it has an orientation: the past only grows. In the latter nineteenth century, Ernst Mach and Ludwig Boltzmann proposed that this asymmetry expresses the second law of thermodynamics, the so-called entropy principle. In other words, they proposed to identify temporal passage with the down-gradient glide of the universe to entropic disorder. The ever-growing past is the ever-growing entropy of the universe. This assumes that the universe is a closed thermodynamic system whose entropy ineluctably rises, tending to the disappearance of all process and what Arthur Eddington described as "the final running down of the universe."[60] Gilbert Newton Lewis demonstrated the mistake in this thinking. An isolated system does not necessarily move to equilibrium: "It will move toward it and move away from it, and in the long run as often in one direction as in the other."[61] If that is not enough, what must finally refute the identification of temporal passage with entropy is the unexpected discovery that the universe has already very nearly attained maximum entropy. The point is worth a closer look.

About half a million years into the Big Bang, the early universe was sufficiently cool for atoms to stay formed. From that point, all the electrically charged matter (protons and electrons) is locked in stable, electrically neutral atoms. Electromagnetic radiation (photons) does not interact with electrically neutral particles, so atomic matter and radiation decouple, and the photons fly to the end of the universe. This primordial radiation has been receding and cooling ever since. It now pervades all space in a cosmic fog of photons reaching to the horizon of the universe, with a temperature three degrees above absolute zero.[62]

This cosmic background radiation is very old, nearly as old as the universe. It is (almost) without structure, having (almost) the same temperature and intensity across the entire volume of the universe. And there is a lot of it. For every particle of baryonic matter (protons and neutrons), which composes the mass of macroscopic bodies, there are 10^9 photons in the background radiation. There is so much of it, so nearly homogeneous, that most of the energy of the universe is already in this degraded state of cold photon radiation. As we go back in time, total entropy remains nearly constant. All the stars burning out would contribute only a fraction to the total entropy already realized in an early phase of cosmic evolution.[63]

The cosmic background radiation was discovered and measured in the 1990s. It was subsequently determined that it is the largest pool of entropy in the universe only if we ignore gravity and the entropy of black holes, which, if taken into account swamps the background photons.[64] In any case, the lurid image of a universe sliding into entropic heat-death is fantasy, not physics. No inexorable cosmic tendency exists for energy to degrade, and it is untenable to attribute time's anistrophy to this source.

Bergson is of course unaware of these findings, but he was already cautious about equating anisotropy with thermodynamic entropy. He views entropy as a phase shift in the evolution of matter, when bodies melt back into continuous extensity. He compares the evolution of the universe to a falling weight: the weight tends to fall, energy tends to dissipate, but like any tendency it is not unopposed. What opposes it is the counter-entropic tendency of life. That is why James Lovelock could argue that there was no need for a landing to determine whether life exists on Mars. All one need do is measure the entropy of the atmosphere, which is an infallible detector of planetary life. Anywhere that atmospheric entropy is remotely as low as the earth, planetary life exists to a certainty.[65]

The evolution of life and the entropic de-evolution of matter are two interpenetrating passages of time, two tendencies leaning into the future, each opposing the other. That is what life and matter are for Bergson—tendencies. Matter tends to determinism and life tends to individuality. We cannot know that life will overcome entropy, but it retards it very effectively. Bergson's alternative to the entropic death of the universe is evolution unlimited and irreversible. The cosmic struggle is not between order and chaos or empty and full but between mechanical order (including entropy) and vital finality (CE 226). Local regression is possible, even catastrophic extinction, but the eventual death of life is not a foregone conclusion.

Psychological duration and organic evolution are irreversible, indeed all concrete (not abstract and closed) genesis is irreversible.

A process is time-invariant, or reversible, if it can be reversed (conceptually) by reversing the signs of the motion variables. I mentioned (Chapter 1) that Émile Meyerson thought mechanical reversibility was purely ideal and real change is irreversible.[66] It would be a mistake to confuse the formal time-reversibility of equations with a dynamic reversibility of the processes they describe. Just because mathematically consistent solutions exist when signs in equations are reversed does not mean the reverse process is physically possible.[67] The temporal reversibility ascribed to a system in a box cannot be extrapolated to the open universe, which has not stopped expanding and continues to grow, making irreversible temporal passage a cosmological predicament.

Chaos and Nonbeing

We tend to suppose a concept that serve us well (for instance, in science) is more than an advantageous contrivance. Why would it work so well, if not for the adequacy and truth of its disclosure? Isn't that the best explanation? Not only does this argument aggrandize the preference of a contingently evolved neurology. The error is not innocent, being a fertile source of pseudo-problems in philosophy. Some philosophers, including Bergson, think philosophy is flush with such problems and needs thorough laundering before serious work can recommence: "I believe that the great metaphysical problems are in general badly stated, that they frequently resolve themselves of their own accord when correctly stated, or else are problems formulated in terms of illusions which disappear as soon as the terms of the formula are more closely examined" (CM 77).

Ludwig Wittgenstein was another who found nothing in philosophy but pseudo-problems. Philosophy has nothing to say of its own, being at best a mode of therapy for problems that never should have been raised and can only be analyzed into dust and made to float away: "The results of philosophy are the uncovering of one or another piece of plain nonsense and of bumps that the understanding has got by running its head up against the limits of language."[68] Bergson disagrees with the diagnosis and dispenses with the therapy. Philosophy's pseudo-problems are not delusions of grammar; they flatter our amour-propre and reify unconscious utilitarianism. The pseudo-problem of determinism arises from this source, as do problems concerning chaos and nonbeing. The idea of chaos raises problems when we assume disorder is the original condition and order something added, the problem being *how*. And if order ultimately comes from nothing, what prevents it from lapsing back? Why is there something, anything, not nothing at all?

Einstein once said the most incomprehensible thing about the universe is that it is comprehensible. Years later someone prompted him to explain: "A priori one should expect a chaotic world which cannot be grasped by the mind in any way."[69] Why that should be the default expectation he does not say. Perhaps he thought that order is something more than disorder, something positive, emerging from or added to primitive chaos. While order can appears to us as *fact*, disorder, "which appears to us to be less than order, is, it seems, of *right*" (CE 231). An idea of cosmic birth from chaos appears in many traditions, for instance Hesiod: "Assuredly, at the very first, came the Abyss, then followed Earth with its wide bosom, ever sure foundation for all." Plato reformed the myth for philosophy: "Before it came into its present order as a universe it was an utter chaos of disorder . . . a bottomless abyss of unlikeness."[70] Descartes observed that "it does not agree so well with the sovereign perfection of God to make him the author of confusion rather than order."[71] Order is more, better, higher.

Bergson regards this entire line of thought as erroneous, the error arising from the habit of spatializing time and reifying utility. He begins with the disorder familiar from practical life—say, the shocking disorder of the hotel room you just rented. What does disorder mean in such a case? Mechanically, geometrically, the order of the room is impecable. Everything is where antecedent causes determine it to be, though the room is a mess, hardly what you expect. Obviously, this disorder is the absence of one order and the unexpected prominence of a different order to which one is indifferent. Let us therefore suspend all regular causality and imagine laws of nature randomly violated. Against the spontaneous emergence of predictability, we might introduce a demon to randomize incipient regularity. Still, we are far from chaos. What we have instead is an artfully contrived and extremely, even excessively improbable order. It is improbable that anything should be so improbable. Randomness is not the essence of disorder and does not mean no order; it means the equal probability of a range of orders. Shuffling cards produces an improbable order, not a disorder.[72]

Bergson concludes that *disorder* cannot be thought absolutely. Order and disorder cannot shake their anthropomorphism. Order is nothing positive, nothing inherent, and what we call disorder is merely order of an unexpected or irrelevant sort. Einstein was wrong to think (if he did) that disorder is simpler, more basic or given than order. The reverse is true; there is not less but more in disorder than in order, namely, some idea of order plus its negation. Things are in order when we perceive expected affordances to our action: "Reality is *ordered* exactly to the degree that it satisfies our thought," that is, our expectation (CE 223).

Bergson reaches what was also Spinoza's conclusion. Spinoza thought that the right understanding of divinity precludes divine purpose in nature. Only a finite being has purposes, which imply a lack to be overcome by an instrument and are thus unthinkable for God. So we should not regard nature as a divine purpose, but more than that, we should not regard nature as in any respect *ordered*. The idea of "natural order" is a prejudice, a shadow of our practice, a product of imagination, and a fallacy in philosophy. The Demiurge of Plato's *Timaeus* reasons in the way Spinoza criticizes: "Finding the visible universe in a state not of rest but of inharmonious and disorderly motion, the god brought it to order from disorder, as he judged that order was in every way better."[73] It is this order absolute, an order *in* nature in advance of perception and interest, which Spinoza condemns as errant imagination, refuting those who believe "that there is an order in things . . . as if order were anything in nature more than a relation to our imagination."[74] Or as Bergson said, our expectation.

Why is there something, not nothing at all? Some philosophers think this is a profound question.[75] It seems to present an alternative—something, anything, or nothing at all. But do we understand this "nothing at all"? We can imagine emptiness outside—a spaceship drifting in extra-galactic space—but that assumes fullness within. Or we can imagine fullness outside and empty within—an empty jar sealed and tossed into the sea. But who can imagine empty inside and out, nothing but empty? Any "nothing" that we imagine is relative to something, a relative absence.

Well, isn't that the limitation of imagination? We cannot *imagine* nonbeing because what we imagine is what we can perceive and we cannot perceive what is not. However, a concept is not logically remiss for being unimaginable. Who can imagine square roots? Nonbeing is a logical concept and must be thought, not imagined. Since any given entity might be annihilated, the idea of *nothing* is the limit of annihilation. Annihilate *a*, annihilate *b*, annihilate *c*, and run all the way to the end and annihilate everything, leaving nothing. Of course, we would have to assume that this is a well-defined series converging on a unique limit, which seems unlikely. It is in any case a fallacy to infer that because this or that can be annihilated, therefore everything can be annihilated. Any parent could be a father but all parents cannot be, any coin or bill could be counterfeit but not all of them.

What is it to think nonbeing? On Bergson's analysis it is to think a thing to be possible but not actual. The golden mountain and the unicorn do not actually exist, though there is no logical contradiction in their concept and they can be described as possible existence. To think nonbeing is to think such possibles contingently excluded from actuality. These possibles are not nothing.

The logical space of possibility is an ideal limbo created by reason to lodge all the sign-combinations that logic cannot fault but experience does not confirm, like golden mountain, unicorn, and so on. What we think does not exist *does* exist as a possible. Possibility is not a robust, concrete mode of existence but neither is it sheer nonbeing. It is the possibility of a combination of signs, a syntactic possibility, an ideal, intentional *ens rationis*, not physical or natural. Democritus might call it *nomos*, "convention."

Whatever you say about possibilities, do not call them virtual. Virtual existence is dynamic, which distinguishes it from Aristotelian potential, and it is obscure, which distinguishes it from possibilities, with their precise address in logical space. It may seem that possibility is fundamental, since before something actually happens, it must be possible. That is correct when it means there must be no insurmountable obstacle to its occurrence. But this *no obstacle* condition does not imply that the event enjoys preexistence as a clear and distinct logical possibility. Bergson argument resembles that of Francisco Suárez, for whom the only "logical possibility" is what he calls *potentia logica* and explains as non-repugnance. "Non-repugnance of being ... is usually called 'the logically possible.' " This logical possibility "does not consist in any simple and real faculty [i.e., power or positive reality], but in the mere non-repugnance of the extremes." It is a creation of the mind, belonging "to the composition and division of the mind that logic is concerned with."[76]

No possibility of *Hamlet* existed until *Hamlet* was created. Once created, we imagine that it was always possible, even though that very possibility was unimaginable until the thing happened. Its "possibility" is a shadow cast by the present over the past, an operation Bergson calls the "retrograde movement of the true," that is, from actual truth back to a fallaciously induced antecedent possibility. "Backwards over the course of time," he writes, thought carries out "a constant remodeling of the past by the present, of the cause by the effect" (CM 84–85). As a result of the future, the past has changed, containing now a logical possibility that it did not before the seventeenth century. That is what Bergson described as a shadow that the historical *Hamlet* casts over the past. The important lesson in all of this is that not even logical possibility escapes temporal becoming.

A desperate nihilist or believer in nothing might argue that the concept of nonbeing can be constructed by the logical operation of negation. We simply negate everything: *For all x, not x*. If we can think this logical form, then nothingness is possible. The argument seems to depend on the logical power of negation, yet there is more to negation than logic. On Bergson's analysis, to negate is implicitly to affirm that something is possible and that something else, known or unknown, prevents the possibility from actually being the case. "Not all swans are white" analyzes as "It is possible that all swans are white, but the fact is otherwise." Contrary to the spirit Hegel vested in logic, negation creates no new content. It introduces nothing beyond the affirmation it judges and puts aside.

Negation presupposes existence twice over, the existence of possibilities and the extant actualities that exclude them. C. S. Peirce also made this point: "*Not* means *other than*, and *other* is merely a synonym of the ordinal number *second*. As such it implies a first." He thinks of negation existentially, like a death. "The nothing of negation is the nothing of death, which comes *second* to, or after, everything."[77] A comparable thesis has been argued with much subtlety: "There is no negative content to negative predication over and above that which is provided by the occurrence of the positive predication within it." The *negating* is not in the logical form but in how it is presented dialogically: "Negative predication is the display, through an assertoric gesture, of the positive predication inside the context of negation."[78] This is comparable to Bergson's idea that negation is not about things but about people's statements. "The cat is black" is about a cat. "The cat is not white" is about somebody's statement that a cat is white. What we negate is typically what somebody else affirms, and we negate not a content but its affirmation.

Bergson concludes that an absolute concept of nonbeing is as incoherent as an absolute concept of disorder. What we call *nothing* is always *something*, just not what interests us. As for why there is anything at all, the question takes concepts that are only functional on a human scale for a human purpose and creates an unconditional opposition. There is no "nothing at all," so the alternative is specious and the question either confused or sophistical.

The theme of Bergson's philosophy is continuity. Life and matter, body and mind, quality and quantity, space and time—these are not categorically different; they are continuous, each becoming the other under different conditions. In *Time and Free Will* he denied contact between the extended and nonextended (TFW 70). Then he said they meet in perception (MM 202). Only a difference of degree separates being and being perceived (MM 30): "Matter, as grasped in concrete perception, which always occupies a certain duration, is in great part the work of memory" (MM 237). Spatial extension is temporal tension (interpenetration) interrupted by sense-induced discontinuity. Perception punctuates natural continuity to distribute figures over a ground. That is the work of perception, any perception, and it is work perception cannot complete without memory. So even virtual and actual are continuous, which explains an otherwise puzzling remark: "There is no virtuality, or, at least, nothing definitively virtual; whatever exists is actual or could become so" (*Il n'y a pas de virtualité, ou du moins rien de définitivement virtuel dans les choses. Tout* CE *qui existe est actuel ou pourra le devenir*; (ME 235). That *could become* is crucial. I take the remark to deny an absolute virtual, a heavenly virtual sequestered from actuality. Instead, the virtual ceaselessly tends to actuality and the message once again is continuity.

* * *

This chapter began with Bergson's ideas about body, image, and perception. He defines matter as an aggregate of images. Perception perceives these same images formatted for evolved, species-specific interaction. To say that matter is an aggregate of images is to say that bodies are stabilities which organisms perceptually detect and are relative to their form and scale of life. A thing, a body, "necessarily participates in the immobility of a *point of view*" (CM 157). A body, a material form, is a center of relations created by perception, not found in matter, which is all continuity, no boundaries, no forms, or species, only fluctuation, rhythm, and resonance. Though body is relative, duration and its phenomena are absolute. A movement, for instance, is an undecomposable, qualitative duration, as different from another as red from blue.

The images we perceive are in the environment where we interact with them and not in our eyes or brain. The brain does not create images; it is one of them, and the molecular motions of nervous tissue that accompany perception do not create images but prepare action. Perception is virtual action, a motor phenomenon, and memory is virtual experience, tending to become actual experience as a supplement to perception. The brain does not create images, neither does it store them; memories are temporal and require no storage. Neurology is a channel and filter, selectively initiating attention to the virtual images of memory. The brain and nervous system afford past images a means by which they lend their experience to choice.

Spirit temporalizes unity, which makes it endure. Its efficacy is that of tendency, the efficacy of a final cause, contributing immanent finality to efficient causes. Life and matter, body and mind, quality and quantity, duration and extension, actual and virtual—with time these all pass into each other.

Bergson advances a distinctive panpsychism. Most panpsychism follows Leibniz to identify consciousness with perception and perception with representation or sense content ("what it is like"). For Bergson, perception presupposes memory and it is the power of memory, not sense or representation, that distinguishes consciousness. Distinguishes it, but also makes it ubiquitous in matter and in the cosmos.

3
Élan Vital

Bergson introduced the idea of *élan vital* because he became convinced that Darwinism was a dead end. Schematically his argument is as follows. Darwinism is the strongest version of biological mechanism since Democritus; therefore, the refutation of Darwinism delivers the coup de grâce to mechanical biology. As for the refutation, in thinking about evolution we must not forget time's irreversible, anisotropic quality, which as an event or process biological evolution inherits and which excludes mechanical causation. Mechanical causation is reversible, life and evolution are not, and nothing irreversible can be the effect of a reversible cause. With biological mechanism a dead letter, Bergson unfolds the rest of his argument.

The evolution of terrestrial life is a single movement, understanding movement as an indivisible, qualitatively singular duration. This movement began some four billion years ago and remains ongoing, a movement that has yet to reach its end. This movement is *vital* because it begins with the origin of terrestrial life and has evolved to the present. Bergson describes it as an *élan* because this ancient, ongoing event has the impetuous quality of tendency, striving to become all that it can be. The originating impetus of life "is finite and it has been given once for all" (CE 254). Life at the origin already has all the tendency ever to be expressed in terrestrial evolution.

Élan vital is thus an event, datable to the origin of terrestrial life, and it is the process or movement thereby initiated, which remains active, with an immanent, internal finality. *Élan vital* is the final cause of terrestrial life. Not the efficient, moving cause but the final one, that is, the tendency, the immanent cause of evolution's trends. That is most of the argument on which I'll expand in this chapter. Additionally, since biological evolution is a phase of cosmic evolution, I'll review Bergson's ideas in light of scientific cosmology. Unfolding his thought on evolution and the human future is an opportunity to compare ideas with Nietzsche, another pioneer in evolutionary epistemology and ontology.

The Vitalist Canard

Bergson explained matter as the aggregate of images. What about *living* matter, organisms? Are other animals mere anthropocentric images of our potential interaction? Organisms seem organized not for *our* action but for *theirs*. Acknowledging this, Bergson writes, "As we rise from the inorganic to the organized, we find ourselves in the presence of facts that are more objectively willed as facts by nature itself," that is, accomplished by nature, with natural finality.[1] When he ascribed this finality to a vital *élan*, the idea became a red flag for critics, who gleefully added *vitalist* to his outrages.

The controversy around vitalism is as old as Aristotle's disagreement with Democritus.[2] Is life's a higher kind of being than that of the inanimate? Aristotle thought it was and located the difference in a power of self-movement, which he identified with soul (*psuche*). That is vitalism in a nutshell. Life requires a principle whose action is a final rather than efficient or material cause. There had been talk of vital principles in medicine for a long time, but no *vitalism* until the beginning of the nineteenth century, when Charles-Louis Dumas, a medical professor at Montpellier, introduced the neologism *vitalisme* to epitomize a Montpellier teaching associated with Théophile de Bordeu and Paul-Joseph Barthez.[3]

This approach to medicine emerged in the 1730s, inspired by then new work of Georg-Ernst Stahl, who was writing against Cartesian medicine and the reduction of life to mechanical action.

Stahl thought living beings are wholes with parts internally related; the whole is efficient and the parts cooperate. He observed that while ablated organs rapidly rot, disease is an exceptional condition; and protoplasm, being fat and water, is poorly mixed and easily corrupted, yet flesh is stable and vital. It seems that everything merely chemical or mechanical about vital processes tends only to their dissolution. Stahl inferred a further factor, an extra-chemical, extra-mechanical, immaterial spirit of life that resists degeneration. This *anima* gives the soul a power to do what it apprehends to be necessary for survival.

The Montpellier physicians pay homage to Stahl, but they silently drop his equation of the vital principle with an apperceptive *anima*. Where Stahl was an "animist," the Montpellier physicians are "vitalists," with a vital principle that operates independently of the body but also independent of consciousness, that being the difference from Stahl.[4] These first vitalists aspire to reunite humanity and nature from Cartesian exile, creating a medical language of reciprocity, sympathy, and synergy to express the threads of relation that bind them. Living things are distinguished from inanimate bodies by reciprocal interaction and economic rapports. The vital force is a force *sui generis*, independent of corporeal structure, and purposeful in the preservation of health. Barthez emphasized purposiveness in his explanation of the vital principle's watchful independence, admiring how it suspends normal chemical affinities and responds with finesse to all of life's requirements.

By the end of the eighteenth century, the long-awaited Cartesian physiology had failed to materialize. Far from finding anything mechanically simple, living systems revealed new complexity the closer researchers probed. Vitalist ideas began to attract attention beyond medicine, in physiology and chemistry. Researchers were only then acquiring the basics of biochemistry; blood groups, enzymes, vitamins, and hormones were all new ideas. The vitalists of this generation felt the need of a principle to make the leap (as it seemed to them) from inorganic chemistry to the biochemistry of vital processes. For instance, chemists introduced vital forces to form and maintain organic compounds, which combine against the affinity of their elements; and facts from embryology were thought to justify a vital principle in physiology.

By the mid-nineteenth century, a vitalist could be expected to adduce experimental grounds in support of an extra-physiochemical cause or agent, either a special substance peculiar to living things or a special property peculiar to tissue. This line of thought reached its apex in the research of plant physiologist Justus von Liebig. He proposed that the organization of matter in tissues generates a *Lebenskraft*, a power of life, which explains why chemical operations are so different inside and outside a living body. Different forces are acting. For instance, outside the body, organic compounds spontaneously oxidize, yet inside the tendency is resisted, as life requires. Liebig felt enough confidence in his idea to write, "It must be admitted as a law demonstrated by experiment that plants elaborate proteinaceous compounds, and that it is these compounds that are molded by the vital force under the influence of atmospheric oxygen and the components of water, to create all the numerous tissues and organs of the animal economy."[5] Notice that this vital force is local, an efficacious agent in an organism's internal economy. This will be important when we come to Bergson.

Vitalism was still vital in Bergson's time, prominently in the work of Hans Driesch.[6] He distinguished an old vitalism, from Stahl to Liebig—the vitalism relentlessly criticized by Lotze, Bernard, Helmholtz, and others—and his new vitalism. The old vitalism emphasized powers of finality or teleology, but the new vitalism emphasizes individuality and autonomy. Driesch postulates an individualizing causality that he calls *entelechy* to regulate cellular action. He takes the term from Leibniz, for whom entelechy is "something analogous to soul, whose nature consists in a certain eternal law of the same series of changes, a series which it traverses unhindered."[7] That makes entelechy good for synthesizing subordinated elements. Driesch thinks biology requires entelechy because under pure mechanism an individual is impossible even though living nature consists of nothing else. A material assembly is an inert accumulation, a heap. It cannot evolve or develop, there is no life in it.

He draws evidence of entelechy from embryology. "Embryological becoming is 'vitalistic' . . . it is impossible to comprehend it by the laws of physics and chemistry."[8] In experiments with sea-urchin eggs he found that cells isolated at the two-cell stage of development did not grow into two half-embryos but rather two complete individuals. Driesch concluded that the cells were pluripotent. Their development is not determined by spatially preformed physical or chemical structures, but rather by an entelechy that endows cellular factors with differential tendencies to form. He also enlisted phenomena of regeneration, as in Trembley's polyp or Driesch's own experiments with the regeneration of the lens in larval salamander eyes, which demonstrate the entelechy at work safeguarding the integrity of organisms and their organs.

Progress in experimental physiology and biochemistry has made these arguments superfluous. Along the way, "vitalism" became a term which, now devoid of denotation remained rich in connotations, all bad. However, the facts to which vitalists appealed are robust and were acknowledged by their critics, for example Claude Bernard:

> In the animate body there is an arrangement, a sort of ordering, that should not be overlooked, for it is truly the most salient trait of living beings. I admit that the idea of this arrangement is ill expressed by the term *force*. But here the word is of little importance; sufficient to say that the reality of the fact is beyond dispute.[9]

Death, disease, and the capacity for recovery are characteristics that distinguish life from mere existence. "Philosophical physicians and naturalists have been deeply struck by the tendency of organized beings to reestablish their form . . . and thus to demonstrate their unity, their morphological individuality."[10] Nevertheless, Bernard firmly resists vitalism, which he describes as a medical superstition and blames for promoting ignorance and quackery in the profession.

Where in all of this is Bergson? *Creative Evolution* singles out Driesch, then the first name in biological vitalism, for criticism. Neither the finality of the old vitalism nor the autonomy or individuality of the new one actually exist. The elements of a biological individual have their own individuality and each could claim a vital principle—a principle for human beings, another for their liver, a third for liver-cells, another for the cellular mitochondria— clearly an untenable proliferation. As for autonomy, no organism is isolated from its heritage or environment, secure in its own autonomous vital principle. Every animal buds from a parental body. Where would the vital principle of the individual begin or end?

The disagreement with Driesch is just the beginning of Bergson's argument with *vitalisme*. All the various vitalists were researchers who adduced experimental evidence in support of an extra-physical cause, either an agency peculiar to living things, like Driesch's entelechy, or a property peculiar to tissue, like Liebig's *Lebenskraft*. Bergson objects to the localization of finality, localizing the final cause in the organism and restricting finality to individual living beings, as both Liebig and Driesch do. Bergson argues that since each individual is "united with the totality of living being by invisible bonds," it must be a mistake "to restrict finality to the individuality of the living being. If there is finality in the world of life, it includes the whole of life in a single indivisible embrace" (CE 43).

A second argument criticizes the "superficial vitalism" of medical vitalists (for instance, Barthez), who locate in the living body a force capable of directing physical changes for the needs of life, "ever repairing faults, correcting effects of neglect or absentmindedness, putting things back in place" (CE 225). Allying himself with

Claude Bernard, he writes against "the superficial vitalism of those doctors and psychologists who affirm the existence, in the living being, of a force capable of battling against the physical forces and thwarting their action" (CM 173).

Bergson's most interesting argument criticizes an assumption shared by vitalists and the mechanists they oppose. Both look on organisms as fabrications and dispute whether mechanical causation is adequate or a vital supplement required. Descartes reassured his many readers that a mechanical explanation of vital form and function is just around the corner. With greater frankness, the vitalists explain these things *obscurum per obscurius* as the work of a vital principle. Yet these vitalists are still mechanists if we understand mechanism broadly. They want a force acting locally to cause the difference between bodies living and dead.

Machines are a byproduct of life and not something to which living beings are aptly compared. E. S. Russell, a wildlife biologist discreetly sympathetic to Bergson, elucidates his argument by contrasting an egg and a machine: "Man makes the parts of his constructs separately and fits them together. The egg works from within outwards; it proceeds by growth and self-differentiation, based upon directive metabolic activity, taking from the outside only raw materials which it builds into its own substance; there is no fitting together of prefabricated parts."[11] This is immanent finality, the organism acts on itself with a distinct tendency expressed in a life cycle.

The idea that organisms are assembled from parts draws plausibility from technology and our long acculturation to the use of tools.[12] To counteract the bias, Bergson updates Spinoza's argument against divine providence. To look on nature as mechanically complex, like our machines only more so, is a fallacious anthropomorphism. Such complexity is imaginary, a schematized perception modeled on our own action. It is a fallacy to regard organisms as marvels of complexity and worse to argue that their activity requires an extra-physical cause.

Bergson's *élan vital* is not another entry in the dreary catalogue of vitalist principles. It is not a local cause acting in an organism's life cycle, nor a cause that keeps the organism viable despite injury or lesion or cures it of disease. The scene and scale of the vital *élan*'s action is entirely different. This *élan* is the final cause of the evolution of life on Earth. This evolution is an event and like any event its eventuality has material and efficient causes and also a final cause, which is the tendency it expresses, and that is Bergson's *élan vital*. It is the immanent final cause of the evolution of life on earth, but it does not operate locally as a cause of organic action. Life is not a test tube process that might happen in an isolated pond of the primordial earth. It is a planetary process, depending on the existence of an ocean, climate stability, an appropriate atmosphere, vulcanism, and mineral surfaces.[13] Organisms are traces of the tendentious finality vitalizing the *élan*'s explosive and still-evolving movement.

Bergson's conception of a vital *élan* does not emerge from the context of medical or physiological vitalism. A better context is Bergson's place in the history of philosophical teleology, though to explain that requires a somewhat involved prolegomenon.

Finality or teleology was a topic of philosophical discussion from Anaxagoras in the sixth century BCE down to the end of Greek antiquity. In *Timaeus*, Plato synthesized the threads of a long argument among earlier philosophers, bringing everything into one system.[14] With Anaxagoras, he makes Mind (*Nous*) the source of finality in the cosmos, and external or extrinsic to the order it introduces. With Empedocles, this super-mundane creative source is imagined as an artisan, a demiurge. With Dionysus of Apollonia, Plato's creator acts for the best, and with Socrates he takes the order of nature to prove its intelligent cause.

Aristotle sets almost all of that aside. Natural substances have characteristic ways of changing, tendencies to their species-specific final ends. This tendency is an immanent final cause, a direction things have by their nature (*phusis*). Finality is built into individual natural substances, the power to be the form they are, directed by what is nature in them. This immanent principle does everything that Plato required a supernatural demiurge to persuade matter to do. Aristotle's rationale for immanent finality over Plato's supernaturalism is its consistency with an eternal world, which he holds against Plato's creationism.[15] The eternity of the world implies that no internal disharmony can lead to cosmic destruction. If the world *could* be destroyed, then given endless time it *would be* destroyed. Since the world exists it must always have existed. For the same reason, this eternal world must be organized for the best, with the species of life, their parts, and mutual relations optimized for the good of each. If a species *could* become extinct, then given endless time it *would be* extinct. Since infinite time has passed, the species of life must be optimally adapted to their conditions of existence.

The locus of Aristotelian finality is the *phusis* (nature) of the individual organism, and it was no doubt remembering this that later vitalists made the vital force local. Without the Unmoved Mover in its appointed place Aristotle's system of nature would collapse, but this Mover is not the final cause of organisms.[16] They have their finality immanently, given by *their* nature, which *complements* the system energized by the attraction of the Unmoved Mover, but is not *for* that system. Nothing about organisms is *for* anything except their being what they are. Motion is eternal and nature is the principle of motion in substances, so the substances, including the species of life, are eternal, and what makes them eternal gives them a finality or teleological tendency which defines their natural end and best activity.

Stoics sought to reconcile differences between Plato and Aristotle. In teleology, they merged Aristotle's immanent finality with an inventively reimagined *Timaeus*-style cosmology. Finality is immanent and belongs to nature, as Aristotle said, but it is not local, not inscribed in the nature of individual beings. Instead, the divine intelligence from which Plato's cosmos drew its finality is *also* immanent and fills the world with its pneuma. What in Plato was extrinsic and super-mundane Stoics bring inside the cosmos, joining Aristotle in setting aside what had been philosophy's oldest principle of teleology, namely, that the source of order cannot belong to the order it inaugurates, which as good as guarantees supernaturalism. Where Aristotle localizes finality in the individual organism, Stoics reconfigure the demiurge Plato stationed beyond creation as the immanent soul of the cosmic organism. The universe is a self-building machine, "not merely craftsmanlike (*artificiosus*)," Cicero wrote breathlessly, "but actually a craftsman (*artifex*)."[17]

Platonism proved amenable to a Christian appropriation that adjusted Plato's supernatural finality to biblical creationism, reinforcing the connection Plato made between finality in nature and a supernatural source. From the Middle Ages, finality in any form is assumed to presuppose purpose, that is, an intelligent cause, neglecting the immanent alternatives in Aristotle and Stoics. It is this Christian-Platonic teleology that seventeenth-century critics of final causes (Bacon, Hobbes, Descartes, Spinoza) refute. Not all of them advocate mechanism, as Descartes did, and Spinoza in particular goes a different way. His argument against final causes is really an argument against divine providence and does not affect the finalism of Spinoza's theory of *conatus*.[18] A *conatus* is not blind impact pushing mechanically from behind; it moves under the direction of a norm or ideal, namely, the essence of the finite mode. *Conatus* is a mode's tendency to endure. This is finality, tending to an end, though the end is not an intelligent design or purpose. The finality is immanent, the end simply to be what the thing essentially is.

Unlike Descartes, Spinoza allows finality in nature. What he denies is purpose, that is, finality by design, by an intelligent cause, or divine providence. Spinoza criticizes the medieval teleology that entrenched the Platonic equation of finality with intelligent purpose. His theory of *conatus* refutes the idea that finality requires purpose, which is also what Aristotle achieved against Plato with his theory of *phusis*. Every least mode of substance actively maintains its form with all its power, which is teleological, goal-directed activity and lodges finality deep in nature. *Conatus* may seem like another localization, but it is not, for it is not Spinoza's primary locus of finality, as the organism was for Aristotelian *phusis*. The power to exist, to maintain a form, which Spinoza ascribes to *conatus*, flows to the finite modes from the one substance, *Deus sive natura*, which is the ultimate source of finality, and as the being whose essence is to exist, the divine substance has no use for a *conatus*. Spinoza's is a Stoic model teleology, not Aristotelian.[19] For Aristotle the primary locus of finality is the individual organism, its *phusis*, while for the Stoics and Spinoza that locus is nature, the universe, and that, to come full circle, is also Bergson's idea.

The biological vitalists of the eighteenth and nineteenth century handled final causes amateurishly. They look for a nonmechanical mechanism, an immaterial force exercising a material effect. Bergson says life is not the work of a part, agent, or force operating locally but is instead a tendency, though not of individual organisms but of the *élan vital*, of which life's species are the trace. Bergson deviates from vitalist theories because he rejects their Aristotelian localization of teleology in the organism and even more their waffling notions of efficient and final causes. He develops a position in the line of philosophical teleology from the Stoics to Spinoza, replacing local finality with the terrestrial teleology of *élan vital*.

Among theories of evolution, Bergson criticizes finalist theories (Lamarck) no less than mechanical ones (Darwin) and proposes his alternative. He says mechanism and finalism are mirror-images of each other; "finalism is an inverted mechanism" (CE 41). But of course everything depends on the explanation of these textbook terms, and it turns out that the finalism Bergson repudiates is Platonic-style extrinsic finality, which is also what Spinoza refutes in his critique of divine providence. The biological finality Bergson rejects as inverted mechanism is a Platonic teleology of design. Both theories, mechanism and providence, are hostile to time and obstacles to taking time seriously. On their terms, biological evolution is either a mechanical impulse transmitted from the past or a magnet-like attraction to a prefigured future; in either case, all is given. Time and evolution are denied creative power.

Bergson's refutation of *that* finalism is consistent with his view that the evolution of life expresses a tendency and therefore has a final cause. He says "there has not, properly speaking, been any project or plan" (CE 265), adding elsewhere that the evolution of life "takes directions without aiming at ends" (CE 102). A direction, then, that is immanent and active without antecedent purpose. That describes the finality of tendency and tendency is what is *élan*-like about the vitality that appeared on the earth some four billion years ago.

Bergson did not call himself a vitalist and criticized all modern versions of vitalism. Furthermore, the biologists who were interested in Bergson's work were not vitalists or interested in Bergson because of vitalism. Bergson's biological readers saw him as having raised the status of biology, not by integrating it within physics, but by giving it a philosophical significance.[20] Writing independently in 1911, British biologists E. S. Russell and John Arthur Thomson both cite Bergson to make the same point. Russell says, "In organisms, the past is always interwoven to a certain extent with the present; we could say, borrowing Bergson's expression, 'the past is extended into the present.' Therefore, living beings must be explained by their history." He adds that "this fundamental fact alone is enough to absolutely distinguish between the biological and the physical sciences."[21] Thomson says nonliving things "do not trade with time. We do not need to remember their history in order to understand their present operations." However, "in the organism as Professor Bergson says, the past is prolonged into the present. Thus, we pass on to a new level of explanation or interpretation which is historical."[22]

These biologists acutely identify what Bergson thought was his important point against mechanism in biology. He says, "The essential argument I aim at mechanism in biology is that it does not explain how life unfolds a *history*, that is to say, a succession in which there is no repetition, in which every movement is *unique* and bears in itself the representation of the whole past."[23] Bergson continues to interest a later generation of biological philosophers dissatisfied with Modern Synthesis cant. "Biology is not done with Bergson."[24] Ideas formerly dismissed as vitalist are now welcome as nonreductive, including Bergson's animadversions against mechanism, which these philosophers turn against the new mechanism of molecular genetics.[25]

Darwinism

Evolutionists distinguish between the fact of evolution and the cause, which answer different questions. Like modern natural historians from Buffon to Lamarck and including his grandfather Erasmus, Charles Darwin affirms evolution (descent with modification) as a fact. What distinguishes him in this company is his hypothesis that natural selection, or survival of the fittest, is the principal cause. If true, that explains the history of life without recourse to supernatural creation, fulfilling the aspiration of materialism since Democritus. However, no few self-described Darwinists sided with Darwin only on the question of fact, and took different views of the cause. T. H. Huxley was one, Bergson is another.[26]

Bergson understands Darwin's theory to be an antiteleological, mechanical one of a sort that Hobbes or Descartes might approve. The maladapted are mechanically destroyed, the fit fortuitously survive and reproduce their heritable advantage. Let this mindless algorithm operate some millions of years and the diversity of terrestrial life is the result. Bergson probably exaggerates Darwin's aversion to teleology, but plenty of avowed mechanists read Darwin as Bergson did, including Huxley, who said that what struck him most forcefully when he read Darwin's book "was the conviction that Teleology, as commonly understood, had received its deathblow."[27] In Bergson's day, August Weismann's so-called Neo-Darwinism militantly advocated for the omnipotence of mechanical selection in the evolution of life.

Bergson counts it against Darwinism that it has no explanation of the origin of life. This is not an interesting criticism since the omission was deliberate and well considered. Darwin thought life's origin cannot be treated scientifically, at least not at his time, and as a scientist he had nothing to say about it. Bergson raises a more serious problem when he addresses the source of variation. Natural selection cannot operate until there are variations to select. Where do they come from? The answer of Darwinists then and now is that they are random products of chance. "I have spoken of selection as the paramount power," writes Darwin, "yet its action absolutely depends on what we in our ignorance call spontaneous or accidental variability."[28] Today we hear of copying errors and mutations and suppose the business is better understood but it is not. The efficacy of mutation for speciation is speculative. Why are we sure it is the sufficient cause of all the variation in the history of life? Especially when it would take a miracle for random variation to endow mutants with a cumulative differential mortality while protecting them from unfavorable mutations.[29]

Since the consolidation of biology's Modern Synthesis, it has been understood that natural selection can keep variation in populations, so in case of need no one has to wait for a favorable mutation but merely draws on the pool already in the population. The question though is where that pool came from, and random mutation still seems an unsatisfactory answer. Bergson's idea that mutations are not random but biased has reemerged in genetics, fortified with evidence that "propensities of evolutionary change reflect propensities of mutation."[30] One conclusion returns biological philosophy to where Bergson was before the Modern Synthesis. "Evolutionary change is not always composed of infinitesimal increments, and the character and dynamics of variation influence the rate and direction of evolutionary change."[31] This is Bergson's argument. Tendencies born with the vital *élan* are expressed in variations and bias the direction of evolution.

Bergson agrees that the cause of variation is probably individual differences in what Weismann called the germ line, meaning the sex cells, but he disputes the Neo-Darwinist claim that these differences are random relative to the evolution of life. Life is not sheer contingency or a lurching series of accidental equilibria. Life is an enduring, symphonic movement-in-motion. We can be sure that its cause is not a mechanical one. Mechanical thought symbolizes time in calculations but allows passage no efficacy. Bergson thinks that should embarrass evolutionists because evolution *takes time*. There is no better proof of time's efficacy than the facts of geology and evolutionary biology, and if time makes a difference, evolution cannot be the effect of a reversible mechanism.

This rather dialectical argument ignores the empirical aspect of evolution—the evidence, the history of life. In response, Bergson builds an empirical case against Darwinism relying on the evidence of convergent evolution. It sometimes happens that practically identical characteristics, including complex organs like eyes, evolve by different paths in distant lineages, with no common ancestor expressing the convergent form. An example is the convergent evolution of eyes, specifically the so-called camera eye (not a compound eye like a fly), which appears with practically identical anatomy in vertebrates, mollusks, and some snails and spiders. Darwin proposed that adaptations arise through the gradual accumulation of many small, chance variations. Bergson thinks the evidence of convergent evolution refutes that hypothesis and takes biological mechanism down with it. Eyes just once are improbable. Now add that accidental causes occurring in an accidental order repeatedly come to the same complex result in distant lineages. Is anything more unlikely? Evolution must depend on causes beyond those Darwin identified.

This is an important argument for Bergson and for us; understanding it helps place him in relation to biology and philosophy in his time and ours. I cannot say Bergson's argument is completely successful, though its merit is greater than appreciated by those content with a facile denunciation of his notorious vitalism.

Convergent Evolution

The most discussed case of convergent evolution is a camera eye in vertebrates and cephalopods, though there are many not less unlikely examples.[32] Camera eyes convergently evolved in three gastropod (snail) species. Cubozoans, a primitive jellyfish, have eight camera eyes. *Dinopis*, a net-casing spider, also has eight camera eyes, somewhat anomalously since arthropod eyes are usually compound, as in flies and bees. Another arthropod with camera eyes is the *Portia* genus of jumping spiders. They too deploy eight camera eyes, six for low-level peripheral motion detection and two primary, combining telescopic vision with a narrow visual field. Their vision is said to be more acute than all other arthropods and even birds. These are all cases of anatomically complex organs whose fine-grain structure is virtually identical with our own eyes.

One wonders whether these diverse species share qualities of lifestyle that might explain the convergence of their eyes. Most live a fast-paced predator's life. The *Portia* spiders are famous killers, "cats with eight eyes." The cubozoan jellyfish, also with eight camera eyes, is an agile swimmer, capable of fast, directionally accurate responses, and effective predation, despite this creature having no brain, none at all. Gastropods, including the proverbially slow-moving snail, may seem an unlikely match for the ecological profile of camera eyes but in fact they almost clinch the case. While snails of the genus *Strombus* are usually slow-moving herbivores, they are also notably acute in avoiding predators, of which they have many. Visually sensing the predator, they perform a series of rapid leaps, showing what an expert describes as "some of the most specialized and effective escape responses known among the gastropods."[33]

Camera eyes do not merely converge phylogenetically in these species. They converge ontogenetically in individual development too, when entirely different embryonic processes produce the same structure. For instance, in vertebrates the retina grows from out of the brain and is an extension of the nervous system to the periphery. In mollusks the retina grows in from the ectoderm (Figure 3.1). Additionally, the cephalopod eye lacks a cornea, which is present in all vertebrates, and the topology of nerves and photoreceptors is reversed, light passing through nerves to the photoreceptor layer in the vertebrate eye and impinging directly on photoreceptors in cephalopods. Finally, remember that a camera eye is merely one example of convergent evolution. There are hundreds if not thousands of cases of evolution converging on the same form.[34]

Simon Conway Morris is natural history's most profound student of convergent evolution. One of his ideas is that convergence is evolution's way to navigate the combinatorial immensity of biological space, skirting, for instance, all the chemically possible but biologically inert proteins and amino acids. To get an idea of the

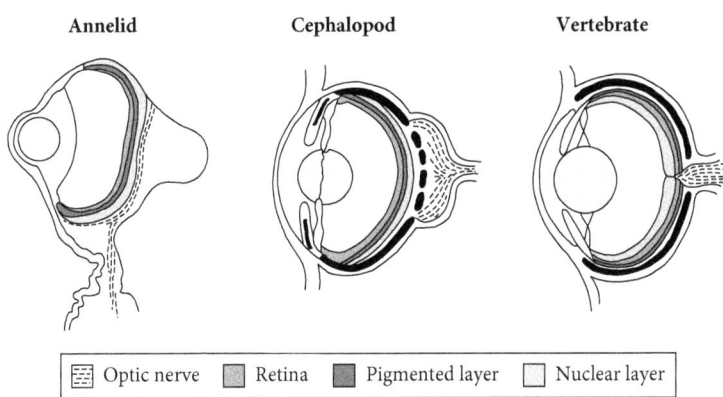

Figure 3.1 Convergent Eyes. From Simon Conway Morris, *Life's Solution: Inevitable Humans in a Lonely Universe.* Cambridge: Cambridge University Press, 2003, 152.

problem, consider that all proteins are a combination of twenty different amino acids. Even a short chain of just three amino acids can be arranged 8,000 different ways, with each arrangement having unique biochemical properties. Most proteins chains are much longer. The possible arrangements of a chain of one hundred amino acids are 10^{130}. Many proteins have thousands of amino acids; for instance, the hemoglobin protein combines ten thousand amino acids and is not the largest or most complex such molecule. If natural selection had to test these one by one, we would still be waiting for the first metazoan. There must be some bias, some attractor, some tendency, *some final cause*.

Conway Morris thinks that convergence occurs because once found, points of ecological stability become such attractors, "by which evolutionary trajectories are channeled toward stable nodes of functionality."[35] They become favored evolutionary endpoints, a final cause and source of tendency. Not everything is biologically possible and what is possible has usually been arrived at more than once. The convergent evolution of camera eyes should not be a surprise. With viable biological properties as attractors in the phase-space of evolution, convergence is practically inevitable.

Conway Morris draws two conclusions from convergence. One is that time matters. Life on Earth is somewhat more than four billion years old, and a lot can happen in a billion years. With millions of opportunities, a one-in-a-million chance moves from unlikely to inevitable. The second conclusion reaffirms Darwin's thesis that adaptation is the engine of evolution. He thinks the importance claimed for alternative causes, including exaptation (so-called spandrels), is exaggerated. "The great majority of the examples [of convergence] are almost certainly the result of selective processes operating in the context of adaptation."[36]

He alludes to Steven Jay Gould's thought experiment of rerunning the tape of life's evolution. Gould concluded that a rerun would produce an entirely different evolution: "Any replay of the tape would lead evolution down a pathway radically different from the road actually taken.... Alter any early event, ever so slightly and without apparent importance at the time, and evolution cascades into a radically different channel."[37] That is his intuition. The contingency of evolution, its ultimate chanciness, is a principle of Darwinism. Darwin spoke of chance to signify the causal independence of variation from subsequent adaptation; variations do not come into being *for* anything. Emphasizing this contingency makes Gould's conclusion plausible, though Conway Morris thinks that "what we know of evolution suggests the exact reverse: convergence is ubiquitous, and the constraints of life make the emergence of the various biological properties very probable, if not inevitable."[38]

These conclusions inspire Conway Morris to a bracing speculation. He says it is consistent with the evidence to conjecture that there is a "deeper fabric to biology in which Darwinian evolution remains central as the agency, but the nodes of occupation [of viable biological space] are effectively predetermined from the Big Bang."[39] He is impressed by the evidence of very primitive creatures which, without anatomical expression, already have most or all the genetic architecture of more advanced species.[40] Units of complex structure are evidently available well before they are recruited to the struggle for existence. I think the conjecture is that from a very early point of cosmic evolution, astronomical eons before terrestrial life, these attractors become established as virtual tendencies. What begins as obscure yet distinct virtual tendency evolves into actual trends in life's evolution.

We tend to see convergent evolution as improbable. Conway Morris and Bergson both want a way to understand the facts that makes it seem unsurprising and even likely. For Conway Morris, convergence confirms Darwin's idea that adaptation and its discovery by natural selection are the primary cause of evolution. For Bergson the same evidence refutes the Neo-Darwinist mechanical theory of evolution.

Bergson introduces a somewhat elaborate analogy (CE 94).[41] Imagine an invisible hand thrust into a sack of fine iron filings. The spatial organization of the displaced filings is a trace of a simple motion. Geometry can define the structure but tells us nothing about the event that produced the order it describes: "If we took into account only what we saw, the simple act of an invisible hand plunged into iron filings would seem like an inexhaustible interplay of actions and reactions among the filings themselves in order that they might effect an equilibrium" (TS 46). We express the same naivety when we consider the eye and think it is composed of parts.

> What we call a series of means employed is, in reality, but a number of obstacles overcome; the action of nature is simple, and the infinite complexity of the mechanisms which it seems to have built up piece by piece to achieve the power of vision is but *the endless network of opposing forces which have cancelled each other out to secure an uninterrupted channel* for the functioning of the faculty. (TS 45–46, my emphasis)

The improbable spatial arrangement of the filings is a relic of the opposing forces that canceled each other in response to an impulse or energy passing through them. The form of the filings is a *trace*, a *form of resistance*, not a synthesis. This is a parable of life. The "parts" of an organ like an eye are not parts at all, not assembled to obtain a function. They are resistances to resistance. At the origin of life, the vital *élan* is a simple, undivided movement passing through pre-individuated continuous extensity, leaving as traces of its passage the tendencies we call species. This is what Bergson means by *nature*. "Nature—let us repeat it—is the name we give to the totality of compliances and resistances which life encounters in raw matter," that is, continuous extensity (TS 300).

Bear in mind that life and matter are tendencies, not substances, which makes them more like currents, melodies, or rhythms, and lets them interact in ways that solid blocks cannot; for instance, they can interpenetrate, which is what an organism is. That is how I understand Bergson when he describes life as "consciousness launched into matter," or when he says that a current of consciousness "penetrate[s] matter, loaded, as all consciousness is, with an enormous multiplicity of interwoven potentialities" (CE 181). These statements describe the interaction of tendencies, which are virtual, temporal entities. For life or consciousness to penetrate or be launched into matter is like oceanic currents flooding through each other, like the currents of the Bosporus, the narrow strait linking the Black and Aegean Seas. The two bodies of water differ in temperature and salinity, and the narrow passage is laced with treacherous reversing currents. The relation between the tendency of matter (entropy) and the tendency of life (individuality) is like that.

Another lesson of Bergson's invisible hand is to expose the complementary errors of mechanism and vitalism. Proponents of both views look on an organism as something complicated—many parts externally related. That is like marveling at the architecture of the iron filings: "How could mere natural causes do *that*?" It is a fallacy to regard organisms as marvels of complexity, and amazement at the evidence of convergence redoubles the trouble. We should not expect evolutionary biology to explain how a very complicated and unlikely convergence arose, because a camera eye in multiple species is not an improbable convergence. It seems like one because we look at it from the perspective of our own action and think of it as something that had to be assembled from parts.

Two million years of co-evolution with tools has made our sapient species born artisans (it was Bergson who coined the expression *Homo faber*).[42] Design appeals to the technician in us, and from experience with technics we appreciate a difference between qualities and their bearers. In life, that means a distinction between function and mechanism, understanding that different mechanisms might execute the function of vision, just as there are different ways to fletch an arrow. However, this distinction between function and mechanism is an artifact of technical experience and a treacherous piece of unconscious pragmatism. The only way artifice could mimic vision is with a very complicated machine, but that does not mean eyes are very complicated machines, or that causes adequate to mechanical effects might have given birth to living vision.

The organ and the organism, the trends they express, are traces of a still-moving movement, byproducts of a passage that remains open, an enduring duration, an unfinished finality, an open whole. In *Time and Free Will*, Bergson argued (against Zeno) that movement does not instantaneously halt at the points of its trajectory. In *Matter and Memory*, he argued that movement is a duration with no parts. Now he says the same thing about organisms. They are not complex mechanisms assembled from simpler elements, no more than movement is assembled from the points of a trajectory. Manufacture is not a good analogy for nature (as Hume also observed).[43] Commenting on the inevitable example, Bergson says, "The eye, with its marvelous complexity of structure, may be only the simple act of vision, divided *for us* into a mosaic of cells, whose order seems marvelous to us because we have conceived the whole as an assemblage" (CE 90).

Artifice works methodically from many to one, from parts to whole. Life develops explosively from center to periphery, beginning from almost a point and moving out in waves over embryological and terrestrial space and time. A part is a body, and a body is an image, so, to recall the argument of Chapter 2, all division of parts is the work of perception and relative to a form of life. The beginning of life is the beginning of "parts" or individuated, discontinuous bodies. Without life, without perception, these bodies melt into continuous extensity.

Envisioning the Octopus

I mentioned the criticism, not original with Bergson, that Darwinism cannot account for the variations natural selection requires. This is where Bergson thinks his hypothesis of a vital *élan* makes a contribution: "This impetus, sustained right along the lines of evolution among which it gets divided, is the fundamental cause of the variations, at least of those that are regularly passed on, that accumulate and create new species" (CE 92–93). It also accounts for convergent evolution: "We do not see how otherwise to explain the likeness of structure of the eye in species that have not the same history" (CE 86). He is saying that something about the vital *élan* makes it the source of the trends he detects in evolution and explains both the variation on which natural selection acts and the phenomena of convergence. It is a huge claim, and the argument is not easy to make out.

As one interpenetrating duration, every phase of the evolution of life enjoys continuity with every other: "Even in the latest channel there would be something of the impulsion received at the source"; hence "life may manufacture the like apparatus, by unlike means, on divergent lines of evolution" (CE 54). But why so selectively? Why aren't *all* eyes the same? The gist of the argument seems to come in this sentence:

> No matter how distant two animal species may be from each other, if the progress toward vision has gone equally far in both, there is the same visual organ in each case, for the form of the organ only expresses the degree in which the exercise of the function has been obtained. (CE 96)

If the form of the organ expresses the degree to which the function is obtained, then we are wrong to focus on the form; we should pay attention to the function, of which form is the expression. No matter how distant from each other two animal species may be, if in respect of some power (some function) they are equal, we should expect the organ that expresses the power to have the same form. There is more to Lamarck than "form follows function," but so far Bergson takes a page from Lamarck.[44]

I'll rephrase Bergson's argument so we can focus on it. No matter the phylogenetic distance separating two species, if the quality of their vision achieves a given level, we can expect the same form in the visual organ, and where we find the same organ, we can expect comparable visual functionality. Vertebrates and octopuses had their last common ancestor in a sightless worm of the Ediacaran era, more than five hundred million years ago. Today, their eyes are the same in detail (Figure 3.1). Bergson says this similarity indicates that the "progress toward vision" has gone equally far in each case. Presumably that means vertebrates and cephalopods have evolved a comparable level of coordination between differences visually detected and potential action, especially controlled limb movement. Let ME summarize some of the evidence.

All the cephalopods have large brains and well-developed sensory organs, powers they evolved independently of their genesis in vertebrates.[45] Octopuses offer the sole examples of cleverness, playfulness, and invention outside of mammals. Their sophisticated behavior has as much to do with their limbs as their brain, which in their case are difficult to distinguish, since no less than *60 percent* of an octopus's neurons are in the tentacles, not in the brain at all. A large octopus can have sixteen hundred suckers on those tentacles, each one capable of voluntary control, including the formation of a pincher grip like our thumb and forefinger, and each equipped with as many as ten thousand neurons for taste and touch. Sixteen hundred clever fingers and tongues!

All the cephalopods enjoy what researchers call a high-performance lifestyle. They are fast-moving animals in a complex environment, predators that are also prey, and visually guided hunters, each eye swiveling independently. Researchers describe their predation as a fast, accurate, ambush-like strike, with their tentacles shooting out to seize prey. We saw evidence that camera vision facilitates a predator lifestyle, but it has other prerequisites too, for instance the capacity for a rapid burst of activity, which places demands on heart, blood pressure, and arteries. Cephalopods and vertebrates again converge, for as Conway Morris observes "only in the cephalopod and vertebrate is the circulatory system completely enclosed in vessels and so capable of operating at high blood pressures."[46]

For the octopus as for us, perception is virtual action. Quality of vision depends on quality of motor control and vice versa. It is unsurprising that octopuses are clever (aquariums have legends), and it is appropriate that convergent camera eyes in arthropods appear in spiders, with their nimble legs, and net-casting, jumping spiders at that. Whether camera-eye vision is adaptive for a species does not merely depend on an environment. It depends on the neurology and morphology required to make this eye virtually adaptive. A viable outcome becomes one of Conway Morris's attractors in life's evolutionary phase-space. Such attractors must be virtual.[47] They have no spatial existence and are not efficient causes, their causality being that of tendency, a final cause.

Bergson said that no matter how distant two species may be, if visual functionality is comparable, we should expect a comparable form, "for the form of the organ only expresses the degree in which the exercise of the function has been obtained" (CE 96). This is the Lamarckian argument that so-called form merely reifies an organism's habits. A mollusk with camera eyes is one that, in its way, in its environment, with its body type, uses that quality of vision as adaptively as do vertebrates. It is a matter of the quality of vision. To have that quality you must have that organ: "Vision will be found, therefore, in different degrees in the most diverse animals, and it will appear in the same complexity of structure wherever it has reached the same degree of intensity" (CE 96).

Bergson may suppose that camera eyes express a qualitative difference of vision compared to compound or other types of eye, which is not impossible. To correlate camera eyes with a specific intensity of vision implies that octopuses and jellyfish (which have such eyes) experience vision more intensely than ants and flies (which do not). There is some evidence of superior acuity for camera over compound eyes, and their distribution seem to correlate with the availability of nimble limbs. It used to be thought that compound eyes were better at detecting motion, though apparently this is a mistake. The real difference is that camera eyes resolve significantly better than compound eyes, where vision is marred by diffraction and poor photon capture in the array of small lenses.[48]

Bergson's conclusion may not be that far from Conway Morris. The idea of the organ, the virtual organ, attracts evolving tendencies and therefore tends to repeat whenever the tendencies into which evolution has divided approach this island of adaptation. It may seem improbable that humans and octopuses have convergent eyes, but less improbable that vertebrates and mollusks do, and it is perhaps not at all improbable that, having evolved, camera eyes should prove convergent. Older than the struggle for existence among organisms is a struggle for materialization among tendencies. When a point arises where this quality or intensity of vision would be adaptive, a channel opens for the tendency to pass from virtual to actual, though nothing guarantees the successful establishment of a new character. Virtuality acts in the evolution of life as it does in personal memory. Memories cannot to be searched out. They press of their own accord toward the present and remembering often requires only the opportunity to supplement perception with their experience. In a similar way, the opening to adapt a species is another conduit for virtual tendencies to find actual expression. The adaptive potential provides a path to materialization for a tendency that may be as old as life itself.

Writing in another context Bergson explains a law to the effect that when a tendency splits, each derived tendency preserves and develops everything of the ancestral tendency that is compatible with the new differentiation (CE 119).

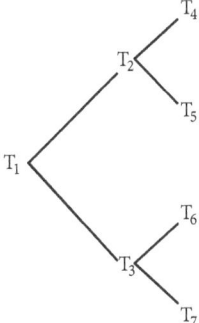

In the above figure, T_4–T_7 have as much of the tendentious virtual potency of T_1 as is consistent with whatever bifurcations differentiate them, each tendency preserving a kind of selective inheritance as they materialize. Bergson suggests that this law illuminates convergent evolution. The tendency that produced a camera eye in one line could be quite old *as a tendency* (not an actual character) and could share this virtual lineage with many other conventionally (spatially) "distant" species.

Bergson's idea is consistent with the new sort of homology introduced by molecular developmental biology. Originally, "homology" referred to similarities of adult structure. In this sense, the convergent eyes of cephalopods and vertebrates could only be an analogy, not a true homology, since the eyes evolved after their last common ancestor. But embryology and molecular biology have discovered new modes of homology, not in anatomy but in ontogenesis. Organs that seem merely analogous can be outcomes of genetically homologous developmental processes.[49] Eyes are again a prominent example. The same regulatory gene plays a role in eye-formation in vertebrates and arthropods, being expressed in all the components of the developing vertebrate eye as well as the compound eye of most arthropods. This gene evolved before the separation of arthropods and vertebrates in the Cambrian Period some five hundred million years ago. Present-day arthropod and vertebrate eyes are thought to be modified descendants of a light-sensitive cell in a Precambrian metazoan or multicellular organism. Those eyes are not classical, anatomical homologies but their *genesis* is a *developmental* homology, and a true inheritance across this vast difference of lineages from an ancient common ancestor.[50]

Convergent camera eyes may be homologies after all, which would mean convergence could not be the refutation of Darwinism that Bergson expects. It is a paradoxical tradition among vitalists to offer hostages to fortune when they declare that standard biology cannot possibly explain this or that vital phenomenon. Every time the vitalists did this (and they always did), they were eventually refuted by the very inquiry they wanted to redirect down their dead end. Bergson has learned nothing in this regard, staking his case for introducing the vital *élan* on evolutionary phenomena for which he claims, much too rashly, that Darwinian explanation is impossible. Considerations adduced by Conway Morris, as well as the evidence of embryological homology, make convergent evolution no longer especially unlikely, and offer new evidence for the preeminence of adaptation as a cause of evolution, as well as for the existence of evolutionary trends.

The Vital *Élan*

Bergson thinks he has established that Darwin's mechanical theory of evolution is baffled by convergent evolution and unable to explain the variety natural selection presupposes. We have seen the limitations of the former argument, but novelty remains a problem for Darwinism. Whatever a mechanism does it does as long as it operates and no novelty comes out of it. Mechanisms are like crystals, always already everything they can be. Crystals add layers to their surface without internal change, and mechanisms pass from one machine-state to the next. By contrast, life is always infinitesimally new, different, and evolving: "The more duration marks the living being with its imprint, the more obviously the organism differs from a mere mechanism, over which duration glides without penetrating" (CE 37).

In calling his vital *élan* a scientific hypothesis and underscoring the dead-end of mechanism, Bergson implies that biology should rethink the repudiated final causes. Julian Huxley mocked Bergson: "To say that biological progress is explained by *élan vital* is to say that the movement of a train is explained by an *élan locomotif* of the engine."[51] An egregious analogy but let's belabor it. A locomotive is a machine par excellence, and what makes it go must be as mechanical as it is. So, all that Huxley says is that the vital *élan* is not a mechanical cause, which is true but obtuse. Bergson's argument is that mechanical causes cannot explain the evolution of life. Evolutionary science requires final causes, which are active in trends and tendencies, themselves outcomes of the vital *élan*, which is the final cause of terrestrial life.

The evolution of life on earth "continues ... an initial impulsion" (CE 246), creating an "explosive force—due to an unstable balance of tendencies—which life bears within itself" (CE 98). This impulsion "is finite, and it has been given once for all. It cannot overcome all obstacles. The movement it starts is sometimes turned aside, sometimes divided, always opposed; and the evolution of the organized world is the unrolling of this conflict" (CE 254). *Élan vital* is a name for this event and the multiply tendentious movement it rolls out. Life begins with an impetuous singularity, "a continually growing action" (CE 128), defining "a single indivisible history" (CE 37):

> From the bottom to the top of the organized world we do indeed find one great effort. (CE 127)

> All organized beings, from the humblest to the highest, from the first origins of life to the time in which we are, and in all places as in all times, do but evidence a single impulsion.... All the living hold together, and all yield to the same tremendous push. (CE 271)

Referencing the distinction of germ and soma cell lines, Bergson agrees with Weismann that the causes of variation are differences in the germ, with two qualifications. First, these differences are not accidental or individual, being instead "the development of an impulsion which passes from germ to germ across the individuals" (CE 85). Second, heredity does more than transmit characters, "it transmits also the impetus in virtue of which the characters are modified, and this impetus is vitality itself" (CE 231). Here is Bergson's hypothesis: "An *original impetus* of life, pass[es] from one generation of germs to the following generation of germs through the developed organisms which bridge the interval between the generations." He adds that this impetus "is the fundamental cause of variations, at least of those . . . that accumulate and create new species" (CE 87), and elsewhere that it "carries life in a given direction, toward an ever higher complexity" (TS 113).

An evolutionary rise in life's complexity is due primarily "to the necessity of complexity in the nervous system" (CE 251). The broad line of progress, variously displaced by the imperative of adaptation to conditions of existence, is to create and protect a nervous system, make it maximally independent of external conditions, and furnish it with energy to be expended in finely controlled movement. Why a nervous system? It is only a first step. The existence of life is the existence of a tendency and tendencies are distinguished by the limit toward which they lean, so the whole movement of life's evolution should lean toward some limit, which Bergson describes as that of introducing the greatest possible indeterminacy into matter, reversing the tendency of inertia to the unknown furthest extent. In our case, the neurology innervating a morphology of nimble limbs, camera eyes, and organs of speech created what Bergson describes as "a veritable reservoir of indetermination" (CE 126). This or any indeterminacy would be fatal without a power for which it provides an opportunity, and that is consciousness: "The chief office of consciousness is to preside over action and to enlighten choice" (MM 182). Bergson's panpsychism (Chapter 2) prepares us for consciousness wherever there is controlled vital movement: "The humblest organism is conscious in proportion to its power to move freely" (CE 111).

The only way Bergson acknowledges to generate rising complexity is through diversification. "Life does not proceed by the association and addition of elements, but by dissociation and division" (CE 89). Conway Morris observes how the simplicity of early life gives no hint of the illimitable virtuality that has materialized over time, which Bergson sees as the diversity of life becoming more virtual, less actual, looking further back in time: "While, in its contact with matter, life is comparable to an impulsion or an impetus, regarded as itself it is an immensity of *virtualité*, a mutual encroachment of thousands and thousands of tendencies which nevertheless are 'thousands and thousands' only when once regarded as outside of each other, that is, when spatialized" (CE 258).

The origin of life initiates a movement with a quality Bergson describes as an *élan* because of its tendentious character. He likens it to a rocket burning into the entropic night of continuous extensity and exploding in forms (CE 261). The origin of life opens a duration, which is not an event or sequence of events but rather one undecomposable, interpenetrating epoch. Bergson conjures the image of a wave of vitality rolling through extensity, the whole series of the living having become "one single immense wave flowing over matter" (CE 250). If we take the image seriously, we must conclude that "harmony is rather behind us than before," though that harmony was completely virtual, the harmony of tendency that knows only positivity and abides inclinations that cannot actually co-exist, like the virtually innocent Adam's virtual sin. Bergson makes this point against the finalist theory of evolution associated with Lamarck, according to which life should be growing more perfect. He says this point about past and future is something "on which finalism has been most seriously mistaken" (CE 51). For Bergson, the future does not exist, not in plan or idea or in the logical space of possibilities, which is more dynamic, even historical, than Wittgenstein or David Lewis thought.[52]

Bergson describes *élan vital* as an immanent tendency that presses life to all its diversity. His image is artillery shells bursting in the night sky (CE 98). Imagine that each shell burst into smaller ones and those into still smaller ones, a seeming endless cascade of explosive motion and melting form. Returning to the image later, he names consciousness as "the rocket whose extinguished fragments fall back as matter" (CE 261). Consciousness is "the motive principle of evolution" (CE 182). The essential causes operating in the evolution of life are "of [a] psychological nature" (CE 54). In Chapter 2, I explained that consciousness for Bergson is a tendency, not a substance; as such it is marked by distinctive qualities, namely, interpenetration, succession without separation, continuous change, and the persistence of the whole past. Any similarly qualified tendency will also be conscious or like consciousness. The life of the organism is one of these: "Life is of the psychological order, and it is of the essence of the psychical to enfold a confused plurality of interpenetrating terms" (CE 257). Evolution itself is another such tendency: "The more we fix our attention on [the] continuity of life, the more one sees organic evolution approaching to that of consciousness, in which the past presses against the present and makes a new form emerge from it that is incommensurable with its antecedents" (CE 29).

What life and evolution share, prompting Bergson's comparison to consciousness, is temporal interpenetration. The essential quality of consciousness is neither the glancing ray of intentionality nor the unspeakable phenomenality of "what it is like."[53] The essential quality of consciousness is duration, the tense contraction of an enduring temporal organization like a song. Anything with such qualities is conscious or like consciousness, because "it is of the essence of the psychical to enfold a confused plurality of interpenetrating terms" (CE 257). To enfold or hold together (synthesize) temporal phases "implies a real persistence of the past into the present, a duration which is, as it were, a hyphen, a connecting link" (CE 22). Such links are mnemic, expressing a spiritual, pneumatic power of temporal contraction, binding, or synthesis: "The humblest function of spirit is to bind together the successive moments of the duration of things" (MM 295).

In 1936, Bergson wrote about *élan vital* to his nephew Floris Delattre, an accomplished French scholar of English literature, who had written to Bergson for advice on the evolutionary philosophy of Samuel Butler:

> When I relate the phenomena of life and of evolution to an *élan vital* it is in no way an ornament of style. It is even less meant to mask in images our ignorance of the deepest causes, as when the vitalist in general invokes a "vital principle." ... The truth is that philosophy only offers philosophers two principles of explanation in this matter: mechanism and finalism.... Now ... the place to be is somewhere in between these two concepts. How should we determine that place? I have to point to it, to indicate it, since no concept between mechanism and finalism exists. The image of an *élan* is only this indication.[54]

I understand him to say that *élan vital* is not merely a name for our ignorance, which is how he sees the verbose vocabulary of vitalism. Philosophy offers two ways to explain life, mechanism and finalism. Mechanism in the form of Darwin and especially Weismann is a dead end, and finalism, whether as creationism or Lamarck's more discreet teleology, is no better. All of these fail to take time seriously, a notable omission in a theory of evolution, which (with geology) exposes the efficacy of time more than any other science. So philosophy needs a third way and the image of an *élan* is a marker to indicate where it might lie, namely, with an immanent mode of finality between supernatural teleology and mechanism. But this is not the terra incognita Bergson suggests. He finds himself where Aristotle did, seeking an alternative between

Plato and Democritus, and where Stoics were, wanting to reconcile Plato and Aristotle. Later Spinoza was in a comparable position, criticizing Platonic supernaturalism and divine providence while naturalizing immanent finality with his concept of *conatus*. Bergson implies that no conceptual space exists between mechanism and finalism, but there is room for nuance about finalism, which does not *have* to disregard time and assume that "all is given" by a plan or purpose. That is the medieval Christian version of Plato's teleology, but already in antiquity Aristotle and the Stoics introduced profound alternatives both to Plato's supernaturalism and atomism's mechanical antiteleology, and this is the line Spinoza and Bergson continue in modern philosophy. Bergson thinks he replaces finality with impulsion (*élan*), but that impulsion is not an efficient cause and becomes effective only as a tendency, that is, an immanent finality. *Élan vital* does not replace finality with impulse; it replaces external with immanent finality.

Intellect in Evolution

The human intellect "is not at all what Plato taught in the allegory of the cave" (CE 191). Platonic intellect (*nous*) is a faculty of pure knowledge (*episteme*), born to high things, dedicated to higher values than mere survival. This intellect is a power of knowing the truth, the truth of being, whose contemplation is its wellborn destiny. Bergson's alternative understanding of intellect or intelligence is inflected by evolutionary thought and therefore irreconcilable with Platonism. Intelligence adapts our species to diverse environments and serves the satisfaction of needs. It is preeminently a power of technology, which has been a feature of the hominid adaptation since before the first stone tool. Experience with technics teaches that structure is provisional. Once we learn to see things as assembled, we understand that they might be disassembled and reassembled in a preferable configuration. Anyone who can use a tool understands that, and once people have the idea of technical assembly, nearly anything they look at can seem to be made of parts. This is not a fact but a perception and biased by long experience with technics.[55]

The scheme of form-and-matter and the intuitions of Euclidean space are inevitable, though not for the reason Kant explained: they are not a priori conditions of experience. They arise contingently but fatefully from the habit of making and using tools, which is the adaptive specialty of human intelligence. Bergson has a patriarchal notion of intelligence, whose essential qualities are stereotypically masculine—tools and technical problems—rather than stereotypically feminine—language and social relations. This intelligence did not come together gradually by assembly. It is a qualitatively singular tendency, born of the evolutionary bifurcation that also launched instinct into life. Intelligence and instinct are co-differentiated actualizations of one virtual tendency in which they obscurely commingle.

As a result of their differentiation, two lines appear in the history of life, one evolving intelligence and culminating in *H. sapiens*, the other evolving instinct and culminating in the Hymenoptera (ants, wasps, and bees). Intelligence and instinct are complementary trends in evolution, qualitatively different powers, implying thoroughgoing differences in form of life, as different as ants and apes. Nevertheless, common birth makes instinct and intelligence interpenetrating; they haunt each other like a dream and neither occurs in a pure state. Rational people are not without instincts that may baffle them, and the dullest animal is not without wiles. Darwin documented the intelligence of earthworms.[56]

Intelligence is an organ of experiential knowledge, expressed in the learned and habitual movement of nimble limbs (including tongue). Instinct is another sort of knowledge, spontaneous and unconscious. A bee making hexagonal cells expresses instinct's knowledge. The animal seems masterful, the cells exactly made, but give this animal different material or a different task and the appearance of skill falls away.[57] The knowledge is adequate for one effect on one body only. It is knowledge unconsciously lived rather than consciously achieved, knowledge that does not enhance choice but eliminates it. Such certainty comes at the price of freedom and art. Unlike instinct, intelligence is not fixed on specific bodies (forms); it looks past bodies to their qualities and relations. By attending to relations—for instance how the action of one body affects another—intelligence can think its way to new applications. Intellectual knowledge bears on a relational, functional scheme that can be filled by different qualities of different materials. It does not always have to be the same things; it can be the same relation among different things. By looking past particular bodies and considering relations we discover qualities. We discover hardness, tensile strength, sharpness, waterproof. These can become goals of inquiry and experiment, pursuing a harder metal, a sharper blade, a redder dye.

This knowledge is not limited to practical utility, and those who can pose the problem of a boat or a bridge can find the problem of the stars. The capacity for knowledge is adaptative, which explains the existence of cognitive powers in the first place, but knowledge is more than an adaptation because evolved cognitive powers prove capable of more than whatever cognitive function was naturally selected by survival. To reveal potentials for acting on distant things, vision must reveal things (like stars) on which we cannot act. To make its tools, intelligence must be able to think instrumentally about anything, even other people. Human beings are animals with an animal's ways, sleek survivors, clever opportunists. We also have the exapted potential to press faculties beyond the adaptive limits to which habit restricts them. Science is an example.

By turning perceptual and cognitive powers to unselected, nonadaptive activity we take a step beyond what evolution settled for *Homo sapiens*, transcending the determinism that engendered us. Understanding and knowledge are adaptive functions for language-and-tool-using primates, but these powers also have autonomous higher forms in art, science, and philosophy. Intelligence does not distinguish between practical and useless and even has an extraordinary capacity for futile passions like Eldorado. That does not happen with instinct, which has no capacity to express knowledge independently of the struggle to exist. Intelligence thus breaks free of instinct only to succumb to stupidity.

In Bergson's argument, intelligence or intellect are names for spatial and mechanical thinking, implying objects to count and measure. The philosophy Bergson criticizes under the name of intellectualism (or rationalism) sublimates mensuration's mechanical and spatial assumptions into a philosophy of nature, rationalizing the success of its methods as confirmation of nature's rationality. This presumptious rationalism judges ontologically second-rate anything that does not submit to its method, a credo memorably expressed by physicist William Thomson: "When you can measure what you are speaking about, and express it in numbers, you know something about it; but when you cannot measure it, when you cannot express it in numbers, your knowledge is of a meager and unsatisfactory kind."[58]

Bergson describes natural science as a partial view. It is not an absolute view of fundamental parts, but a partial view of the whole through the (spatial) lens of intelligence and subject to experimental control. What makes the scientific view partial is to prescind from the qualitative and continuous despite their evidence in experience. Science follows practice and what matters to practice is what we can act on. It is a mistake to think of science as the philosophers' long-sought Truth of Being. It was this fallacious reification of contingent cognition that William James denounced as intellectualism.[59] Yet Bergson is not a pragmatist. The first part of Bergson's philosophy, the propaedeutic part, is a pragmatic view of concepts and science. The value of both is utility or expediency, anything but what philosophers classically define as truth (*adaequatio intellectus ad rem*).[60] There is no such truth. Bodies are artificial discontinuities that perception introduces into the extensive continuity of physical becoming according to our capacity for adaptive interaction. Nothing exist in itself with a nature to which mind might be true.

So far, Bergson is as pragmatic as the Pragmatists. The value of science is to enhance the efficiency of action, "to foresee in order to act" (CE 330). However, he did not need to read Pragmatist authors to arrive at this idea, and if he is influenced by an earlier thinker I would guess it is Schopenhauer, for whom intelligence "is entirely practical in its tendency."[61] For Schopenhauer, empirical science builds on the practical powers of perception and concepts, though for just that reason these sciences remain bound to perspective, knowledge of how we are affected rather than things in themselves. Acknowledging the discipline this disenchanted view of cognition imposes, philosophy is free to develop its proper material, which is where Schopenhauer, as uninterested in time as philosophers usually are, and Bergson go separate ways. For Schopenhauer, "the principal truth of all philosophy" is that "the same thing exists at all times, all becoming and arising are only apparent, the Ideas alone permanent, time ideal."[62] Darwinism may have eased the way for Bergson to overturn this *philosophia perennis*, though his genius was to retain Schopenhauer's proto-pragmatism for the extensive phenomena, and in place of Will as the source of appearances introduce time and the phenomena of duration.

Humanity in Evolution

Every species is in one respect a success, in another a fragment. The form and habits by which species survive and adapt over geological time are also obstacles that confine the expression of individuality. The vitality of an organism is a tendency to develop toward individuality, yet the effort is compromised by the opposite tendency of the body to repetition. An early milestone in life's unfolding tendency to individuality and self-determination is the evolution of neuron cells and nervous systems. The filigree of dendrites and the variability of synapses make nervous tissue a "veritable reservoir of indetermination" (CE 126). The appearance of the human species is another milestone and current peak of the indeterminacy that life has introduced into matter.

To this point the advance of life has been on the level of species, where vitality becomes locked into an adapted form that simply repeats. All life is a balance of individuality and association. Every individual is haunted by a common form with others of the kind and the compulsion to reproduce life. Life is indifferent to any individuality that is not hereditary, but that could change. Bergson discreetly discloses his idea of the next phase in life's evolution, which is to take a step beyond species, replacing the reproduction of species with individuals creating individuals. Such individuals would be human only in a genealogical sense; we are their ancestors, but they have taken a step to which we can only aspire. They are beyond current humanity, though not a higher *species* since their accomplishment is precisely to have founded a society of individuals unhindered by species-being. Not that they have no species-being, but rather that by the great gift of technology, species being does not make them less individual. Present humanity's singularity is to be the ground on which to launch the aspiration to that future (Chapter 4).

With the evolution of humanity, life achieves true (i.e., effective) individuals. We are not complete and perfect individuals, but we have advanced individuality well beyond any other species, becoming the most individuated organisms in the history of life.[63] We are not absolute individuals because that requires an impossible self-closure. Bergson stands with Stoics and Spinoza against Leibniz and monads. But a tendency to individuality does exist, a tendency of life everywhere, however thwarted. With the evolution of *sapiens*, the obstacles matter presents to individuality are breeched by a species that has outgrown the limitations that define a species, as hands and speech have outgrown whatever function for which they were selected.

Since the rise of metazoan or multicellular life about a billion years ago, the most prolific source of evolutionary change has been individual behavior. Individuality is a phenomenon of phenotypic plasticity, what the genome passively enables individuals to do, and which they do, if at all, by preference and habit. Such individuality creates abundant selection opportunities for evolutionary change. Two evolutionary microbiologists write: "If there has been a progressive theme to metazoan evolution, it has been that organisms have not only improved their responses but have increasingly taken part in the selection." Individualized behavior is the prototype of preference, and its differences "may be the principal mechanism for extending the phenotype to the adaptable limit and continually testing the capacity of the embryological mechanisms to come up with new solutions."[64]

Bergson dismisses microorganisms as insignificant to evolution and assumes that the first major distinction in life is between plants and animals (CE 116–17). Both assumptions are unsustainable against later evidence.[65] Microorganisms are now and have always been the dominant form of life on earth, and the first great division of life is not plant and animal but prokaryotes—bacteria with no nuclear membrane—and eucaryotes, which include all other life forms, all composed of cells with a nuclear membrane. As that suggests, bacteria are the matrix of all other life, dominating subsequent evolution. Life as we know it is impossible without them. It is not clear that Bergson's theory is immune to these facts. If life is a tendency and if tendencies tend with some puissance, why was the vital *élan* stuck in bacteria for three billion years? Simple life emerges early; prokaryotic bacteria appear within a hundred million years of the final cooling of the earth's crust.[66] From that point to the first appearance of the most basic multicellular organisms took *three billion years*. The disparity of time scales suggests barriers to complex life, suggesting in turn that intelligence may be cosmically rare even if life is not.

With multi-cellularity, behavioral individuality becomes the tendency in the subsequent evolution of life. Our position in the history of life has made humanity uniquely capable of "continu[ing] the vital movement indefinitely" (CE 266): "I see in the whole evolution of life on our planet a crossing of matter by a creative consciousness, and [an] effort to [set] free, by force of ingenuity and invention, something that in the animal still remains imprisoned and is only finally released when we reach man" (ME 23). He is not saying that humanity is the *telos*; he says humanity is a condition on further advance toward the *telos*. Bergson carefully defines the singularity he attributes to our kind. "It would be wrong to regard humanity, such as we have it before our eyes, as pre-figured in the evolutionary movement." That is the finalism he refutes. It is, he says, "in a quite different sense that we hold humanity to be the ground (*la raison d'être*) of evolution" (CE 266).

Humanity is the ground for something else. It is as Zarathustra said, we are a bridge, a passage to something higher. Not to a higher *species*—any species is a halting place for a vitality that will not be confined—but a superior individuality for life beyond the differentiation of species.[67] Such beings do not exist and perhaps they never will, but the tendency does. The vital *élan* is that tendency, launched four billion years ago and still pressing to this summit of creative freedom. The universe "is a machine for the making of gods" (TS 317).

As these words suggest, Bergson's thought on divinity is less about God, more about gods to come. What is divine about a thing is not what it *is* but its power of *becoming*, which in mortals goes as far as it can and halts, falling into form and dying the death of its ancestors. To stop this stopping would be divine. At one point in *Creative Evolution* Bergson pauses to ask whether *élan vital* might afford a definition of God. His reply to his own question is evasive. He says that *if* we define God that way, then God "has nothing of the already made; he is unceasing life, action, freedom" (CE 248). We can understand why the Catholic Church was reluctant to embrace Bergson's philosophy (or his soul), yet there is austere consolation in the great resonance of his thought with words from the Daoist *Zhuangzi*: "The blessed stop stopping. Not stopping means galloping while you sit. This is the transformation of ten thousand things, the secret of the ancient sages."[68]

An Evolving Cosmos

The evolution of terrestrial life is a phase of cosmic evolution, especially for an evolutionary thinker like Bergson, and his evolutionism cannot be limited to biology, as Deleuze observes: "Bergson's philosophy comes to completion in a cosmology where everything is change in tension, change in energy, and nothing else."[69] We should bear in mind the poverty of scientific cosmology when *Creative Evolution* appeared in 1907. Einstein's Special Theory of Relativity had just been published (1905), with the General Theory still years away (1915). To Bergson's time, no telescope had resolved another galaxy. When he imagines something astronomically large it is the Solar System, which he describes as "the system most objectively isolated and most independent of all" (CE 10). It would be more than a decade before Edwin Hubble resolved the Andromeda "nebula" and discovered the first exo-galaxy—really, he discovered the first *two* galaxies, for by discovering that Andromeda *was* a galaxy he inadvertently discovered that the Milky Way is one too and not the whole universe floating in otherwise empty space.

Shortly thereafter, in 1929, Hubble discovered and measured the spectral red-shift of distant galaxies, proving that far from floating they are receding in all directions, their recessional velocity increasing with distance from our galaxy, behaving for all the world like the ejecta of an explosion. Hubble was not a theorist and did not suggest the comparison, but his discoveries seemed to point to a universe evolving from a primordial event concentrating matter with almost inconceivable density and temperature. Einstein's equations were shown to be consistent with such a "singularity," which Belgian abbé Georges Lemaître christened the "primordial atom."[70]

Lemaître's cosmology is close to what Bergson suggested twenty years earlier (without Hubble's evidence). Both theories allow only finite time and space and eschew supernatural creation; the universe does not come into existence instantaneously or *ex nihilo*. Instead, it emerges by evolution in a process with a physical sequence. Lemaître stresses the indeterminacy of the future: "If we go back in the course of time we must find fewer and fewer quanta, until we find all the energy of the universe packed in a few or even a unique quantum.... Clearly the initial quantum could not conceal in itself the whole course of evolution; but, according to the principle of indeterminacy, that is not necessary."[71] Not possible, rather. He alludes to Heisenberg, whose principle excludes the fine coordination of space, time, and energy.

Lemaître draws Bergson's conclusion that the future does not exist, that it is not just the past over and over but always new. Ours is a world "where something really happens," the whole story of the world is not inscribed on the primordial atom "like a song on the disc of a phonograph."[72] That "something else" is the freedom that begins with indetermination. In words remembered by a friend, Bergson is said to have said, "If there is the origin of all, if the duration is finite, there is freedom at the beginning of everything and, consequently, in the things themselves. If, on the contrary, there is no origin of the whole, if the duration is infinite and eternal, if there is no absolute beginning, there cannot be freedom within the series itself."[73]

The evolution of the universe can be described in three phases. The first stretches from the unfathomably early time of the first Planck moment (10^{-43} seconds) to the first millisecond (10^{-3}). Astronomer Royal Martin Rees describes this earliest phase, forty orders of temporal magnitude, as terra incognita.[74] The second phase runs from the first millisecond to the first several million years. The Astronomer calls this stretch the easy bit, the physics is well-understood, the cosmological process amounting to a (nearly) smooth expansion with nothing yet sufficiently organized to call structure. Finally, the recent cosmological epoch, characterized by the freezing into place of key constants together with the introduction of intractable complexity, sensitivity to initial conditions, and perhaps most surprising the cosmic reversal, when some ten billion years into the Big Bang the recession of the galaxies began to *accelerate*. For the first eight billion years of cosmic evolution the galaxies were slowing down as we intuitively expect, then against all intuition, they began to accelerate. It is strange that this should happen, reversing the quality that originally suggested the idea of beginning with a bang. To add to the enigma, for technical reasons the energy required for the acceleration cannot have always been present and acting in some other direction. This acceleration has only recently begun to assert itself and why it happened remains a mystery of cosmology.[75]

The universe was no more folded up in the Big Bang than an infant is folded up in a blastula or a bird folded up in a dinosaur. Big Bang cosmology does not propose that all the particles of matter meet at a first moment. Instead, they all spring into existence in one cosmic event, simultaneously but separately, and not with a bang but a shiver. Quantum cosmologist Lee Smolin observes, "What caused our world to exist was probably not so much an explosion as an event that caused a region of the universe to cool drastically and freeze."[76] The t_0 singularity is, of course, unfathomable. Any singularity is, whether the truly singular singularity of the Big Bang or the garden variety singularity of any black hole. Roger Penrose says that "physics comes to an end at such regions. Or, if it does not, then it continues in some kind of universe-structure of a completely foreign character to that of which we have knowledge."[77] If we value Darwin's theory despite its leaving life's origin mysterious, we should appreciate the value of an evolutionary cosmology even if it leaves something very dark.

Physicist Leonard Susskind helpfully explains that what physicists usually mean by the term *exist* is that the object in question "exists as a solution to the equations of the theory." By that criterion, he says, "perfectly cut diamonds a hundred miles in diameter exist. So do planets made of pure gold."[78] Lots of entire universes exist too, even though they do not admit a clock, whether because of thermal equilibrium or being too small or too simple to divide into subsystems. A *temporal* universe must be qualitatively complex, organized, dynamic, and far from equilibrium. Smolin says that "time can only exist in a structured and complex universe, with a sufficient balance of order and variety. There seems to be no viable approach to the problem of time in quantum cosmology that does not lead to this conclusion."[79] He says time requires a universe of a certain quality. The proposition is convertible. A universe that is not merely consistent with equations but actually exists must express time. A universe too simple for time is too simple to actually exist.

Time is not optional to physical existence because actuality is qualitative and change takes time. Qualities take time: red takes time, Bergson had to wait for sugar to melt. Qualitative change propagates through an environment that is ultimately cosmic, and that takes time. A universe of time requires a clock, a movement with which to compare others. It is difficult to identify a clock-process in the very early universe. Current thinking suggests that the notion of timescale disappears at about 10^{-11} seconds, at the quark-hadron phase transition.[80] At 10^{-11} seconds after the singularity, all fundamental particles have zero rest mass, precluding any regular physical process. From this point back, there is no timescale, that is, no ranging of events as earlier or later. This epoch is the pure past, a past that has never been present.

Earlier, we noticed Bergson's argument that pure space, Cartesian coordinates infinite in all directions, is a concept, a diagram, not a reality, and the same goes for pure time. Pure time, by which I mean bottomless interpenetrating continuity, is a concept and an abstraction since we have no experience of that *bottomless*. As long as time exists, it is duration, continuous and interpenetrating, but that does not mean duration exists aboriginally. Quantum cosmologist Carlo Rovelli thinks it is a mistake to assume that time is one thing with one nature, for instance, duration. That's Bergson's mistake: "The mistake is to take the complex experience of time that we have and to assume that all aspects of it are general and must underpin nature in general."[81] When we approach the boundaries of extension, as in quantum physics, especially in quantum cosmology, we should not be surprised to find that duration, which has by this point become a *concept*, is not a helpful one.

Duration commences with the first Planck interval. Not the *absolutely* first, which is the (imaginary) interval from the singularity to 10^{-43} seconds. What I am calling the first Planck duration is the first *upon* the birth of duration, from 10^{-11} seconds. This first interval is a passage, no more fully present than any duration. It contains the virtual memory of its immediate past (the whole epoch from the singularity to 10^{-11} seconds) and fleeting as it must seem the interval is truly a passage, embracing changes of temperature and density due to expansion and some creation of particles from energy. Duration and passage are born in this first Planck interval, and the past already exists (virtually) all the way back to the singularity. Before this interval, all events belong to the pure past, an absolute past in which no event is more or less past than another. At 10^{-11} seconds after the singularity that began to change. The past became temporalized and began to grow.

Physicists can be reluctant to acknowledge time's difference from space (Chapter 1). The issue has been revisited by cosmologists who suspect that like geology and biology their science has to take time seriously. Smolin argues that "time is real and fundamental, and the history of the universe is a necessary part of understanding its present state." In other words, the passage of time is effective on a cosmological scale, no less than terrestrially. Smolin explains cosmological time as "a real present moment," a *now*. To call this *now* "real" implies a cosmic frame of reference with respect to which absolute simultaneity can be defined: "There is a boundary all observers can agree on between the real present and the not yet real future. This implies a universal, physical notion of simultaneity that includes distant events and, indeed, the whole universe."[82] That is not impossible. What cosmologists call the canonical (Lemaître) frame of reference is defined as that in which every galaxy is (almost) at rest and the universe is expanding, not through the motion of galaxies but by the creation of new space between them, so that what looks like a recession of galaxies is actually a flood of new space. Since there is no purely spatial distance, new space is also new time. In this canonical frame, all galaxies have experienced the same interval since the singularity, clocks in any of them read the same time, and they all experience the frontier of the future (*now*) simultaneously.[83]

Experimental physicist Richard Muller thinks the continuous creation of new time is the physical basis of time's arrow. "Every moment the universe gets a little bigger and there is a little more time, and it is this leading edge of time that we refer to as *now*," a cosmological present. This *now* marks "the boundary, the shock front, the new time that is coming from nothing, the leading edge of time." This is not the *now* of McTaggart's A-series, not a movable instant gliding over points including a future that is already given. *Now* is a moment "that has just been created. The time axis for a true space-time diagram does not extend to infinity. Time stops *now*."[84] And immediately starts over, a present that is always beginning again. What Muller describes is a cosmological temporality, a *now* or present that is older than life and not a phenomenon of life. In a cosmos where life may be a stranger and so too life's temporality and the phenomena of duration, there remains a time proper to the universe, a duration-less time of lifeless matter-energy, a present endlessly starting over.

Bergson might say that the present, the now, is an index not of time but of life and consciousness. *Now*, the duration of the present, is relative to an organism and its attention to life: "Our present is the very materiality of our existence, that is to say, a system of sensations and movements, and nothing else" (MM 178). Bergson defines *our* present, a *human* present, in terms of our body. "Our present is, above all, the state of our body" (MM 320). With panpsychism, however, all bodies are conscious, including the universe, which Bergson describes as "a kind of consciousness" (MM 313). In the cosmological theory we are considering, new time and space are created in an expanding region of intergalactic space-time. If it is time that comes into being, this must be a time of interpenetrating continuity. The cosmological *now* is not instantaneous, having instead some internal thickness and sustaining some analogy to the specious present of an organism, a conclusion that Bergson's panpsychism requires and leads us to expect.

The Two Sources of Morality and Religion ends with the statement that the "essential function of the universe" is to be "a machine for the making of gods" (TS 317). The appropriate connotation for "machine" is not mechanism but finality. What is technical about machines is their purposiveness; they are *for* something, with an effectiveness that exceeds their parts separately. Bergson is saying there is something the universe is for, a final cause of the universe, which implies a tendency to this end active throughout cosmic evolution. It may be helpful to review what was said earlier about philosophical teleology. For Plato, the source of finality was external to the order it inaugurates; the demiurge who creates the world is not part of the creation. Aristotle broke with this understanding to introduce the immanent finality of an inbuilt *phusis*-nature for every substance. Philosophers of the Middle Ages set aside immanent finality for a theologically more tractable Platonic theory, according to which the creation of the world proceeded under the determination of an external intelligent cause. Bergson's teleology is in the Stoic-Spinoza tradition, which amalgamates immanent finality with a teleology of the whole: "If there is finality in the world of life, it includes the whole of life in a single indivisible embrace" (CE 43).

The universe is a machine as an egg is a machine. It is a dynamic system of immanent finality tending to a limit, which in the cosmic case is divinity, understood in terms of individuality, freedom, and creative power. *Élan vital* is this still-tending tendency, coextensive with the emergence of life and continuous with the Big Bang. It is one motion with one tendency that has diversified beyond count in four billion years of terrestrial evolution. This tendency is finite and has been given all at once, so it must evolve and adapt and therefore has divided into tendencies of lesser duration, which struggle for actuality. Were life to evolve beings capable of continuing creation forever, then spirit would overcome matter and life would overcome death. That end is the "essential function"—I would say *ultimate tendency* or *immanent finality*—of the universe. It is a tendency, not a design, purpose, or plan, not predetermined, and not unopposed, in this case by the entropic tendency of matter.

Bergson and Nietzsche

Bergson's work was well received in Germany in the early twentieth century and comparisons with Nietzsche were often drawn.[85] In 1909, a German scholar observed that "in Germany a veritable spiritual war was kindled when it was first appreciated just how much [Bergson] put into question and stirred up. . . . He is more dangerous than Nietzsche."[86] A publication by Georg Simmel in 1914 succeeded in getting German philosophers to read these thinkers together. In a widely mooted conceit, Bergson was the French Nietzsche, with Schopenhauer mentioned as a mediator. Thoughtful readers still found the difference unmistakable. In a 1933 lecture on Bergson's *Two Sources* Ernst Cassirer says, "Bergson's ethics does not go down the road of Nietzsche, and his praise of life does not turn into a praise of the will to power."[87]

Bergson himself was cool about association with Nietzsche. He names the German a single time in his books when in 1932 he alludes to "Nietzsche's mistake" (TS 278).[88] The only work by Nietzsche in his library was *La volonté de puissance*, an edition from 1937, thus several years after *The Two Sources of Morality and Religion*. In 1936 Bergson is reported to have said that he had not read Nietzsche because he disliked reading aphoristic works. Jean Wahl remembers him saying, "I cannot read Nietzsche," again complaining of a disagreeable "unstructured" writing. Yet peers whom Bergson respected pressed him to clarify his relation to Nietzsche; for instance, in 1917, Ernest Seilliére, whose work Bergson lauded "for depth and forcefulness beyond praise" (TS 268), wonders whether Bergson will succeed in developing a philosophy of life that could stand as an alternative to Nietzsche.[89] A scholar of Bergson's German reception thinks he did exactly that in his last work.[90]

Scholars have identified points of consilience, beginning with an understanding of life in terms of will, an argument foreshadowed in Schopenhauer.[91] Bergson and Nietzsche also make a similar criticism of Darwinism. Life cannot be understood merely as adaptation to external conditions; there is a drive, an impulsion. Thus Bergson: "[Natural selection] explains the sinuosities of the movement of evolution, but not its general directions, still less the movement itself" (CE 102). And Nietzsche: "Life is not an adaptation of internal conditions to external conditions, but will to power which, from within, always masters and incorporates more of the exterior."[92]

I mentioned Bergson's reference to "Nietzsche's mistake." It is the mistake of thinking we can separate people into two types—strong or weak, master or slave. The dichotomies are odious and everything alive mixes them up. Tendencies to command and obey are in us all, and even if obedience predominates that does not make people sheep. Bergson does not reference titles or pages in Nietzsche, and while I can imagine passages that could leave an impression of the idea he criticizes, it seems to ME that Nietzsche's considered view is closer to Bergson's own. They already share important ideas in ontology, primarily the priority of becoming over being. "All becoming seemed to ME the dance of gods," Zarathustra muses, as does Nietzsche, writing in a note, "A kind of becoming must itself create the deception of beings." That is an epitome of Bergson's theory of images. The Dionysian philosophy that affirms "*becoming* along with a radical rejection of the very concept of 'being' " is no less an epitome of Bergson's polemic against Greek ontology.[93]

For Nietzsche as for Bergson, becoming is primary, original, older than being. "Movement is reality itself, and immobility is always only apparent or relative" (CE 155). Every form is changing "at every moment; or rather, there is no form, since form is immobile and the reality is movement" (CE 302). What we recognize as a "being" (entity, object, thing, species, form) is the perspectival result of species-specific perceptual invariants. This is comparable to Nietzsche's perspectivism, which he describes as "the fundamental condition of all life."[94] They may both be remembering Spinoza: "The human mind does not perceive any external body as actually existing except through the ideas of the modifications of its own body."[95]

Taking time seriously means introducing original becoming, which makes "being" perspectival because, as Bergson says, "it is always the stop which requires explanation, and not the movement," an explanation to be found in the ends of the perceiving organism (TS 312). Perception, evolved and species-specific, introduces these stops, though they are not literally stops but synchronies, rhythms, stable correlations an organism can perceive and act on, making them as good as stops. Where they arise and what action they afford depend on the organism and is not prefigured in the continuity perception samples: "The division of unorganized matter into separate bodies is relative to our senses and to our intellect, and . . . matter, looked at as an undivided whole, must be a flux rather than a thing" (CE 186). Nietzsche reaches the same conclusion. "The world with which we are concerned is false," he writes in a note, explaining that he means "it is 'in flux,' as something in a state of becoming."[96]

For Nietzsche as for Bergson, the rhythm of life is self-overcoming. Becoming means becoming more. "Reality is a perpetual growth," Bergson says, "a creation pursued without end," and a veritable *need* of creativity, because the future does not pre-exist (CE 239). Zarathustra dramatically concurs, "This secret life itself spoke to ME: *Behold*, it said, *I am that which must always overcome itself.*"[97] In early philological studies on rhythm, Nietzsche found his way to *durée* and an idea of time comparable to Bergson's. In a manuscript of 1871, he says, "rhythm (*Takt*) is to be understood as something utterly fundamental, i.e., as the most primary sensation of time, as the very form of time." A contemporary note reads, "Rhythm is an attempt at individuation. For rhythm to exist, there must be multiplicity and becoming. Here, the rage for beauty shows itself to be a motive for individuation. Rhythm is the form of becoming, generally the form of the world of appearance."[98] *Mutatis mutandis*, this is Bergson's *durée*.

Bergson's thought on time casts light on some knotty problems of Nietzsche interpretation. For instance, in a text from 1885 Nietzsche writes dramatically of "my *Dionysian* world of the eternally self-creating, the eternally self-destroying." He describes this world—our world—as "a play of forces and waves of forces, at the same time one and many, increasing here and at the same time decreasing there."[99] Read with Bergson, this "play of forces" is the thwarting and contesting of virtual tendencies at the interface with actuality. The vital movement of the *élan* is finite, which means that growth on one level is senescence on another, syncopating the rhythm of becoming in terms of active-reactive or domination-submission. At every level of form or physical existence, something yields and something imposes, one suffers, another increases and commands: "The interaction of antagonistic tendencies is always implied" (CE 13). Will to power is not as alien to Bergson's thought as Cassirer suggested. A tendency may be thwarted, but unthwarted tendency tends to thwart all thwartable tendencies, for only by this contest can it become what it is.

Deleuze offers the most convincing demonstration of Bergson's value for reading Nietzsche.[100] If we think of time in the usual way, we think of it spatially, as if time were an axis in Cartesian space. With that assumption, Nietzsche's "eternal return of the same" becomes the idea proposed by Pythagoreans and Stoics in antiquity. "There will be nothing different in comparison to what has happened before, but everything will occur in just the same way and indistinguishably, even to the last details."[101] This is repetition in spatialized time, a formal iteration, the same forms one more time. Let us call this Stoic, or geometrical repetition. If this were Nietzsche's thought too, it would hardly be a great new idea; it merely repeats a Pythagorean and Stoic idea well known to scholars. The argument turns out differently when time is understood with Bergson as duration. Reading Nietzsche this way is not anachronistic. We have seen him find his way to a concept of duration, which he understood as essential to rhythm and music. With time as duration, repetition repeats the whole past, which is different every time, making every repetition of duration inherently, qualitatively different. The same over and over means different and different again, eternal return means eternal singularity, a future that is always new.

Deleuze reads the repetition in eternal return, not extensionally, as the circular iteration of forms, but intensively and qualitatively, a Dionysian repetition of power rather than finished form: "Eternal return is linked, not to a repetition of the same but on the contrary to a transmutation."[102] Stoic, geometrical repetition is the nauseating and disowned thought of every form forever returning, the same to the last detail. Zarathustra's joyous idea of eternal return is a qualitative, intensive repetition that is different every time. The third part of *Thus Spoke Zarathustra*, which was the work's original conclusion, ends with a song. At each chorus Zarathustra sings of his "lust for eternity and for a nuptial ring of rings—the ring of recurrence."[103] The song's verses sing of moments when a passion for eternity overwhelms him with longing. It happens when lightning strikes, when dice are rolled, when necessity forces accidents to dance. None of these can happen the same way twice. They are irruptions of the new and can be that only once, never again. Zarathustra longs for the repetition of this *only once, never again*.

When we understand time with Bergson, the new and different is the only concrete form of repetition. That is especially true of life; he says it is the "fundamental law of life" never to repeat in what we called the Stoic or geometrical way (L 23). An organism is different every moment if only for the passage of time. The notion of mechanically repeating an identical form is sheer abstraction; concrete, *passing* time does not run that way. Given that time is duration, the sole respect in which two moments might be the same or repeat is in qualitative terms of intensity or power. To be as intense as something of the past is not to repeat a number of units or do anything that is extensively, quantitatively comparable. Only a creative act can repeat what was creative in the past. That is why Deleuze withholds eternal return from small, petty, reactive lives.[104] Nothing they do is different enough to be the same as what was creatively different in the past. For the herd, the masses, all is given, a qualitative repetition of the all too human, with no invention, no style, no artistry, same old same old. At any moment such lives are all they can be, while others have more futurity. The ethical challenge in the art of life is to become *capable* of repeating and thereby creating futurity.

Time is an eternal return; the future is the same as the past. Understand those words extensively and we understand them as Zarathustra's demon, the spirit of gravity, does, which is Stoically, spatially, as a geometrical iteration of form. Understand the same words with Bergson, and repetition becomes intensive, qualitative, and properly temporal. By the end of his adventures, we understand the choice Zarathustra posed at the beginning between the last human beings (*letzte Mensch*) and the overman. It is a choice of futures. What repetition will the future harbor—intensive or extensive, quantitative or qualitative, Stoic or Dionysian? To ME,

Nietzsche's texts on eternal return make better sense when time is understood with Bergson as duration than spatialized with the Stoics. Nietzsche was a carefully trained specialist in ancient literature, and it is inconceivable that he did not know the Pythagorean and Stoic versions of eternal return or appreciate how rationalistic especially the Stoic version is.[105] If his idea was no different, why did he think eternal return was a great new thought? But if time were duration and rhythm, then Nietzsche's thought on eternal return is Europe's first non-spatializing, properly temporal reflection on creative repetition.[106]

Nietzsche and Bergson could be accused of time worship, the idea that things are valuable not for what they are but for what they become. However, this valuation is defensible when *to be* is an artificial halt imposed by perspective on the continuous extensity of original becoming. How could we worship what a thing *is*, when identity and seeming fullness of form merely reduce an original becoming to an anthropocentric image? There's idolatry for you! The form may be useful, it may be beautiful, but its provenance is all too human. However, to worship what in things is becoming, the *élan*, their tendentious movement, is to worship the single respect in which finite existence participates in the divine. Life's secret, whispered to Zarathustra, is self-overcoming, which is also a rite of Dionysus: "What I called Dionysian is to be oneself the eternal joy of becoming."[107]

Nietzsche's Dionysian teleology follows Aristotle and Leibniz and localizes finality not in the whole cosmos but in the will of the striving individual: "My idea is that every specific body strives to become master over all space and to extend its force (—its will to power:) and to thrust back all that resists its extension."[108] Bergson develops a different line in philosophical teleology, a Stoic teleology of the ensemble. He was never more Stoic or further from Aristotle when he says, "If there is finality in the world of life, it includes the whole of life in a single indivisible embrace" (CE 43). Nietzsche would doubtless scoff at such finality, not because he denies finality per se—how could a philosophy of the will do without finality? Nietzsche's objection would be to the Stoic idea of a totality with a good of its own to which the individual is subordinate.

Bergson takes time seriously in a way neither Spinoza nor Stoics did. The whole is virtual, closure is never more than tendency, moreover a tendency that does not subsume human ends but rather *uses* them to carry forward *its* tendency, which as Bergson said is the creation of gods, many of them, each a maximum of individuality, freedom, and creative will. This may not be so different from the overman Zarathustra envisions, except perhaps for the democracy implicit in Bergson's alternative, as I will explain in the next chapter. While Nietzsche expects individuals to contest and conflict forever, Bergson envisions a cosmopolitan mode of peaceful coexistence.

* * *

Better than calling Bergson a vitalist, call him a teleologist, a philosopher of final causes. None of the recent vitalists (Liebig, Driesch) had been clear on the relation of efficient and final causes or the integration of finality with scientific biology. Bergson's teleology is modeled after the Stoics and Spinoza rather than Plato or Aristotle. He criticizes the compromised and amateurish teleology of modern vitalist philosophy. Disposing of some ill-explained *ummph*, Liebig's *Lebenskraft* and Driesch's entelechy sit awkwardly on the fence between spooky causes and redundant purposiveness. *Élan vital*, the final cause of terrestrial life, contributes not *ummph*, not mechanical dynamism, but tendency or *telos*. By insisting that *élan vital* is a scientific hypothesis Bergson implies that the biological sciences need to rethink the repudiation of final causes. *Élan vital* is only a scientific hypothesis when we allow that teleology cannot be eliminated from life or its science.

Bergson adduces convergent evolution to show that the history of life depends on causes beyond Darwin's ken. This argument is unsuccessful. Embryological and genomic modes of homology make convergent evolution no longer appear fantastically unlikely. Conway Morris even turns it to new evidence for the primacy of adaptation in evolution. Bergson's untenable refutation of Darwinism does not make *élan vital* an untenable or superfluous idea. It represents a philosophical understanding that incorporates Darwinism without being limited by it. It establishes a temporal framework for Darwinian algorithms while qualifying the grandiose claim for their omnipotence, introducing immanent tendencies to the variation natural selection confronts.

Élan vital names the movement or process initiated at the origin of terrestrial life. Like all movement, this has a tendency, which is not an actual, efficient cause but a final one and explains the tendentious variety time presents for natural selection. What becomes available for selection is not random relative to the tendency of life's evolution, which is to introduce the greatest possible indeterminacy into matter. The current summit of this trend is our humble species, a current summit, not the final one, for human beings are not life's evolutionary *telos* but rather a condition of further evolution toward the cosmopolis of open society.

4
Open and Closed

This chapter studies the theme of open and closed in Bergson's last work, *The Two Sources of Morality of Religion*, though I also discuss *Laughter* from 1900, which anticipates and complements the later argument. In this last philosophical statement, Bergson develops expansive theories on morality, religion, magic, mysticism, and technology. I will not summarize or comment on much of this material. I focus on the theme of open and closed, tracing it through Bergson's late statements on social philosophy, aesthetics, and the philosophy of technology.

The philosopher associated with an idea of open and closed society is Karl Popper. What he means by "open" is, roughly, liberalism. *The Open Society and Its Enemies* was a defense of liberal freedoms (economic and political) against the authoritarianism recently witnessed under Hitler and Stalin. Popper's open society is one that cultivates rationality and experiments; "open" means open to criticism, extending reasonableness as widely as possible. Popper's closed society refers to a tribal past, lightly sketched, characterized by "the belief in magic taboos." It was critical rationality that got European civilization out of its closed, tribal, magical past by opening it to criticism and experiments, introducing modern liberty and liberal philosophy: "The closed society breaks down when the supernatural awe with which the social order is considered gives way to active interference [i.e., experiment], and to the conscious pursuit of personal or group interests [i.e., liberal economics]."[1]

Popper thinks Western civilization is and should remain an open society, because that is the most reasonable form of association, closed society tending to relapse into tribalism. Yet this open society is fragile and "has not yet fully recovered from the shock of its birth—the transition from the tribal or 'closed society' with its submission to magical forces, to the open society which sets free the critical powers of man." He invokes this shock, a wobbly age of birthing modernity, as "one of the factors that made possible the rise of those reactionary movements which have tried, and still try, to overthrow civilization and return to tribalism."[2] Open and closed means liberal and authoritarian, which in his mind means rational and tribal. Closed society belongs to that tribal past, having been superseded by a conglomerated Western, open, scientific, liberal society. As for Bergson's idea of open and closed, Popper looked into it and reports "a considerable difference . . . between Bergson's way of using these terms and mine," due, he thinks, "to a fundamentally different approach to nearly every problem of philosophy."[3] Popper's dichotomies, rationalism, and racist anthropology are unappealing, but at least he acknowledges that his ideas have nothing to do with Bergson and it is good to have that cleared up.

Open and Closed Society

A social form of life is not uncommon among vertebrate animals, more common among mammals, and becomes the rule in primates. Lions, wolves, antelope, bison, elephants, whales, and apes are some of the species that have evolved adaptations for social life. These are instinctual behaviors that moderate interaction. Darwin calls them social instincts, which are a behavioral adaptation. Adaptations can be anatomical, like our thumbs, or behavioral, for instance, to sleep at night. *Social* instincts are instinctive or easily learned preferences for peaceful interaction with others, including willingness to sacrifice selfishness for a socially unifying choice. Morality belongs to this social adaptation, as Darwin concluded. "The so-called moral sense is aboriginally derived from the social instincts, both relate at first exclusively to the community."[4] That describes the closed morality of closed society, and Bergson agrees with Darwin that such societies are humanity's evolved tendency. Closed society is the original society, humanity's common social matrix.

Bergson elucidates the thematic difference between open and closed by a system of contrasts (see below figure).

Closed	*Open*
Group	Humanity
Exclusive	Inclusive
Static	Dynamic
Obligation	Aspiration
Social	Individual
Habitual	Voluntary

The columns are not a series of dichotomies. Each term is an element in systematic differentiation and draws its value from the group. Open society is a total package, but it is a package of tendency, a thematic tendency, materializing variations in space and time. It is not Bergson's argument that world society should be open rather than closed. That was Popper's argument. With Bergson, open society is an aspiration and the expression of a creative emotion.

The primary characteristic of closed society is to include some groups and exclude others, while open society is an inclusive society of humanity. Closed society is consistent with a morality of obligations and traditional religion. The religion and morality of open society are personally felt, energized by aspiration rather than obedience. The evolved tendency of our species is for closed societies, and no amount of experience with civilization has changed that. Closed morality is (or was) adaptive, as Darwin suggested; it promoted the durability of a group that everybody individually required for survival, though also guaranteeing intergroup hostility. We cherish our own people more than outsiders, who are meritoriously plundered, enslaved, and killed. Yet closed morality is only half of morality and evolved social instincts are only one of two sources.

Norms of closed society explain judges and gossip but not saints and jeremiads. How should we understand an individual like Jeremiah, who chastises his community for not aspiring to a higher standard? To call his behavior (or our response) adaptive seems bizarre. Individuals like Jeremiah, Gandhi, or Martin Luther King inspire aspiration, communicating the possibility of a new order of life. Bergson calls such people geniuses of the will. "The will has its own genius, as does thought" (TS 58). This genius of the will is an unconscious artist and pied piper who inspires others to ideals they would never aspire to on their own. Their aspiration and our enthusiasm are Bergson's second source. The first source of morality and religion is evolved social instinct; the second is the forward-facing finality of the vital *élan*. This is what followers feel in the presence of those geniuses of the will. Every great agitation for liberty, equality, and justice would have been impossible were it not for the contagious enthusiasm of one or a few who felt in it the intimation of a life more worth living.

To elucidate the operation of this second source, Bergson distinguishes between two kinds of emotion (TS 43–44). One is feeling in consequence of an idea, feeling excited or shocked by a new possibility of thought. The other emotion does not *follow* an idea but is instead the stimulus to new ideas, being an emotion that contains a virtual multitude of ideas and the aspiration to realize them. People love this feeling of aspiration even before they understand the ideas to which they may be committed, and because the emotion does not depend on any specific ideas, the passion survives all refutation.

Closed morality is articulated in terms of obligations, while aspiration is most effective when aroused by a definite person, a moral leader or teacher, challenging the impersonal and habitual and making people feel new. The closed morality of obligations is dedicated to the preservation of one group among other, excluded groups. The open, personal morality of aspiration responds to an exciting feeling of movement and the enthusiasm of growth. Closed society cultivates many virtues—discipline, self-sacrifice, obedience, solidarity, honesty, fairness, loyalty, security, patriotism—and fulfilling closed-morality obligations promotes a feeling of well-being.[5] However, life on such terms is spiritually confined, ritually repeating the past. With this as the human default setting, every step toward open society becomes a test, "a leap forward," Bergson says, "which can take place only if society has decided to try the experiment; and the experiment will not be tried unless society has allowed itself to be won over, or at least stirred" (TS 74). We must be *stirred* out of closed society. Every advance in liberty, equality, and justice begins with such leaders, aspirational geniuses of the will, and grows by contagion.

Living in time is not just consciousness and memory; it is living with others and living on earth. Open and closed are two modes of social temporality, modes of duration in social existence; moreover they are the only two. Living in time is living in social organizations that express variations on these two temporalities. Bergson's argument opposes the kind of sociology Durkheim represented, which explains society with social facts.[6] Bergson says society "is not self-explanatory; so we must search below the social accretions, get down to Life" (TS 91). Closed social forms live time as the repetition of the past, while open forms live time as the invention of the future.[7] The closed tendency is organized by habits in people and instincts in other animals. In closed social forms, all change is a variation on a routine. These are societies of spatial parts; each member is a part, each is a role. Motivation is impersonal, a pressure from outside. The open tendency appeals to the generative principle of life and love beyond family and community. The difference appears not just in human social life but across the species, for instance, in the difference between reproduction and individuation (CE 13). Each species is a composite of these tendencies. From this evolutionary inheritance, human collectives derive tendencies to open and closed forms, the habits and obligations of social life, and aspirations that occasionally break through. These are Bergson's two sources.

Neither open nor closed exist in a pure form; in actual communities they are mixed and, as tendencies, can be expected to interpenetrate.[8] We feel their difference in the contrasting experience of obligation and love, or what Bergson calls feelings of attachment and feelings of release.[9] He explains that open and closed "are but two complementary manifestations of life, normally intent on preserving generally the social form which was characteristic of the human species from the beginning, but, exceptionally, capable of transfiguring it," thanks, he says, to those geniuses of the will, who "represent, as the appearance of a new species would have represented, an effect of creative evolution" (TS 97).

The first source of religion and morality is an aboriginal tendency to social exclusion, a tendency with a surprising ally.

Laughter

In 1900, Bergson published *Laughter: An Essay on the Comic*, which had earlier appeared in serial in the *Revue de Paris*. Coming between *Matter and Memory* and *Creative Evolution*, the work may seem anomalous in Bergson's oeuvre, though once we study the details we see that it is nothing of the kind. The topic of laughter is as large as life and no theory can contain it.[10] Laughter is a universal human response associated with happy feelings and social bonding, but it is also an idiosyncratic behavior. We are not the same in when or how we laugh and uncertainty about who will laugh on what occasion can make laughter difficult to orchestrate. Laughter is energetic, volatile, its physical symptoms vivid, and it has an unstable association with emotions, by turns amiable, antagonistic, playful, or hostile.

One explanation of laughter is an incongruity theory. We laugh at things unexpected, unusual, or out of place. Why are puns funny? A topsy-turvy second meaning barges in like a clown at a prayer meeting. But not any incongruity is funny, and many are not funny at all, for instance parental cruelty or filial ingratitude. Bergson's new idea is to be specific about the incongruity laughter perceives. Humor arises from the incongruity of people unconsciously behaving as if they were machines or as if their body had been taken over by a mechanism, moving not with intelligence but under mindless compulsion. A person caught in a repetitive routine like dancing after the music stops is funny. Frozen postures, a dignity too rigid, irrelevant mannerisms, a dignified pose interrupted by an urgent physical need are funny for the same reason. We laugh at the sudden transformation of person into thing, living action into mechanism, freedom into necessity. Life is infinitely sensitive and constantly changing, while mechanism is the opposite, rigid and clunky. Humor arises from the incongruity of something mechanical where we expected life.

Why should the perception of this specific mode of incongruity make our sides shake? Bergson says we must consider the place of laughter in the economy of life. "Laughter is above all a corrective" (L 96). Its function is disciplinary, punitive, fit chastisement for pomposity, insincerity, and stupidity. It is intended to humiliate, a snubbing slight yet dreaded. Laughter punishes behavior that is inattentive to social nicety and indifferent to common sense. Such behavior threatens social life by making people less predictable. While laughter punishes eccentricity it also reintegrates, provided we can take a joke.

Bergson claims that comic effects are always caused by people, either their appearance or behavior. No landscape is comical, and if anything nonhuman seems comical the amusement is probably anthropomorphic. Another quality of the comic is the absence of feeling. The action we laugh at does not affect us; we do not care what happens to the one at whom we laugh. If we cared we would not laugh: "Laughter has no greater foe than emotion" (L 10). Laughter is cold observation, intellectual appraisal, and a momentary anesthesia of the heart. Laughter is also typically interactive, practically always the laughter of a group, even though no one type of interaction is specially associated with it. Laughter can solidify group bonds; it can persuade or reassure; it can also mock, exclude, attack, and demean; it can be positive, negative, intimate, or public. In all these settings, however, laughter usually anticipates a resonance in the laughter of others.[11]

The social side of laughter prompts Bergson's hypothesis that laughter is a social instinct: "Laughter must answer to certain requirements of life in common. It must have a *social* significance" (L 12). That means an evolved, adaptive function. He begins his analysis by stating what he calls the "fundamental law of life," which is never to repeat (L 23). A pianist cannot strike a key the same way twice. However, sometimes people's behavior appears mechanical, as if their body were taken over by a machine and they succumbed to mechanical repetition. From the law of life Bergson derives a law of laughter: "Any arrangement of acts and events is comic which gives us, in a single combination, the illusion of life and the distinct impression of a mechanical arrangement" (L 40). One face may be unremarkable. Set it beside a closely resembling one and the ensemble makes us laugh. What we thought was the singular visage of a living being suddenly looks mechanical, as if stamped from a mold. To be alive and not a machine means to pay attention, and one who slips on a banana peel or keeps dancing after the music stops is not paying attention. This "deflection of life toward the mechanical" is "the real cause of laughter" (L 24); "the attitudes, gestures, and movements of the human body are laughable in exact proportion as that body reminds us of a mere machine" (L 22).

Merely assembling people stimulates passions. Peaceful, mutually beneficial social existence requires averting passionate expression; hence duties, rules, and the expectation of conformity. Children are born prepared to learn whatever norms adults and peers expect, much as they are prepared to acquire whatever language people speak. These social instincts produce feelings and ideas consistent with common life and dampen what Bergson calls "the inner fire of individual passions" (L 80). In human evolution,

178 LIVING IN TIME

fiery passions would have been counterproductive to group survival. Human ancestors cultivated an aversion to individuality that has left us often happy to be who others think we are. This social self is an adaptation acquired as instinctively as first language. Its value is to ease the social form of life and ensure the reproduction of closed society. Singularity is not advantageous to closed society and society begins closed. Singularity is a kind of deviance that may not be immoral but is seldom without reproach, including the rebuke of laughter.

The social life of closed society requires a balance of tension and flexibility, an alert elasticity. Inflexibility, connoting eccentricity, is devalued, and the group's response to such people and their actions is laughter. Most of us fear this unanswerable opposition, which makes it effective, its work being "to suppress any separatist tendency" (L 87). Dreading laughter compels us to attend to our social surroundings and how we appear to others. Laughter is an agency of closed society and in laughing we do the work of this collective, entrenching its exclusions and reinforcing closure.

Laughter contains Bergson's most sustained discussion of artistry and the arts. He begins with the legacy of evolution. *Homo sapiens* is one species but each individual is deeply different, despite suppressing this individuality in society and scrambling it in reproduction. Common sense demands prosaic attention to life, undistracted by irrelevancies. Things have endlessly many properties, but those we cannot use we tend to ignore. We respond to things not for what they are but in terms of their usefulness to us or the cliches we have heard about them: "We do not see the actual things themselves; in most cases we confine ourselves to reading the labels affixed to them" (L 77). Works of fine art compel attention to the otherwise unnoticed individuality of sensible existence. This art "has no other object than to brush aside the utilitarian symbols, the conventionally and socially accepted generalities, in short everything that veils reality from us, in order to bring us face to face with reality itself" (L 79). That means face to face with palpable individuality. Science seeks the invariant; art discovers the singular. The invariant is relative; the singular, absolute.

Bergson returns to this argument ten years later in a lecture at Oxford. He describes normal life as dominated by "a constant effort of the mind to limit its horizon, to turn away from what it has a material interest in not seeing." He thinks we are "obliged to narrow and drain [perceptions] by our attachment to reality, our need for living and acting" (CM 113). This tendency to closure sacrifices perceptual singularity to the general will. Art has the power to disperse this fog from consciousness. Works of art memorialize singular perception and entice contemplation. Artists dig deep, shun cliche, intuit singularity, and recover the individuality squelched by quotidian perception. The experience can be hypnotic.

Art shows something we were never meant to see, being a use of perception that does not serve species survival, yet which we love and never have enough of. Bergson says philosophy is analogous to art in this quality. Ever since Thales, common people have laughed at philosophers and their useless arguments.[12] Bergson thinks philosophy should follow art in aspiring to "a completer perception of reality by means of a certain displacement of our attention" (CM 114). He explains that "through philosophy we can accustom ourselves never to isolate the present from the past which it pulls along with it. Thanks to philosophy, all things acquire depth. . . . What was immobilized and frozen in our perceptions is warmed and set in motion. Everything comes to life around us, everything is revivified in us" (CM 131–32). Bergson learned this idea from Félix Ravaisson—he calls it "the whole philosophy of Ravaisson"; namely, that "it is the same intuition, variously applied, which makes the profound philosopher and the great artists" (CM 197).[13]

Artistry and philosophy are varieties of the aspiration to open social forms. Yet if laughter serves closed society and artistry is a tendency to the open, we may wonder whether comedy is fine art at all. A painting, sculpture, poem, or symphony is assembled as it is solely for the pleasure of those who perceive it. That applies to comedy too. Why does anyone make a joke if not to give others pleasure? Comedy is less disinterested than fine art, however, having an external purpose, contrary to Kant's admonition.[14] Comedy differs from canonical fine art in what Bergson describes as its "scarcely confessed or scarcely conscious intention to correct and instruct" (L 85). Shakespeare and Goethe did not want to correct and instruct their audience. They wanted to impart lasting, endlessly renewable pleasure, and there is no way to do that without plumbing the depth of individuality. Comedy is not so detached. More is at stake than disinterested pleasure since pleasure for the audience is pain for the target of their laughter. Audiences are aware of the pain and laugh all the same, their pleasure deriving from an unavowed intention to humiliate and correct. Is this still fine art?

Comedy deliberately evades individuality and depicts only stereotypes. A comic character is not a vivid individual like Hamlet, Oedipus, or David Copperfield (Bergson never mentions Falstaff). A comic character is a type, falling into a ready-made category— the Alchemist, the Hypochondriac, the Misanthrope, the Miser; a deviant whose impertinence is repaid with laughter. Individuality is downplayed for comic effect, since the more singular characters become the more audiences care about them, feeling emotions like pity and fear, at which point the comedy is over and a tragedy has begun. Once again, "Laughter has no greater foe than emotion" (L 10).

Bergson expects that once readers appreciate the unconscious significance of laughter, they may feel a "curious pessimism" about their participation in it (L 97). What do we do when we laugh at someone or even at ourselves? We detect deviance and hasten to negate it. Idiosyncrasy breaks through and we laugh to scorn, punishing with humiliation. This is not the outcome of reflective judgment; we can't help laughing, it's a natural thing to do. But can our laughter still be so unconsidered now that we appreciate its exclusionary function? Laughing is fun, it is relaxing, but it also enforces social closure. The more we laugh the less we aspire, since laughter requires an absence of emotion, undercutting creative emotions like aspiration no less than tragic emotions of pity and fear. Everything that keeps us laughing also keeps us stuck in a form, closed and violent.

Arthur Koestler thought he destroyed Bergson's theory with his touché observation that if Bergson were right nothing should be more humorous than a corpse.[15] However, a corpse is not amusing precisely because it is not alive. A character who, though visibly alive, was somehow corpse-like might be funny, though it would take a genius to make us laugh at a zombie clown. That is not to say Bergson's theory is without difficulty.[16] To say that laughter is always chastising overlooks aspects of humor for which it is difficult to account. For instance, the element of play, frivolity, topsy-turvy, extravagance, distortion, and fancy in humor. Lewis Carroll's *'Twas brillig, and the slithy toves did gyre and gimble*; or delirious logic like, *If you come to a fork in the road, take it!* (Yogi Berra), make language mock itself, which is funny. The humor confounds the habit of meaning with no sense beyond the boldness of its nonsense. *If it's feasible, let's fease it!* (P. G. Wodehouse). There is no place for the madcap in Bergson's comic. This other comedy is detached, relaxed, a moment of individuality, and not the punitive scrutiny of others.

Presumably people with little or no experience of machinery still laugh. We might wonder whether Bergson's laughter is European. It requires no ethnographic finesse to see that others are laughing, but to share the laughter can be harder. For instance, the Inuit of Nunavut play a ritual game when a young hunter kills his first bird. As the successful hunter, the boy holds the head while others try to tear body parts away and eat them. A Nunavut elder (2008) remembers: "Every first kill was shared that way and always with laughter and joy. Sometimes the tugging came down to two individuals. The person who caught the [bird] held on to the head and another person held the neck, which was very strong. When two grown men tugged against each other, they could cause one another to lurch forward. Spectators would almost die of laughter. Some were so hysterical that it seemed they were crying."[17]

The right test of Bergson's argument is not whether it captures all and only what is funny. Laughter is not cognition, and its philosophy is not conceptual analysis. What strikes us as funny tends to involve other people, avoid arousing emotions, occur in a social context, and mock eccentricity. Are there counterexamples? Of course. The last point is the least convincing. But counterexamples show only that universalization is inadvisable and in Bergson's case it was never intended: "We shall not aim at imprisoning the comic spirit within a definition. We regard it as above all a living thing. However trivial it may be, we shall treat it with the respect due to life" (L 1). It may be a little thing, but under Bergson's examination we watch it grow to merge with the tendency to social exclusion and see it revealed as an instrument of closed society.

Another Laughter

Nietzsche resists the aspiration of Bergson's open society, though not because he values closed society; disdaining the closed is not the same as aspiring to the open. Closed society laughs and perhaps open society smiles, but both exclude a Dionysian emotion, which is no more to be domesticated by open, dynamic aspiration than by closed and static norms. Dionysus smiles but does not laugh, because this smile defeats all socialization. This god smiles on anything, on everything, but laughs at nothing, punishing no excess. The laughter Bergson describes is a monotonous agent of social closure, while the multi-modal laughter of Zarathustra's experience exposes norms of laughter beyond Bergson's analysis.

One fine morning, Zarathustra left his mountain fastness to go down among the people and teach the overman idea. He does not even make it off the mountain before someone laughs at him. He encounters a hermit who, when Zarathustra explains what he is doing, finds it risible. How little he knows the people, to expect them to harken to that message! Zarathustra's next encounter, when he reaches a town and tries to speak in the marketplace, confirms the hermit's premonition. Zarathustra harangues the indifferent crowd. "We laugh at apes," he shouts at them, "but we ourselves will be a laughingstock [and] painful embarrassment"—to the overman. The people just laughed. "They laugh, they do not understand me." "They look at me and laugh, and in laughing they hate me too. There is ice in their laughter."[18]

That is Bergson's laughter, the laughter of closed society, laughing at eccentricity. Such laughter might be expected from the rabble, but Zarathustra hears another laughter in his dreams. Like the Socratic daimon, this laughter does not tell him what to do; it merely laughs at his pusillanimity. In one dream, the clock of his life speaks to him. "You know it Zarathustra. . . . You know it but you do not speak it!" "I do not want to," he replies. "Then laughter broke out around me. Alas, how this laughter tore my entrails and slit open my heart. . . . Again there was laughing, and it vanished."[19] This passage appears at the end of the Second Part, marking the end of Zarathustra's second sojourn among the people. He had been pretending that he understood why this second effort to unburden himself of his wisdom was a failure as the first had been. He knows it but won't say it, resisting self-knowledge like a petulant child. For that he is laughed at, though by whom we do not know.

Zarathustra himself laughs and thinks he has something to teach with his laughter.[20] A series of passages direct rounds of laughter at modern ideals. He laughs at equality, laughing "my laughter of the heights." He laughs at public education. "I had to laugh! Never had my eyes seen anything so splattered with colors! I laughed and laughed. . . . You seem to be baked from colors and paper slips glued together. Motley, all ages and peoples peek from your veils." He laughs at the radicals, whom he likens to a fire-hound, good for nothing except belching smoke and spreading grime. He laughs at atheists, "My heart convulsed with laughter. . . . Indeed, this will be the death of me, that I choke from laughter when I see asses drunk and hear night watchmen doubting God's existence. . . . Has the time not *long* since passed for all such doubting?"[21] Irrepressible laughter at these modern paragons will be a touchstone for the free spirit.

Zarathustra also laughs at himself. Having aborted his second experiment with disciples, he faces a solitary journey home. Walking alone, mulling his experience, he "laughed at himself with melancholy and bitterness," saying, "Laughable indeed are my folly and my modesty in love. Thus spoke Zarathustra, and he laughed once again." After this second fiasco, Zarathustra will never again descend among the people, but that does not mean his involvement with disciples is over because now they come to him and they're nervous wrecks. He says their problem is their fear of laughter, which as Bergson said is the wrath of the herd against singularity. Their fear of rebuke and laughter is a self-imposed obstacle to becoming the higher men they are: "Learn to laugh at yourselves as one must laugh, you higher men! Oh, how much is still possible!"

> You higher men, your worst part is that all of you have not learned to dance as one must dance—dance over and past yourselves . . . *learn* to laugh over and past yourselves! Lift up your hearts, you good dancers, high! higher! And don't forget good laughter either. . . . I pronounce laughter holy.[22]

In these passages we hear a laughter devoid of social significance, subserving no adaptive function, expressing aspiration, certainly, but not for Bergson's open social forms. There is no place for this exalted laughter in Bergson's theory. Can a genius of the will laugh—at himself? Gurus compromise individuality as well as inspire it. Nietzsche sees a problem in their effect on others, which is also the interpersonal dynamic with which Zarathustra struggles in relation to disciples. Charismatic geniuses of the will have no evolved, adaptive social function; instead they are a creative force working against closure and fixity, aspiring to something infinite. Nietzsche might place Bergson's genius of the will among those he calls "the teachers of the purpose of existence," where he finds a functionality that Bergson neglects, namely, priestly service to the resentful herd of society's slaves.[23] These teachers promote faith in life, stilling a slave's tendency to doubt the value of life, and offering something at which it is forbidden to laugh.

Zarathustra associates laughter with courage: "Courage wants to laugh. . . . Who among you can laugh and be elevated at the same time? Whoever climbs the highest mountain laughs at all tragic plays and tragic realities." Another association is beauty, "the holy laughter and trembling of beauty." Beautiful things lighten the soul to the point of laughter; the best are even born laughing. In the terrible vision of a shepherd choking on a snake, he bites the horrid thing and is transformed.

> No longer shepherd, no longer human—a transformed, illuminated, *laughing* being. Never yet on earth had I heard a human being laugh as *he* laughed. Oh, my brothers, I heard a laughter that was no human laughter—and now a thirst gnaws at me, a longing that will never be still. My longing for this laughter gnaws at me.

A heart made light by laughter draws the body into dance: "All good things laugh . . . whoever approaches his goal dances." Such laughter is joyous, not punitive. It is a creator's laughter at a work's fruition. This dancing laughter expresses the dance-like quality of existence, as Zarathustra recounts in a vision: "All becoming seemed to me the dance of gods and the mischief of gods and the world seemed unloosed and frolicsome." From the dream, he learned to count as a loss any day "on which we did not dance once! And let each truth be false to us which was not greeted with one laugh!"[24]

Bergson emphasizes a single side of laughter, its evolved, adaptive side, the laughter of closed society with its exclusionary function. Remember that open and closed are tendencies in social existence and pull everybody more or less. But if one withholds punitive laughter at norm-violation, at what *does* one laugh? Open-society aspirations are no laughing matter. Bergson almost implies that we might give up laughter as we have abandoned other archaic barbarities. Nietzsche goes another way. Suppose we grant what Bergson says of laughter, grant his whole argument and the conclusions too. Yet as we can do things with our hands for which hands did not evolve, so we can do things with laughter that are more and different than its evolved function of social exclusion.

The multimodal laughter of *Thus Spoke Zarathustra* shows what can be made of a tendency to laugh when disciplined by a will free of subordination to the norms of closed society. In a later work, Nietzsche calls masters of such a will *sovereign individuals* and explains their freedom in terms of conscience.[25] If your will is free, then there are things you will not do, things that are against conscience. Can the voice of conscience laugh? Rousseau never described such a thing, nor Nietzsche explicitly, but is that not the laughter Zarathustra hears in his dreams?[26] And if conscience laughs, what would it laugh at if not ego's temptations to stop, hold back, resist, or deny what one is becoming? The laughter that haunts Zarathustra's dreams and the rueful laughter he directs at himself are conscience laughing at the hypocrisy by which he evades knowledge of the discrepancy between his aspiration and his acts.

Bergson's genius of the will is a charismatic source of aspiration. Nietzsche might observe that only those who have no aspiration need the stimulus. He dreams of an elite aspirational culture that lives on the back of slaves reproduced by the closed society they master. Bergson dreams of overcoming closed society, not in a sovereign elite but in an open society of fraternity and human rights. Nietzsche shuns the appeal of fraternity and values only the best, but Bergson will not disavow his neighbors so lightly.

Mystical Technology

The terrestrial evolution *of species* ceased its forward movement with *Homo sapiens*. Earth will never see a more advanced *species*. The human body is "the most complete thing nature [has] found it possible to produce," and at that point, Bergson says, "the evolution of life stopped" (TS 301). Higher forms of life may appear in the future, but they will be individuals, not species. They will have been carried by the vital *élan* to a higher point than current humanity. Actually, they have been among us for some time. They are the great mystics that appear in world traditions. He calls them "the culminating point of evolution" (ME 32). "The great mystic is to be conceived as an individual being, capable of transcending the limitations imposed on the species by its material nature, thus continuing and extending the divine action," that is, the vital *élan* (TS 220–21). Bergson explains that the "mystic love of humanity" aspires "to complete the creation of the human species" (TS 234). The tendency of this mystical love "is exactly that of the vital impetus; it *is* this impetus itself, communicated in its entirely to exceptional men who in their turn would fain impart it to all humanity" (TS 235).

To his detractors, approbation of mysticism confirmed Bergson's toxic irrationality. However, there is nothing either mystical or irrational about his argument. He is interested in mystics as others have been interested in saints or ascetics. There are mystics in every world tradition. Who are these people, why do they appear, how do they attract followers? (These were Nietzsche's questions about ascetics.) Bergson is objective nearly to the point of behaviorism about mystics, whom he identifies not by what they say, how they think, or their consciousness, but by the effect of their action on others. He looks for the mystical effect of personality that sweeps over people and draws them in as music can. He stresses the personal connection; there is no mysticism at a distance. A mystic's genius is not in the intellect but in the will, the aspiration to which they have the audacity (the genius) to dedicate their life.

Such mystics are found everywhere, which suggests that they have a social significance, though Bergson denies it. Mystics serve life in a completely different way, serving not adaptation but advancement, mobilizing the action that continues life's unfinished movement. The same force that advanced the human species over others "also acts later and indirectly, through the medium of privileged persons, in order to drive humanity forward" (TS 42). He says that the ultimate end of mysticism is "the establishment of a contact, consequently of a partial coincidence, with the creative effort which life itself manifests. This effort is of God, if it is not God himself. The great mystic is to be conceived as . . . continuing and extending the divine action" (TS 209).

Bergson's mystics still have growing to do. We have not yet seen a complete mysticism; mysticism has not finished learning from different traditions. In this connection Bergson discusses Jewish prophetism. Unlike Greek and Eastern mystics, who remained contemplative, the prophets take the step to action. Their "passion for justice" requires it (TS 255). Wisdom is inadequate to overcome injustice; it is necessary to act. This is not a movement from closed to open but from static to dynamic, an active mysticism, and we can expect this sort of activism in the mature or complete mysticism for which Bergson hopes, whose aspiration will be to break through the limits of the present and expose a new and more hopeful horizon.

Bergson's mystics are all the same, as rational beings are all the same for Kant. Their sayings count for little because what they must communicate is not an idea but a creative emotion, one that can change everything in people's lives, which they do not by the content of their ideas but by their presence. Bergson does distill a message, though, and we cannot say it is obscure: "God is love, and the object of love: herein lies the whole contribution of mysticism" (TS 252). The political expression of this love is democracy. "Democracy is evangelical in essence . . . its motive power is love"

(TS 282). In this way, Bergson assimilates the mystic's wordless aspiration to his idea of open society, politically articulated in terms of democracy and human rights.[27]

Human rights are more than an extension of political rights to a wider community, as Durkheim thought, claiming that "family, nation, [and] humanity repeat different phases of our social and moral evolution, stages that prepare for and build upon one another."[28] Bergson finds no continuity between closed and open society. They interpenetrate but remain different in kind, qualitatively different, not steps in a continuous ascent. That may be something Bergson learned from his experience of the First World War (he served as a diplomat).[29] He was shocked to see long-standing commitments to human rights evaporate in time of war. He seems to have concluded that tribalism is not overcome by enlarging the perimeter; the principle of power remains exclusion despite the latitude of obligations, which are more labile than Bergson had assumed.

To exclude exclusion, open society must refuse essential, tribal, closed definition, for only if there is no *us* can there be no *them*. Open society remains open to definition and does not know in advance how it is composed or who its members are.[30] Such openness is not natural; indeed it is contra-natural (natural human sociality tends to closure), and therefore requires effort, which is why open society cannot be an extension of closed society. As humanity's evolutionary default position, nothing is easier or more natural than closed society. The tendency to open social norms aspires to a qualitative transformation, overcoming social closure with cosmopolitan fraternity. The mystics among us help the rest overcome the hurdle: "The task of the great mystic is to effect a radical transformation of humanity by setting an example" (TS 239). The message of mysticism is the message of open society, and the aspiration to open society is itself mystical.

For another perspective, let us compare Bergson and Kant. In "Idea for a Universal History with a Cosmopolitan Aim," Kant describes his cosmopolitan ideal of a civil constitution and a global federation of like-constituted states. He expects this world-system to arise in step with the historical progress of rationality, and he allocates to philosophy a part in this great history: "Philosophy can also have its chiliasm; but one the bringing about of which is promoted by the very idea of it."[31] Philosophy's chiliasm, a hoped-for millennium, is an *idea*. Kant is saying that philosophy has a right to this idea, and while philosophical consciousness is inadequate to its realization in time, making people conscious of the idea is already movement toward realization. Never before has humanity collectively and consciously *done something* for its own advancement. Kant thinks that with the European Enlightenment this is set to change. Humanity is set to begin taking over a direction that has so far reposed unconsciously in an unseen pattern of historical advance.

Kant's ideal is one of rationality; what is ideal about action is the universality of its maxim. Under the constitution, the administration of justice is universal, in accord with principles that any rational being must endorse. Bergson's open society does not make rationality the highest norm, which is instead individuality, though rationality is good for arriving at mutually beneficial arrangements. This was also the Epicurean evaluation, for while pleasure is the highest good, friendship and law are good too, though like justice they are instrumental ends.[32]

Kant views the Enlightenment as an opportunity for humanity to take its future in hand and do something to advance the progress of reason.[33] He anticipates philosophy stepping in, becoming an actor in the human drama, and by the suasive example of its lucid rationality take over the teleology that has so far unfolded unconsciously in history. By contrast, Bergson anticipates technology stepping in and taking over a teleology that has been unconsciously unfolding in terrestrial evolution, the *telos* of the *élan vital*, which is to introduce into matter the greatest possible indeterminacy. Bergson anticipates the progress, not of rationality but individuality, another word for freedom, and expressed in creative action, another word for the future. He looks to technology to do what biological evolution has done to this point, which means taking over the *telos*, becoming the new source of direction in future evolution, an evolution no longer of species but of individuals.

Bergson and Kant differ in their understanding of autonomy. We might view them as developing different strands of Rousseau's ample legacy. One of Rousseau's ideas is that freedom is autonomy, understood as accord with the general will. This is the legacy Kant develops. Another idea from Rousseau is that freedom means not depending on the will of others. This is the legacy Bergson develops. In Rousseau, of course, these were supposed to merge. The way to eliminate dependence on particular wills is to place oneself under a general one. That was the theory, although the effort to establish this general will introduced two new words to Europe's political vocabulary—terror and totalitarian.

Kant anticipates as the *telos* of history the fullest development of humanity's rational powers. However, fully developed rational powers assimilate people and do not individuate them; the more rational we are the more we coincide in the universal. Universalization is needful, however, only when we seek proof that action is autonomous, as Kant must in light of his determinism; I mentioned (Chapter 1) his argument that with adequate knowledge we could "calculate a man's conduct for the future with as great a certainty as a lunar or solar eclipse."[34] It would take a special sort of proof to justify the evaluation of an action—an event in nature— as unconditioned by special interest or antecedent causality at all, and that is what universalization promises.

But if Bergson is right and determinism is refuted, then we do not require proof that we are free, which diminishes the value of universalizability or a general will. For Bergson (as for Nietzsche), autonomy is individuality, being unconditioned by the will of others, and is confirmed by a feeling of dominating power. We are as autonomous as we feel, and do not require the talisman of a universal maxim. Could an agent be deluded? Yes, in cases, but not massively, the way arguments for determinism imply. The problem is not that we tend falsely to think we are free; it is that we tend to live and die "without having known true freedom" (TFW 166).

Bergson expounds most of his philosophy of technology in the final chapter of the *Two Sources*, entitled "Mechanics and Mysticism." Philosophers are stimulated to think about technology when something in its practice begins to seem problematic, and Bergson is no exception. Let me sketch the place of his thought in the history of philosophy's interaction with technology. The first such reflection arose in Greek antiquity, when Plato and Aristotle came to view their tradition's high evaluation of *techne* (technical art and knowledge) as an obstacle to their idea of science (*episteme*). They discuss *techne* with the purpose of explaining how debased it is, unworthy of a virtuous man's attention. For Plato, to work with one's hands is a reproach. Aristotle wanted to revoke the artisans' citizenship, a political status that should "belong only to those individuals who are released from occupations which provide the necessities for life."[35]

This devaluation of *techne* was a revolt against the philosophers' own tradition. In the epoch before philosophy, the arts and technologies were honored as indispensable gifts that lift people above the animals and make a good life possible. Odysseus bragged about being the carpenter of his own bed.[36] Antiphon epitomizes this older, pre-Platonic evaluation: "We master by *techne* what we are conquered by in nature."[37] Classical philosophy's devaluation of technology was favorably received among the elite of the ancient world, who associated tool-use with slavery. What Plato and Aristotle decided about technology was thus long unchallenged, though by the mid-eighteenth century, philosophers were feeling the injustice of the traditional evaluation, and technology emerged again as a philosophical question.[38]

The *Encyclopedia* of Diderot and D'Alembert displayed the unity of technical arts as never before. Guild secrecy was breeched; technologies that had operated in isolation were seen as cogs in a greater machine; plans were projected for the rationalization of industry. European Enlightenment discovers a new expectation of progress in technology envisioned not as discontinuous or revolutionary, but as a smooth glide to ever-improved tools and instruments and ever more rational procedures. That was all *before* the Industrial Revolution, which despoiled the once-happy prospect of technology's future. It fell to Karl Marx to expose the problem in this new phase of technology. In a chapter of *Capital* on Machinery and Modern Industry, he writes,

> Darwin has interested us in the history of nature's technology, i.e., in the formation of the organs of plants and animals, which organs serve as instruments of production for sustaining life. Does not the history of the productive organs of man, of organs that are the material basis of all social organization, deserve equal attention? . . . Technology discloses man's mode of dealing with nature, the process of production by which he sustains his life, and thereby also lays bare the mode of formation of his social relations, and of the mental conceptions that flow from them.[39]

This expresses the materialism and determinism for which Marx's name became a byword in twentieth-century criticism. Technology expresses our capacity to modify natural conditions, which we do by the processes that reproduce our life. Tools, technologies, industries—any means of production—not only sustain people's lives, they also condition ("determine") social relations and mental conceptions.

Following the Industrial Revolution, the next decisive crisis for European technology came with the First World War. Science and technology were greatly scaled up. Industrial in-house research laboratories proliferated; scientific research was integrated into national economies; and different epistemic networks meshed the contributions of firms, military, research institutions, and regulatory authorities. It was the dawn of Big Science, that is, scientific research on an industrial scale.[40] Writing in 1932, Bergson is an innovator in this phase of philosophical reflection on technology, and his work inaugurates a line in French philosophy of technology from Andre Leroi-Gourhan, Gilbert Simondon, and Raymond Ruyer to Bernard Stiegler and Bruno Latour.[41]

Bergson acknowledges toolmaking as the chief expression of intelligence, and tools afford endless new functions beyond the rationale that attends their invention. In this way tools retroact on users, providing them with new organs that prolong and expand their potential for action. Technology "reacts on the nature of the being that constructs it; for in calling on him to exercise a new function, it confers on him, so to speak, a richer organization, being an artificial organ by which the natural organism is extended" (CE 141). By opening environments to choice in ever wider respects, technical mediation introduces a far-reaching indeterminacy. An organism creates freedom for itself by accumulating potential energy, then kinetically expending it in a preferred action. All life does this in proportion and higher animals are the pinnacle of the tendency. What people add is technical mediation, that is, tools and technologies. Organs (e.g., limbs) are natural instruments and instruments are artificial organs; a tool extends and continues the body and technology extends and continues the species-body, yielding a greater body which "calls for a higher soul" (TS 309).

Bergson hopes for mysticism to overtake science and engineering and bring religious devotion to the technology that will make open society work. He says that "machinery will find its true vocation again," and once more "render services in proportion to its power," only when it breaks an alliance with war and capitalism, and finally becomes what it always tended to be, which is an instrument of freedom (TS 310). The challenge facing the aspiration to open society is to get technology on side, so that humanity can grow with it, instead of being made to suffer alienation from our tools. How can a technology captured by capitalism be induced to rejoin the aspiration to open society?

Bergson acknowledges grievances against technology—that it multiplies artificial needs, fosters luxury, destroys countryside, widens inequalities, and drives the working class to militancy. What went wrong? Was it the machines, their inhuman logic? Or science, Faustian and reckless? Perhaps human nature, our inveterate selfishness? Bergson rejects all these answers. There is no blame; it is coincidence, an accident of history. The scientific and industrial revolutions fortuitously coincided with a time when Europe was entering a phase of aspiration to material ease, which inadvertently drew science and technology into a frenzy of consumption. It was this contingent concurrence that made technology the ambivalent force it has become. In a society differently configured, technology could overcome this diversion and rejoin humanity as a power for freedom.

Technology does not inevitably produce superfluity and artificial needs. Mechanical invention has evolved in the *Homo* genus since the first stone tools, and its capture by capitalism is a diversion of this ancient alliance with freedom. The aspiration to ease is not universal; Bergson says it was little in evidence (in Europe) before the fifteenth century, earlier times being more indifferent to conditions of daily life. On the verge of scientific and technological modernity, however, Europe was swept into an adventitious alliance with rising affluence (especially from American metal) and birthing global commerce. These tendencies could come apart again. Austerity could become normative again, even if in a new way. Science and technology could be uncoupled from capitalism and the war machine and infused with the aspiration to open society, bending their efforts to make it real and make it work. All of that is suspended though, while we wait for the mystical genius who will touch the hearts of scientists and engineers and inspire this new creative emotion in their work: "Let a mystic genius but appear, he will draw after him a humanity already vastly grown in body [i.e., technology], and whose soul he has transfigured" (TS 311).

Bergson dared to think this was possible. Along with philosophers Henry Sidgwick, William James, C. D. Broad, and H. H. Price, Bergson served a term as president of the Society for Psychical Research, a field for which he had outsized expectations. He thought this research might confirm an afterlife and normalize parapsychological phenomena like telepathy, and he expected its results to play a role in shifting global consciousness toward simplicity and away from convenience and complexity. He may even have found the way to imagine the end of capitalism: "If we were sure, absolutely sure, of survival, we could not think of anything else" (TS 317).

Bergson thinks technology is on the verge of mastering "the force which is enclosed, or rather condensed, in the slightest particle of ponderable matter" (TS 312). In our terms, nuclear energy. His expectations for this technology are unrealistic; he goes so far as to suggest the possibility of cost-free energy. Liberate the energy condensed in the least particle of matter, he says, and human power "will be altogether limitless. . . . The material barrier then has well-nigh vanished" (TS 312). It sounds wonderful and he is just starting. He associates cost-free energy with mastery of material conditions, as if costless energy inspires the technology that makes optimal use of it. Mastery of the energy condensed in the least particle of matter would enable what he calls "a very special 'will to power'" (TS 309). He means a technological domination over *things* so far reaching as to make political domination over *people* superfluous, thus eliminating the scourge of tyranny and war.[42]

To read him in the light of later experience with nuclear energy may be unfair. He is writing a decade before the first controlled nuclear chain reaction (1942), trying to envision a future that was only birthing and perhaps still is. Before 1900, the idea of limitless energy was laughable. Thermodynamics had sung its threnody to a universe winding down. Einstein and Bohr changed that. With mastery of matter at the atomic level, we accede to the mystical energetics of $e = mc^2$. Now that we know nuclear energy is possible, Bergson calls on science and engineering to instrumentalize it for the future of humanity. Only effortless mastery of material conditions can eliminate tyranny, which arises from the scarcity that cost-free energy will overcome. Saving us from ourselves is important because there is a future for which humanity is collectively responsible. The creative power (*élan vital*) at the origin of life is now concentrated in humanity and if the evolution of life continues at all it passes through us.

Behavioral individuality, implying some degree of consciousness, memory, experience, and preference, is already a tendency in the early evolution of multicellular life.[43] A billion years later, life is poised for a transformation in evolution's *modus vivendi*, from advancing phylogenetically through higher *species* to advancing ontogenetically through *individuals*. There will be life on earth after *H. sapiens* is extinct. Vegetal and microbial forms and various animal kin will endure for some millions of years before an expanding sun engulfs the Earth, but this life is residual and has no tendency to advance. All the forward movement of life, all the *élan*, now concentrates in humankind and to us falls the responsibility of "continu[ing] the vital movement indefinitely" (CE 266). After rededicated science and engineering have eliminated tyranny with cost-free energy, the next challenge is to "deliver [humanity] from the necessity of being a species at all", for as he explains, "every species is a halt, and complete existence is mobility in individuality" (TS 311).

Bergson urges philosophers to stir up elite enthusiasm about this possible future, a future that depends on their decisions. Kant saw the Enlightenment as humanity's first experiment in doing something for its own progress, while Bergson calls for collective action to save humanity from the same progress: "Mankind lies groaning, half crushed beneath the weight of its own progress." People should understand that "a decision is imperative" and "their future is in their own hands" (TS 317). What must we do? "Humanity must set about simplifying its existence with as much frenzy as it devoted to complicating it" (TS 307). His language is voluntaristic, staging a choice between the closed, which we have always been, and the open, which is uncertain and requires an aspiration that can only be described as mystical. Shall we do as we always have, though now on a global scale, and drive ourselves to an ignominious extinction, fighting neighbors for the last fresh water? Or can we be moved by mystical aspiration to the love of humanity and nudge the future on another course?

Bergson uneasily combines the voluntaristic mode with something he seems to expect to happen anyway. He sees a historical oscillation between asceticism and consumption, from one extreme to the other, independent of anything else in history.[44] He offers it as an example of the dichotomous dynamics of tendency: "Organized matter has a limit of expansion that is very quickly reached; beyond a certain point it divides instead of growing" (CE 99). He even proposes a so-called law of twofold frenzy, which requires dichotomous tendencies to actualize to their very end. For instance, referring to "general tendencies which determine the trend of a society" (TS 296), he says, "there *is* really oscillation between two opposites. This is when a tendency, advantageous in itself, cannot be moderated otherwise than by the action of a countertendency" (TS 295). Such a tendency "pushes further and further afield, often stopping only on the very brink of disaster. The countertendency then steps into the place that has been vacated; alone, in its turn, it will go as far as it can go" (TS 296). He describes this as "progress by oscillation" (TS 299), though it sounds a bit providential, especially the part about the brink of disaster.

As Bergson reads the history, Europe got caught in a frenetic oscillation when in the fourth century Christians took on ascetic garb and retreated to the desert. Following the law of twofold frenzy, this asceticism intensified through the Middle Ages, until it was overtaken in early modern times by an opposite frenzy of consumption and complexity. From that point, Europe became committed to the capitalism that derailed science and technology and which Bergson ventures to hope is losing intensity, duly to be overtaken by its opposite. "We should," he thinks, "expect, after the ever-increasing complexity of life, a return to simplicity" (TS 299).

If that happens, we'll be fine, no melodramatic decision to make. But what if it does not happen or happen soon enough? Then something really would be up to us. I cannot imagine what would decouple science and engineering from capitalism and war. People cannot "decide" for or against open society. If one feels the aspiration, the decision has been made, and for those who do not, no decision will produce it. The aspiration Bergson conjures is a creative emotion stirred by mystics of open society. What the future depends on, then, is not the wisdom or courage of a collective decision; it is the imponderable advent of those mystics. Will they arrive? Will they be allowed to lead? Will we know them from charlatans?

I don't want to overlook difficulties in Bergson's philosophy of technology, starting with cost-free energy. Bergson refuted the concept of nothingness, so he should not think nuclear reactions would be emission-free. Perhaps he simply assumed that future engineering would have solutions to routine problems like waste. Such thinking is sadly refuted by experience; we still lack a happy nuclear technology and may never have one, placing that "very special 'will to power'" Bergson expects out of reach.

To argue that nuclear-powered technology can eliminate tyranny and oppression assumes that these scourges are rational and instrumental, so that removing their utility will bring them to an end. That is the reasoning of a reasonable person asking why anyone would resort to violence and finding the sane answer, namely, as a means only and a dire one. But what will cost-free energy avail the despot who craves to see others suffer, or who lies and manipulates people to begin wars for reasons no one understands? For some tyrants it seems there is just never enough, and they will plot for more as long as there is someone they can lord it over. The imagination is fertile with reasons to hate others, and the *tendency* of closed society will be with us as long as we are human.

Bergson thinks the alliance between technology and capitalism is accidental and already beginning to disintegrate. This seems less true every year. Our most powerful, productive, and popular technologies are held as legal property by private corporations, and they are not going to give them over to mystics. Bergson does not explain how technology might disengage from capitalism, saying only that it can be expected in light of his law of twofold frenzy. I will not say this law is ad hoc, though it does seem speculative and offered without much account.[45]

His claim that there was no aspiration to luxury in Europe before the fifteenth century is vague. Aspiration by whom—the ruling class, the higher prelate, city folks? Fernand Braudel observes, "It is often thought that hardship increases the further back towards the Middle Ages one goes. In fact, the opposite is true."[46] The authors of *A History of Private Life* speak of constant progress in domestic amenities and claim that from the thirteenth century Europeans enjoyed greater comfort than ever before.[47] On Bergson's account, that period was the wretched maxima of medieval asceticism.

Bergson imagines a mystical movement so compelling that it turns scientists and engineers away from their entanglement with capitalism, bending their work to the enhancement of open social forms. It seems unlikely, but mystical aspiration would, wouldn't it? Can we expect so much from a spiritual revolution? That was Christianity when it took over the Roman empire, so one cannot say Bergson's hope is hopeless, though it is, like life itself, the stuff dreams are made on.

* * *

This chapter discussed the theme of open and closed in Bergson's last work. These terms name tendencies, not finished forms, and as tendencies they interpenetrate, sustaining a zone of conflict as old as humankind. Closed society is our evolved social adaptation, the default tendency of *sapiens* social life. The opposite tendency for open social forms was little heard from before Christianity and not prominent before the Enlightenment. The tendency to open social forms includes democracy, which Bergson understands in terms of fraternity and human rights, but it includes more, even humanity's liberation from species-being.

Bergson refers to two sources of religion and morality. The first is social instinct understood with Darwin as evolved adaptive behavior. As social mammals we have social instincts that keep group life more beneficial than not. Bearing in mind Bergson's idea of evolution (Chapter 3), the first source, social instinct, is what the vital *élan* left behind as a trace of its passage through matter. The other source, the aspiration to expansive life, expresses that *élan* itself, the movement initiated four billion years ago at the origin of terrestrial life, or perhaps 14 billion years ago at the origin of everything.

The laughter Bergson describes is an agent of closed society. By contrast, the multimodal laughter in Nietzsche's *Thus Spoke Zarathustra* is both *not closed*, that is, not tribal, and *not open*, that is, not democratic, rather aristocratic, including only the best. If laughter is the ally of closed society, then technology is the ally of the open, or would be were it not diverted by capitalism and war. Technology becomes the ally of open society with the new will to power Bergson expects nuclear energy to introduce, enabling a technical domination over materials so far reaching that the tyranny of peoples becomes superfluous. His hope is that science and engineering will advance human beings to this higher level of life, inspired by a mystical aspiration that reorients the norms of science and technology on the growth of freedom.

Conclusion

Time comes first in a review of ideas I have explored in Bergson's philosophy. It is the key to everything else and the only point where he had an important change of mind. His argument is that time is real and best understood as duration. To say time is real means, first and negatively, that time is not an abstraction, not a geometrical dimension of space, not a pure form of intuition; and positively, it means that time is effective, a power of tendency. If time is real, meaning effective, then the past must be real and effective too, and that again is *tendency*, which is the efficacy of the past, how the past haunts the present with unfinished final causes. Memory is the tendency of past perception to fund present perception with its experience, and tendency is itself a form of memory, which is the effectiveness of the past. If a thing tends, it must have tended in the past, and that past remains effective in present tending, which is memory.

To understand time's effectiveness, we delved into Bergson's ideas on memory and virtual existence. Virtual existence qualifies the existence of tendencies, past images, or recollections, also of generality, habit, and the Thirds of C. S. Pierce. Perception is virtual action, that is, not acting but tending to; and memory is virtual experience, not present but tending to supplement present perception, enhancing acuity and prudence. Memories are as virtual as the past they recall. They are not traces, they are not actual, and do not exist in space, only in time, in the past. Memory is not a record of the past, it *is* the past and how the past survives, that is, remains effective.

The discontinuity of molar bodies, their perceptual organization as figure and ground, is relative to scale and form of life. In a laboratory, materials can be experimentally probed at *their* scale rather than our own, and it is then that we discover the quantum-scale granularity that seems to be inherent to physical existence, constraining duration's continuity. Life is not a completely new thing added to an inanimate universe; it does not start with the right lifeless molecules accidentally meeting in a tidal pool. The existence of life is a planetary event that has not stopped happening, like an earthquake that continues to rumble, its movement still evolving, like unfinished music. Life does not start or cease, but intensifies and diminishes, at the limit vanishing into virtuality, which is still not nothing. Life on earth is a planetary intensification of tendencies as old as time.

Life is a word for something European languages do not handle well, since it is not a category, kind, or concept but instead a singular movement: an unfinished, planetary-scale, counter-entropic tendency to individuality. The English language classifies "life" as a general noun and we may think we know it when we see it, but there is no logical concept of life just as there is no logical concept of Mozart. These are individuals, not types or kinds. If life were a concept, there should be instances and we should be able to name them, but there aren't. Anything we mention will be an organism and an instance of its species. These are not *instances* of life because they do not *instantiate* conditions necessary and sufficient for anything except their species (if that). Because life is a single developing movement, its necessary and sufficient condition does not yet exist.[1]

Bergson's deviation from Darwinism is his idea that organisms are expressions (traces) of a vital tendency which, like any tendency, *tends*, *inclines*, with an immanent finality that introduces bias to the variations available for natural selection. These biases are the trends Bergson finds in life's history, such as the differentiation of plants and animals, vertebrates and arthropods, *Homo* and the Hymenoptera. Bergson does therefore introduce finality or teleology, though it is immanent rather than supernatural, Stoic rather than Platonic-Christian, and implies no purpose or design. He introduces finality because he introduces tendency, which is the efficacy of the virtual, and tendencies *tend*, expressing the immanent finality Spinoza called *conatus*, a will to act and become what it (virtually) is.

The future will not exist until it happens, that is, becomes present. The existence of events is their existence when they happen, and future events when they happen are present, not future. A future emerges from the past in the cosmic contest among tendencies that activate the cosmos with their impetus to actuality. The character of future time is a problem for enduring entities. What will actualize, what nexus of tendencies will dominate? This is the adventure of being in time. As for humanity, our default tendency is closed social forms, yet there is no future in closed society, which shuts down avenues of growth and tends to a nihilistic mode of repetition. Open society is the tendency of life, of growth, and self-overcoming, but no more than a tendency, thwarted on all sides.

Concluding his elegant monograph on Bergson, Leszek Kolakowski writes, "No matter how infrequently he is quoted or referred to, Bergson's presence has not been eradicated from our civilization; once he appeared, philosophical life could never be the same again."[2] This is generous, perhaps to a fault. In Analytic philosophy it seems to me that everything happens as if Bergson never existed.

Perhaps some of the ideas are outré, but to evoke that response he must touch something unquestioned in our thought. Consider for example his distinction between science and philosophy, and his claim that metaphysics investigates a reality inaccessible to scientific methods. Since Bacon, since Locke, since Russell, and Quine, Anglophone philosophy leans hard the other way. The tendency has reasserted itself under the name of "naturalism," a term whose current prestige derives from W. V. Quine, writing influentially of "epistemology naturalized." "Epistemology, or something like it, simply falls into place as a chapter of psychology and hence of natural science." He says this position "is a naturalistic one; I see philosophy not as an *a priori* propaedeutic or groundwork for science, but as continuous with science."[3] All the new naturalists concur.[4]

Bergson is not a naturalist in philosophy, not when that means making philosophy continuous with natural science. Consider how Quine frames the alternative. Philosophy is either an a priori groundwork for science, presumably a foundational epistemology like Descartes's, or it is continuous with science. Bergson offers a third way. That word "continuous" sounds innocent, but how is it possible for philosophy to be continuous with science yet not *be* science? And if a discourse owes its consistency to science, how philosophical can it be? Bergson's alternative to Carnap's erstwhile foundationalism and Quine's naturalism is a new idea of metaphysics, a metaphysics not of being or substance but of time. This metaphysics is not continuous with natural science; it is instead a complementary supplement, matching quantitative intelligence about space and matter with qualitative intelligence about the phenomena of duration.[5]

It would be wrong to speak of Bergson's ontology if that meant a consciously elaborated and textually indicated thesis. Bergson writes with seeming disregard for system in his several books, though systematic currents run in many directions and receive development in other books and papers. One of these currents I call ontology, meaning a theory of the modes of being. In Bergson, these modes are three, though they only operate relative to each other, sliding over each other, offering each an interface with the others.

The first mode is virtual reality. This is extensity without form and without actual existence. Deleuze and Guattari call it the "Body without Organs" (BwO), in other words, "the unformed, unorganized, nonstratified, or destratified body and all its flows: subatomic and submolecular particles, pure intensities, prevital and prephysical free singularities."[6] This BwO has been widely discussed in Deleuzo-Guattarian theory, often without appreciating its roots in Bergson's concrete extensity (*l'étendue concrète*), which is extensity without individuation, without parts, organs, or actual existence, an entirely virtual being, not material but tending to materialize.

Virtual reality is not another world, not a world of Ideas, or a logical space of possibility. Whatever exists virtually tends to actual existence. It may never materialize but materialization is the tendency, the *conatus*, the immanent finality of the virtually real. Hence, a second mode of being, actuality or actual existence. This is nature, *natura naturata*, the phenomena, cosmic natural history from the Big Bang to now.

The third mode of being is vitality. With life we have perception, preference, expectation, an effective past. Life presupposes memory but more decisively life *uses* memory, instrumentalizing the effectiveness of the past. That was missing in earlier epochs. Matter is not actually animated until the memory it bears becomes adaptive for centers of perception, which are organisms. The more lucid the memory, the more elastic and artful the tension by which it coordinates the interpenetration of durations different from its own, amplifying and extending adaptive action. Perception grows more acute, attention more penetrating, organisms more individuated and autonomous.

The modal scheme recalls ideas from Stoic philosophy that also reappear in Leibniz and this is unlikely to be a coincidence. On the Stoic theory, original matter (*hyle*) is passive and formless, without cohesive force (*sunektike dunamis*). Natural forms appear when a fiery pneuma introduces tension (*tonos*) into the formless mass, making all portions continuous. We have these words from Chrysippus, "The tension of pneuma . . . binds bodies together so that they both have continuity in relation to their own parts and are connected with the bodies adjacent to them."[7] Pneuma is corporeal because it acts, which is the Stoic criterion of body, though pneuma is less matter than force, a tension interpenetrating formed matter and causing interaction.[8] Reaching to the limit of the cosmos, pneumatic bonds make the whole a single living being.

Leibniz develops this Stoic line. Primary matter is passive force, a primitive force of resistance that does nothing except make each body an obstacle to every other. We cannot say primary matter (*moles*) is without force, though all it can do is resist the force of everything else, which leaves it always as it is or, as Bergson says, always starting over. Secondary matter (*massa*) comprises a dominant entelechy and a multitude of subordinate entelechies or substantial souls.[9] These are the living bodies of natural history. To activate the passive primary bulk and explain its transformation into the many material bodies, Leibniz requires a primary principle of activity, like the Stoic active principle (*arche*). In Stoic theory, the principle is a body and thus a force. Leibniz knows of compressive and elastic forces and adds a *plastic* force that he variously names substantial form, conatus, nisus, soul, and entelechy.[10] He says of substantial forms (i.e., entelechies), "Their nature consists in force, and . . . from this there follows something analogous to sensation and appetite, so that we must conceive of them on the model of the notion we have of *souls*."[11] This is the modern foundation of panpsychism and a conceptual affiliate of the Stoic *pneuma*, the tendentious spirit that tenses matter with immanent finality.

Bergson lectured on Greek philosophy in 1894–95, revealing his interest in Stoicism and noticing points of convergence with his argument in *Time and Free Will*, from five years earlier. He describes *tonos* (tension, interpenetration) as the key to Stoic ontology, remarking that for them, "God is, above all, active force, tension, *tonos*."[12] *Tonos* is the divine tension that reaches throughout the (finite) cosmos and makes all parts interpenetrate. Bergson's virtual mode is analogous to Stoic-Leibniz primary matter. To call it formless does not mean it is homogeneous. The virtual mode is endlessly heterogeneous, a qualitative multiplicity obscurely differentiated by uncountable tendencies which, although thwarted on all sides, do tend, lean, verge, and incline by immanent finality to actual existence.

Actuality is like the fiery birth of the Stoic cosmos or our Big Bang. Actualization, duration, and memory are inseparable because physical existence is melodic, like consciousness, a qualitative multiplicity enduring for a while without being for an instant. Vitality is not an addition but instead an intensification of the pneumatic spirit, virtual and tending since the beginning of time but swamped by countervailing tendencies. Virtual existence is eternal. Tendencies exist when matter or energy exist and even in the vacuum, when matter and energy do not exist. Actual existence presupposes virtual existence, which is what we cannot think away when we try to think nonbeing. Nonbeing is nonactual, not nothing *at all*, because even a vacuum is not empty of tendency. Virtual tendency cannot not exist. It is *causa sui, aeternum, aionios*, the deathless BwO.

Despite this intrusion of the eternal, Bergson's philosophy qualifies as what Peirce calls a genuine evolutionary philosophy, "that is, one that makes the principle of growth a primordial element of the universe."[13] Virtual existence, timeless as it is, tends to materialize, and when it does it tends to evolve. Individuality and freedom are effects of such evolution, and the roots of conscious freedom lie in mindless necessity. Bergson's philosophy is also a kind of empiricism, the kind William James called radical empiricism, meaning a more consistently empirical empiricism, more impatient with rationalism and nominalism than were Locke, Hume, Mill, or Spencer.[14] Bergson values intuition as a source of experience superior to sense. The images of sense are relative to our form of life and have no reality in themselves, but the intuition of duration and its phenomena, including movement and development, is not perspectival or anthropocentric, being an experience of time as it is absolutely. Taking intuition seriously prompts Bergson to an empiricism for which duration is the only given, and which overcomes the utilitarian prejudices that vitiate earlier empiricisms, passing beyond what makes experience adaptive for a species and limits perception to the virtual rehearsal of its action. Intuition is not offered as an alternative to intellectual knowledge but as an enlargement of it, to create a hybrid knowledge unimpeded by anthropic prejudice.

* * *

I had been teaching philosophy for twenty-five years before I read a book by Bergson. I'd heard of him of course, but remembering Russell's jibes and Rorty's jaunty dismissal, nothing made me want to look closer. It was only after I began to grapple with Deleuze's work that I came to appreciate how deeply and beautifully thought-out Bergson's ideas are. The point that gripped me was how he placed time at the center of everything in philosophy, evaluating concepts and arguments by the test of taking time seriously. This for him is more important than any "naturalism." Elucidating time leads to a theory of duration and the question of time's mode of existence, which is when we discover the value of the virtual. Time is the matrix of figural beings or bodies; extension is tension interrupted, made discontinuous from a ground, its continuity punctuated by living perception. If time is real and real means effective, then the passage of time is efficacious and changes things, which is evolution, cosmic and geo-biological. Taking time seriously implies reversing the usual order of being and becoming, rendering being a kind of accident of becoming, as Nietzsche proposed, while understanding time with Bergson as duration makes Nietzsche's "eternal return of the same" a qualitative repetition of intensity, not an extensional repetition of form.

I could go on, unfolding all the arguments I have canvassed and others I passed over. Bergson may be too larded with heresy to appeal to orthodox minds, but for others his work reminds us of why we love philosophy.

Notes

Introducing Henri Bergson

1. See R. C. Grogin, *The Bergsonian Controversy in France 1900–1914* (Calgary: University of Calgary Press, 1988).
2. Mélanie Weill, "The Phantom Presence of War in Bergson's *Two Sources of Morality and Religion*," in *The Bergsonian Mind*, ed. Mark Sinclair and Yaron Wolf (London: Routledge, 2022), 284.
3. Good examples of early Anglophone work on Bergson are A. D. Lindsay, *The Philosophy of Bergson* (London: J. M. Dent & Sons, 1911); and A. A. Luce, *Bergson's Doctrine of Intuition* (New York: Macmillan, 1922). William James's principal discussion of Bergson is *A Pluralistic Universe*, ch. 6; see also my "William James's *Pluralistic Universe*," in *Understanding James, Understanding Modernism*, ed. David H. Evans (London: Bloomsbury, 2017), 75–92. For recent Anglophone scholarship on Bergson, see *Interpreting Bergson*, ed. Alexandre Lefebvre and Nils F. Schott (Cambridge: Cambridge University Press, 2020), and *The Bergsonian Mind*, ed. Mark Sinclair and Yaron Wolf (London: Routledge, 2022).
4. John Mullarkey, "Forget the Virtual," *Continental Philosophy Review* 37 (2004): 469–93; also T. M. Murayama, "Bergson on Virtuality and Possibility," *Bergsonian Mind*, 202–15. On the concept of virtual in Deleuze and Bergson, see the thematic issue of *Deleuze Studies* 11, no. 2 (2017).
5. I say accomplished in science on the basis of having won first prize in mathematics for the Concours Général (1877), and the following year publishing his solution to a problem left unsolved by Pascal. He entered École Normale expecting to study mathematics. For a withering refutation of Bertrand Russell's gratuitous attack on Bergson's mathematics see Robin Durie, "The Mathematical Basis of Bergson's Philosophy," *Journal of the British Society for Phenomenology* 35, no. 1 (2004): 54–67.

Chapter 1

1. Herbert Spencer, *The Principles of Psychology*, 2 vols. (1855; New York: Appleton, 1910), 1: 150, 155–56.

2. Immanuel Kant, *Prolegomenon to any Future Metaphysics*, trans. James W. Ellington (1783; Indianapolis: Hackett, 1977), §10. On Bergson and Kant, Camille Riquier, "The Intuitive Recommencement of Metaphysics," *Journal of French and Francophone Philosophy* 24, no. 2 (2016): 62–83.
3. Robin Durie, "The Mathematical Basis of Bergson's Philosophy," *Journal of the British Society for Phenomenology* 35, no. 1 (2004): 54–67.
4. The best effort to explain two bodies in the same space is by Chrysippus of the Old Stoa, who argued that two bodies can occupy the same space when they are thoroughly blended. The reasoning is geometrical. Suppose we had a thorough blend of two bodies. Then no matter how small a sample we select, it contains both bodies occupying the whole region, and we therefore never reach a region where both are not mixed in the same space. Despite occupying the same space, the two bodies still express their differences through distinctive effects from the same center. See John Cooper, "Chrysippus on Physical Elements," in *God and Cosmos in Stoicism*, ed. Ricardo Sales (New York: Oxford University Press, 2009), 98. The argument appears circular, with the conclusion built into the definition of "thoroughly blended." According to Stobaeus, Stoics define that as the condition in which "two entities are mixed together to the point that every part of the mixture contains both of the original entities, yet each of the original entities retains its own distinctive properties and can in theory be extracted from the mixture." In John Sellars, *Stoicism* (London: Routledge, 2014), 89. This simply assumes that in the limit two bodies can occupy the same space.
5. Deleuze thinks narrative film presents images of time Bergson did not anticipate, and which illuminate his ideas of movement and image. See D. N. Rodowick, *Gilles Deleuze's Time Machine* (Durham, NC: Duke University Press, 1997).
6. Michel Georges-Michel, "Henri Bergson Talks to Us About Cinema" (1914), *Cinema Journal* 50, no. 3 (2011): 79–82. Bergson was the first philosopher to write about cinema; see John Ó. Maoilearca, "The Cinematic Bergson," *Journal of French and Francophone Philosophy* 24, no. 2 (2016).
7. Bertrand Russell, *Mysticism and Logic* (New York: Norton, 1929), 128, 129.
8. See J. J. Gibson, *The Ecological Approach to Visual Perception* (Boston: Houghton Mifflin, 1979).
9. Aristotle, *Physics*, 239b. This and all references to Aristotle follow *The Complete Works of Aristotle. Revised Oxford Translation*, ed. Jonathan Barnes, 2 vols. (Princeton, NJ: Princeton University Press, 1984). See also Gregory Vlastos, "Zeno of Elea," in *Encyclopedia of Philosophy*, ed.

Paul Edwards (New York: Macmillan, 1967), 8:369–79; Richard Sorabji, *Time, Creation and the Continuum* (London: Duckworth, 1983), 321–35; Vere C. Chappell, "Time and Zeno's Arrow," in *Bergson and the Evolution of Physics*, ed. P. A. Y. Gunter (Knoxville: University of Tennessee Press, 1969), 253–74; and Émile Meyerson, *The Relativistic Deduction: Epistemological Implications of the Theory of Relativity*, trans. David A. and Mary-Alice Sipfle (1925; Dordrecht: D. Reidel, 1985), 171–72.

10. Walter Porzig, *Das Wunder der Sprache* (1950), in Jean-Louis Dessalles, *Why We Talk: The Evolutionary Origins of Language*, trans. James Grieve (2000; Oxford: Oxford University Press, 2007), 246.

11. Émile Meyerson, *Relativistic Deduction*, xxxvi; also, *Identity and Reality*, trans. Kate Loewenberg (1908; London: George Allen and Unwin, 1930), 227–30. Bergson admired Meyerson's work; see "Rapport sur un ouvrage de Émile Meyerson, *Identité et réalité*" (1909), *Écrit et paroles*, ed. R. M. Moussé-Bastide (Paris: Presses universitaires de France, 1959), 2: 311–12.

12. This resonates with conclusions of Jacques Derrida, for whom "the history of metaphysics, like the history of the West, is the history of the metaphors and metonymies . . . [whose] matrix . . . is the determination of being as presence." *Writing and Difference*, trans. Alan Bass (1967; Chicago: University of Chicago Press, 1978), 279.

13. Einstein, response to Bergson, Paris, 1922, in *Bergson and Evolution of Physics*, 133. See also Jimena Canales, *The Physicist and the Philosopher: Einstein, Bergson, and the Debate that Changed Our Understanding of Time* (Princeton, NJ: Princeton University Press, 2015).

14. Laurence Sklar, "Time in Experience and in Theoretical Description of the World," in *Time's Arrows Today*, ed. Steven F. Savitt (Cambridge: Cambridge University Press, 1995), 226, 228.

15. See J. M. E. McTaggart, *The Nature of Existence* (Cambridge: Cambridge University Press, 1927); and Matyás Moravec, "A Bergsonian Response to McTaggart's Paradox," in *The Bergsonian Mind*, ed. Mark Sinclair and Yaron Wolf (London: Routledge, 2022), 417–31.

16. Richard T. W. Arthur, *The Reality of Time Flow: Local Becoming in Modern Physics* (Cham: Springer, 2019), 53.

17. Hermann Lotze, in Milič Čapek, ed., *The Concepts of Space and Time, Their Structure and Development* (Dordrecht: D. Reidel, 1976), 1.

18. A. S. Eddington, *The Nature of the Physical World* (Cambridge: Cambridge University Press, 1928), 97.

19. Steven Savitt, "A Limited Defense of Passage," *American Philosophical Quarterly* 38, no. 3 (2001), 268.

20. Gilles Deleuze, *Cinema 1: The Movement-Image*, trans. Hugh Tomlinson and Barbara Habberjam (1983; Minneapolis: University of Minnesota Press, 1986), 16–17, 9.
21. F. C. T. Moore, *Bergson: Thinking Backwards* (Cambridge: Cambridge University Press, 1996), 15. On the melody model of time, see Milič Čapek, *Bergson and Modern Physics* (Dordrecht: D. Reidel, 1971), 318, 325. Edmund Husserl also emphasized the music model for temporal consciousness; see *The Phenomenology of Internal Time-Consciousness*, trans. James S. Churchill (1928; Bloomington: Indiana University Press, 1964). A still good discussion of Bergson's idea of duration is Karin Costelloe, "What Bergson Means by Interpenetration," *Proceedings of the Aristotelian Society* (n.s.) 13 (1912–13): 131–55.
22. Julius T. Fraser, *Time the Familiar Stranger* (Amherst: University of Massachusetts Press, 1987), 92.
23. Gaston Bachelard, *The Dialectic of Duration*, trans. Mary McAllester Jones (1932; London: Rowman & Littlefield International, 2000), 20. See also Jean François Perraudin, "A Non-Bergsonian Bachelard," *Continental Philosophy Review* 41 (2008): 463–79.
24. Bergson, *Mélanges* (Paris: Presses universitaires de France, 1972), 353–54; translation by Matthew Gardhouse.
25. Gaston Bachelard, in Teresa Castelao-Lawless, "Is Discontinuous Bergsonism Possible?" *Agathos* 1, no. 1 (2010): 33.
26. Bachelard, *Dialectic of Duration*, xiv. He repeats the point two years later: "Time acts through repetition more than through duration." Gaston Bachelard, *The New Scientific Spirit*, trans. Arthur Goldhammer (1934; Boston: Beacon Press, 1984), 79.
27. Bachelard, *Dialectic of Duration*, 29.
28. Bachelard, *Dialectic of Duration*, 112.
29. Bachelard, *Dialectic of Duration*, 111.
30. Bachelard, *Dialectic of Duration*, 112.
31. Max Horkheimer, 1934, in Suzanne Guerlac, "Mis/Reading Bergson—On Time and Life and Matter," in *Reassessing Bergson*, ed. Matyáš Moravec, Frédéric Worms, and Caterina Zanfi. *Bergonsoniana*, 1 (2021): 101–17.
32. Bachelard, *Dialectic of Duration*, 71.
33. Louis de Broglie (1941), in Castelão-Lawless, "Discontinuous Bergsonism," 33.
34. De Broglie, in Castelão-Lawless, 34. On Bergson and de Broglie, see Čapek, *Bergson and Modern Physics*, ch. 13.
35. Mark Sinclair, *Bergson* (London: Routledge, 2020), 52 (emphasis added), citing Bergson, *Mélanges*, 349.

36. Jean-Marie Guyau. *La genèse de l'idée de temps*, ed. Félix Alcan (Paris: Ancienne librairie Germer Bailliere et cie, 1980), 20; translation by Matthew Gardhouse.
37. Bergson, *Mélanges*, 353–54; translation by Matthew Gardhouse.
38. "Everything Bergson has to say about it comes down to this: duration is what differs from itself." Gilles Deleuze, "Bergson's Conception of Difference," in *Desert Islands and Other Texts*, trans. Michael Taormina (2002; Los Angles: Semiotext(e), 2004), 37.
39. Arthur O. Lovejoy, *Bergson and Romantic Evolutionism* (Berkeley: University of California Press, 1914), 15.
40. This is the argument later associated with Poincaré's geometrical conventionalism. "One geometry cannot be more true than another; it can only be *more convenient.*" Henri Poincaré, *Science and Hypothesis*, trans. George Bruce Halsted (1902; New York: Science Press, 1929), 65.
41. Milič Čapek, "Bergson's Theory of Matter and Modern Physics," *Bergson and Evolution of Physics*, 303–04.
42. John Venn, *Principles of Empirical or Inductive Logic* (London: Macmillan, 1889), 20.
43. Michael Faraday (1844), in Martin Meisel, *Chaos Imagined* (New York: Columbia University Press, 2016), 347; Werner Heisenberg, "Development of Concepts in the History of Quantum Theory," *American Journal of Physics* 43 (1975): 393. On Borel's calculation, Leon Brillouin, *Scientific Uncertainty and Information* (New York: Academic Press, 1964), 24–25.
44. Zygmunt Zawirski (1934), *Bergson and Modern Physics*, 285.
45. Svante Arrhenius, Presentation Speech, December 10, 1922, in Canales, *Physicist and the Philosopher*, 4.
46. Einstein, in Canales, *Physicist and Philosopher*, 373n26.
47. Adolf Grünbaum, *Philosophical Problems of Space and Time* (New York: Knopf, 1963), 329; Hermann Weyl, *Philosophy of Mathematics and Natural Science* (Princeton, NJ: Princeton University Press, 1947), 116.
48. Meyerson, *Relativistic Deduction*, 76–77.
49. Einstein, Review of Meyerson, in *Concepts of Space and Time*, 366–67.
50. Čapek, *Bergson and Modern Physics*, 252. See also Čapek, "The Inclusion of Becoming in the Physical World," in *Concepts of Space and Time*, 501–24; Tim Maudlin, "Remarks on the Passing of Time," *Proceedings of the Aristotelian Society* 102 (2002): 259–74; and Howard Stein, "On Relativity Theory and the Openness of the Future," *Philosophy of Science* 58, no. 2 (1991): 147–67.

51. Steven Savitt, "What Bergson Should Have Said to Einstein," *Reassessing Bergson*, 89–99.
52. C. Hafele and R. Keating, "Around-the-World Atomic Clocks: Predicted Relativistic Time Gains," *Science* 177, no. 4044 (1972): 166–68.
53. Savitt, "What Bergson Should Have Said," 96. Milič Čapek already drew this conclusion; see *Bergson and Modern Physics*, 252.
54. Daniel C. Dennett, *Elbow Room: The Varieties of Free Will Worth Wanting* (Cambridge, MA: MIT Press, 1984), 6. On the emergence of "free will" as a topic of philosophical discussion, see Michael Frede, *A Free Will: Origins of the Notion in Ancient Thought*, ed. A. A. Long (Berkeley: University of California Press, 2011).
55. Immanuel Kant, *Critique of Practical Reason*, trans. T. K. Abbot (1788; London: Longman, Green, 1909), 193.
56. Pierre Simon Laplace, *A Philosophical Essay on Probabilities*, trans. Frederick Wilson Truscott and Frederick Lincoln Emory (1812; New York: John Wiley, 1902), 4.
57. "Philosophers have said before that one of the fundamental requisites of science is that whenever you set up the same conditions, the same thing must happen. This is simply not true; it is not a fundamental condition of science. The fact is that the same thing does not happen, that we can find only an average, statistically, as to what happens." Richard Feynman, *Six Easy Pieces* (1963; New York: Basic Books, 2011), 35. William Unruh describes this result as "one of the most disconcerting aspects of the theory [General Relativity] and the world." "Time, Gravity, and Quantum Mechanics," in *Time's Arrows Today*, 38.
58. D. H. Mellor, *Real Time* (London: Routledge, 1981), 109. Also James Clerk Maxwell: "The difference between one event and another does not depend on the mere difference of the times or the places at which they occur, but only on differences in the nature, configuration, or motion of the bodies concerned." *Concepts of Space and Time*, 232.
59. Sophocles, *Antigone*, l. 646, trans. Friedrich Solmsen.
60. I draw from Karl Popper, "Indeterminism in Quantum Physics and in Classical Physics," *British Journal for the Philosophy of Science* 1, nos. 2–3 (1950): 117–33, 173–95; David Bohm, "Inadequacy of Laplacian Determinism," *Concepts of Space and Time*, 547–49; Andrew van Melsen, *The Philosophy of Nature* (Pittsburgh: Duquesne University Press, 1961), 247–49; and Brillouin, *Uncertainty and Information*, 91.
61. The Stoic and Christian origin of "free will" is well exposed in Frede, *Free Will*.

62. Hermann Weyl, *Concepts of Space and Time*, 561.
63. On anomalous monism, see Donald Davidson, "Mental Events," *Essays on Actions and Events* (Oxford: Oxford University Press, 1980), 207–27. On the "mysterian" thesis, see Owen Flanagan, *The Science of the Mind* (Cambridge, MA: MIT Press, 1991), 313.
64. One neuroscientist claims to have done this very thing, see Benjamin Libet, "Do We Have Free Will?" in *Oxford Handbook of Free Will*, ed. Robert Kane (New York: Oxford University Press, 2002), 551–64. For a range of criticism see Daniel C. Dennett, *Freedom Evolves* (New York: Viking, 2003), ch. 8; and Mark Balaguer, *Free Will as an Open Scientific Question* (Cambridge, MA: MIT Press, 2010).
65. Robert Kane, "Some Neglected Pathways in the Free Will Labyrinth," *Handbook of Free Will*, 432.
66. Robert Nozick, *Philosophical Explanations* (Cambridge, MA: Harvard University Press, 1981), 313.
67. J. S. Mill, cited by Bergson, TFW 174.
68. Peter Pesic, *Seeing Double: Shared Identities in Physics, Philosophy, and Literature* (Cambridge, MA: MIT Press, 2002).
69. Friedrich Nietzsche (1883), *Nietzsche on Freedom and Autonomy*, ed. Ken Gemes and Simon May (New York: Oxford University Press, 2009), 45; and Pindar, *Second Pythian Ode*, line 72.
70. Most of Kant's references to intellectual (or nonsensible) intuition occur in the second edition of the First *Critique*. Immanuel Kant, *Critique of Pure Reason*, trans. N. Kemp Smith (London: Macmillan, 1933), B 72, 307, 311.
71. Bergson introduces intuition in "Introduction to Metaphysics" (1903). It is referred to intermittently in *Creative Evolution* (1907), then subject to a major exposition in "Philosophical Intuition" (1911). Both papers are collected in Bergson's last publication, *The Creative Mind* (1934).
72. Leszek Kolakowski, *Bergson* (Oxford: Oxford University Press, 1985), 101.
73. Maine de Biran is an important exception to modern empiricism's indifference to inner experience. See Philip P. Hallie, *Maine de Biran, Reformer of Empiricism* (Cambridge, MA: Harvard University Press, 1959).
74. "We cognize relations through feeling." William James, *The Principles of Psychology*, 2 vols. (1890; New York: Dover, 1950), 1:247.
75. Bergson's philosophical entomology is partially challenged and partially defended by French philosopher of life sciences Raymond Ruyer. See "Instinct, Consciousness, Life: Ruyer Contra Bergson," trans. Tano S. Posteraro, *Angelaki, Journal of the Theoretical Humanities*, 24, no. 5 (2019): 124–47.

218　NOTES

76. On the equation of adaptations with knowledge, see Henry Plotkin, *Darwin Machines and the Nature of Knowledge* (Harmondsworth: Penguin, 1994).
77. See F. C. T. Moore, *Bergson: Thinking Backwards* (Cambridge: Cambridge University Press, 1996).
78. On embryology, see CE 25, 363.
79. On the ethological concept of instinct as devoid of agency, see Vinciane Despret, "From Secret Agents to Interagency," *History and Theory* 52 (2013): 29–44. For a comprehensive critique of classical ethology, see Dominique Lestel, "What Capabilities for the Animal?" *Biosemiotics* 4 (2011): 83–102.
80. Gilles Deleuze, *Bergsonism*, trans. Hugh Tomlinson and Barbara Habberjam (1966; New York: Zone Books, 1988), 32–33.
81. On ancient medical empiricism and Bergson's radical empiricism, see my *Empiricisms: Experience and Experiment from Antiquity to the Anthropocene* (New York: Oxford University Press, 2021).
82. Bergson, "Psychophysical Parallelism and Positive Metaphysics" (1901), trans. Matthew Cobb, in *Continental Philosophy of Science*, ed. Gary Gutting (New York: Wiley-Blackwell, 2005), 68.
83. *Zhuangzi*, ch. 2, in *Readings in Classical Chinese Philosophy*, ed. Philip J. Ivanhoe and Bryan W. Van Norden, 2nd ed. (Indianapolis: Hackett, 2001), 13–24. I discuss this text in *Empiricisms*, §107. On Daoist philosophy, see my *Vanishing into Things: Knowledge in Chinese Tradition* (Cambridge, MA: Harvard University Press, 2015), ch. 2.
84. *Classical Chinese Philosophy*, 217; see also *Vanishing into Things*, 82–84.
85. *Classical Chinese Philosophy*, 217 (translation modified).
86. *Classical Chinese Philosophy*, 242. I discuss this text in *Striking Beauty: A Philosophical Look at the Asian Martial Arts* (New York: Columbia University Press, 2015), 14. See also Livia Kohn, *Sitting in Oblivion: The Heart of Daoist Meditation* (Dunedin, FL: Three Pines Press, 2010).
87. *Vanishing into Things*, 180, 189, 197, 224.

Chapter 2

1. The best effort to imagine a cephalopod ontology is Vilém Flusser, *Vampyroteuthis infernalis: A Treatise, with a Report by the Institut Scientifique de Recherche Paranaturaliste*, trans. Valentine A. Pakis (2011; Minneapolis: University of Minnesota Press, 2012).
2. Bergson's idea is comparable to the theory that perception is not an internal relation of perceiver and intentional content but rather an

external relation between perceiver and object. See Anil Gupta, *Conscious Experience* (Cambridge, MA: Harvard University Press, 2019). Bergson's conception of perception as virtual action rather than interior image has even been confirmed in insects (bees). "Visual patterns are not stored as images at all, but, for example, as the motor patterns that flying along the pattern's edges induce a bee to perform." Lars Chittka, "Bee Cognition," *Current Biology* 27 (2017), 1052.
3. A. W. Moore remarks of Bergson's virtual that it is "a concept which in the form in which he introduced it had no real precursor in the history of Western philosophy." *The Evolution of Modern Metaphysics* (New York: Cambridge University Press, 2012), 599. Bergson used a concept of virtual earlier in *Time and Free Will* (TFW 4, 13, 84, 204), which is identifiable as that of *Matter and Memory*, though the earlier usage places no special demand on virtual existence, which comes with the theory of perception as virtual action in *Matter and Memory*.
4. William James, *The Principles of Psychology*, 2 vols. (1890; New York: Dover, 1950), 1: 254. For a different idea of the virtual in perception, see Alva Nöe, *Varieties of Presence* (Cambridge, MA: Harvard University Press, 2012).
5. See J. J. Gibson, *The Ecological Approach to Visual Perception* (Boston: Houghton Mifflin, 1979).
6. On epistemic affordances, see Mohan Matthen, *Seeing, Doing, and Knowing: A Philosophical Theory of Sense Perception* (New York: Oxford University Press, 2005).
7. This idea of memory is near to psychology's "episodic memory"; see Mark A. Wheeler, "Episodic Memory and Autonoetic Awareness," *Oxford Handbook of Memory*, ed. Endel Tulving and Fergus I. M. Craik (New York: Oxford University Press, 2000), 597–608. What Bergson says about memory is not supposed to be a comprehensive theory. It goes to the core of diverse mnemic phenomena to identify what makes memory memory, namely, being some way in which the past remains effective.
8. "The Idea is necessarily obscure insofar as it is distinct, all the more obscure the more it is distinct. Distinction-obscurity becomes here the true tone of philosophy, the symphony of the discordant Idea." Gilles Deleuze, *Difference and Repetition*, trans. Paul Patton (1968; New York: Columbia University Press, 1994), 146.
9. On modes of existence, see Étienne Souriu, *The Different Modes of Existence*, trans. Erik Beranek and Tim Howles (1943; Minneapolis: Univocal, 2015). Among the modes Sourieu distinguishes are actual and virtual, both equally real, equally existing, and so too the

passage between them, which is becoming. He describes virtual existence as *l'intermonde*, on the margin of being. "A particularly rich mode of existence with a multitude of presences that are absences," as, for example, when a broken arch virtually outlines the missing section (156–57). Filling out this French-philosophical lineage is Bruno Latour, *An Inquiry into Modes of Existence: An Anthropology of the Moderns*, trans. Catherine Porter (2012; Cambridge, MA: Harvard University Press, 2013).

10. Gilbert Simondon says virtuality "is a theoretical and objective modality, because it corresponds to that which is not within the power of man, and is nevertheless a power," which he understands in terms of tendency: "Tensions and tendencies can be conceived as really existing in a system: the potential is one of the forms of the real, as completely as the actual. The potentials of a system constitute its power of coming-into-being." *On the Mode of Existence of Technical Objects*, trans. Cécile Malaspina and John Rogove (1958; Minneapolis: Univocal, 2017), 168–69, 213.

11. I draw from C. B. Martin, "Power for Realists," *Ontology, Causality, and Mind*, ed. John Bacon, Keith Campbell, and Lloyd Reinhardt (Cambridge: Cambridge University Press, 1993), 175–86.

12. Aristotle, *Metaphysics*, 1050a. "The priority of act assures the absolutely dominant role of form, for Aristotelian act and form are understood to coincide." Joseph Owens, *The Doctrine of Being in the Aristotelian "Metaphysics,"* 3rd ed. (Toronto: Pontifical Institute of Medieval Studies, 1978), 409. See also T. S. Champlin, "Tendencies," *Proceedings of the Aristotelian Society* 91 (1990–91): 119–33.

13. Gottfried Wilhelm Leibniz, "On the Correction of Metaphysics and the Concept of Substance," *Philosophical Papers and Letters*, ed. and trans. Leroy E. Loemker, 2nd ed. (Dordrecht: D. Reidel, 1976), 433. Leibniz came into focus for French philosophy with Maine de Biran. See Jeremy Dunham, "A Universal and Absolute Spiritualism: Maine de Biran's Leibniz," in Maine de Biran, *The Relationship of the Physical and the Moral in Man*, trans. Darian Meacham and Joseph Spadola (London: Bloomsbury, 2016), 157–92. The history is usefully reviewed in *Dispositions and Causal Powers*, ed. Max Kistler and Bruno Gnassounou (Aldershot: Ashgate, 2007).

14. Descartes, *Le Monde*, trans. Michael Sean Mahoney (New York: Abaris Books, 1979), 63. On nominalism, see my *Empiricisms* (New York: Oxford University Press, 2021), §§29–32.

15. John Stuart Mill, *System of Logic*, 3.10.5; *Collected Works* (1872; Toronto: University of Toronto Press, 1967), 4: 445.

16. Nelson Goodman, *Fact, Fiction, and Forecast*, 3rd ed. (Indianapolis: Hackett, 1979), 40.
17. W. V. Quine, *The Ways of Paradox* (Cambridge, MA: Harvard University Press, 1976), 73; *The Roots of Reference* (La Salle: Open Court, 1973), 10, 13.
18. Mauro Dorato, "Dispositions, Relational Properties, and the Quantum World," *Ontology, Causality, and Mind*, 270. For a searching development of this point, see Lee Smolin, *Three Roads to Quantum Gravity* (New York: Basic Books, 2001).
19. Nancy Cartwright, *Nature, The Artful Modeler* (Chicago: Open Court, 2019), 41.
20. Nancy Cartwright, *Nature's Capacities and their Measurement* (Oxford: Clarendon Press, 1989), 181.
21. Cartwright, *Nature's Capacities*, 188–91.
22. Nancy Cartwright, *The Dappled World* (Cambridge: Cambridge University Press, 1999), 73; and Martin, "Power for Realists," 181.
23. The interaction of memory and experience is a theme of my *Empiricisms*.
24. J. Pokorny et al., "Duration Thresholds for Chromatic Stimuli," *The Journal of the Optical Society of America* 69, no. 1 (1979): 103–06.
25. Andrew G. van Melsen, *The Philosophy of Nature* (Pittsburgh, PA: Duquesne University Press, 1961), 204; also 201–02.
26. "That the mind, which is incorporeal, can set the body in motion . . . is one of those self-evident things that we only make obscure when we try to explain them in terms of other things." Descartes to Arnauld, in Paul S. MacDonald, *History of the Concept of Mind* (Aldershot: Ashgate, 2003), 288.
27. See *The Routledge Handbook of Panpsychism*, ed. William Seager (New York: Routledge, 2020); *The Mental As Fundamental: New Perspectives on Panpsychism*, ed. Michael Blamauer (Frankfurt: Ontos Verlag, 2011). This development in analytic philosophy amuses "those anthropologists who have tried for years to make academic philosophy take animism and panpsychism seriously, that is, to retrieve them back from the dustbin in the history of philosophy and accept them as metaphysical positions big with future." Déborah Danowski and Eduardo Viveiros de Castro, *The Ends of the World*, trans. Rodrigo Numes (2015; Cambridge: Polity, 2017), 148.
28. Spinoza, *Ethics*, 2P13S; *A Spinoza Reader*, Edwin Curley, ed. and trans. (Princeton, NJ: Princeton University Press, 1994), 124. The details of this history are well documented in Seager, ed., *Handbook of Panpsychism*.

29. Seager, "Panpsychism Manifesto," *Handbook of Panpsychism*, 1. I draw extensively from this useful overview of arguments.
30. "Each scientific statement can in principle be so transformed that it is nothing but a structure statement"; "all objects of knowledge . . . can be represented as structural entities." Rudolf Carnap, *The Logical Structure of the World*, trans. Rolf A. George (1928; Berkeley: University of California Press, 1967), §§16, 66.
31. This is the argument of Max Newman, "Mr Russell's Causal Theory of Perception," *Mind* 37, no. 146 (1928): 137–48.
32. Arthur Schopenhauer, *The World as Will and Presentation*, vol. 1, trans. Richard E. Aquila (1818; New York: Pearson Longman, 2008), 143.
33. See Thomas Nagel, "What It Is Like to be a Bat," *Mortal Questions* (Cambridge: Cambridge University Press, 1979), 165–80.
34. William Seager, *Theories of Consciousness*, 2nd ed. (London: Routledge, 2016).
35. Stefano Mancuso and Alessandra Viola, *Brilliant Green: The Surprising History and Science of Plant Intelligence*, trans. Joan Benham (2013; Washington, DC: Island Press, 2015), 131. See also Anthony Trewavas, *Plant Behaviour and Intelligence* (Oxford: Oxford University Press, 2014).
36. Mancuso and Viola, *Brilliant Green*, 140. For a case against plant consciousness, see Jon Mallatt, Michael R. Blatt, Andreas Draguhn, David G. Robinson, and Lincoln Taiz, "Debunking a Myth: Plant Consciousness," *Protoplasma* 258 (2021): 459–76.
37. Nagel, "What It Is Like to be a Bat," 166.
38. Nagel, "Panpsychism," 194. See also Joseph Levine, "Materialism and Qualia: The Explanatory Gap," *Pacific Philosophical Quarterly* 64 (1983): 354–61.
39. From Bergson's 1903-04 lecture course on theories of memory, cited in *Bergsonian Mind*, 162.
40. See Betty Jo Teeter Dobbs, *The Janus Faces of Genius: The Role of Alchemy in Newton's Thought* (Cambridge: Cambridge University Press, 1991); and Ernan McMullin, *Newton on Matter and Activity* (Notre Dame, IN: University of Notre Dame Press, 1978).
41. Galileo, Letter to Piero Dini, in William R. Shea, "Galileo's Atomic Hypothesis," *Ambix* 17, no. 1 (1970), 20–21.
42. Samuel Sambursky, *Physics of the Stoics* (London: Routledge and Kegan Paul, 1959), 5.
43. On Bergson and French spiritualism, see Giuseppe Bianco, "What Was 'Serious Philosophy' for the Young Bergson?" in *Interpreting Bergson*, ed.

Alexandre Lefebvre and Nils F. Schott (Cambridge: Cambridge University Press, 2020), 27–47; and F. C. T. Moore, "French Spiritualist Philosophy," in *Nineteenth-Century Philosophy*, ed. Alan D. Schrift and Daniel Conway (London: Routledge, 2010), 161–75.

44. On trace-theories of memory see Sarah K. Robins, "Memory Traces," *The Routledge Handbook of Philosophy of Memory*, ed., Sven Bernecker and Kourken Michaelian (London: Routledge, 2017), 76–87; and Lynn Nadel, "The Demise of the Fixed Trace," *Science of Memory: Concepts*, ed., Henry L. Roediger, Yadin Dudai, and Susan M. Fitzpartick (New York: Oxford University Press, 2007), 177–81. The principal alternative to a trace-theory is Frederic Bartlett, *Remembering: A Study in Experimental and Social Psychology* (Cambridge: Cambridge University Press, 1932); see Brady Wagoner, "Frederic Bartlett," *Routledge Philosophy of Memory*, 537–45. On Bergson and the psychology of memory, see James Burton, "Bergson's Non-Archival Theory of Memory," *Memory Studies* 1, no. 3 (2008): 321–39.

45. The state of the art in memory research at Bergson's time was Théodule-Armand Ribot, *Diseases of Memory* (1881), a work Bergson often refers to in *Matter and Memory*. Ribot classifies aphasias as diseases of memory and discusses them at length.

46. Bergson, "Psychophysical Parallelism and Positive Metaphysics" (1901), trans. Matthew Cobb, *Continental Philosophy of Science*, ed. Gary Gutting (New York: Wiley-Blackwell, 2005), 62.

47. St. Augustine, *Confessions*, trans. R. S. Pine-Coffin (New York: Dorset, 1986), 11.14.

48. Chrysippus, in Philip Turetzky, *Time* (London: Routledge, 1998), 40. The thesis continues to find a defense; see C. Bourn, *A Future for Presentism* (Oxford: Oxford University Press, 2006); and Akiko M. Frischhut, "Presentism and Temporal Experience," *The Routledge Handbook of Temporal Experience*, ed., Ian Phillips (London: Routledge, 2017), 249–61.

49. Bergson, *Matière et mémoire*, in F. C. T. Moore, *Bergson: Thinking Backwards* (Cambridge: Cambridge University Press, 1996), 62. Husserl too finds the attempt "to set forth what is past as something not real or not existing" as "very questionable." Edmund Husserl, *The Phenomenology of Internal Time-Consciousness*, trans. James S. Churchill (1928; Bloomington: Indiana University Press, 1964), 39.

50. On body memory, see Antonio Damasio, *The Feeling of What Happens: Body, Emotion, and the Making of Consciousness* (London: Vintage, 2000), 133–67.

51. Quantum cosmologist Lee Smolin rediscovers this idea: "Motion is absolute.... Einstein was wrong. Newton was wrong. Galileo was wrong." Bergson was right. "There is no relativity of motion." *Time Reborn* (Toronto: Knopf, 2013), 163.
52. Bertrand Russell, *The Principles of Mathematics*, §446, in *The Concepts of Space and Time, their Structure and Development*, ed. Milič Čapek (Dordrecht: Reidel, 1976), 253.
53. William Ockham, *Tractatus de successivis*, *Philosophy in the Middle Ages*, ed. A. Hyman and J. J. Walsh, 2nd ed. (Indianapolis: Hackett, 1987), 687; and Dennis Des Chese, *Physiologia: Natural Philosophy in Late Aristotelian and Cartesian Thought* (Ithaca: Cornell University Press, 1996), 33. For a lucid explanation of Ockham's idea of motion, see Anneliese Maier, "The Nature of Motion," *On the Threshold of Exact Science*, ed. and trans., Steven D. Sargent (Philadelphia: University of Pennsylvania Press, 1982), 21–39.
54. Steven Harnad, "To Cognize Is to Categorize," *Handbook of Categorization in Cognitive Science*, ed. Henri Cohen and Claire Lefebvre (Amsterdam: Elsevier, 2005), 19–43.
55. Erwin Schrödinger, "What Is an Elementary Particle?" (1950), *Interpreting Bodies: Classical and Quantum Objects in Modern Physics*, ed. Elena Castellani (Princeton, NJ: Princeton University Press, 1998), 205. See also Milič Čapek, *Bergson and Modern Physics* (Dordrecht: D. Reidel, 1971), 78, 266, 267, 310; and "Bergson's Theory of Matter and Modern Physics," *Bergson and the Evolution of Physics*, ed. P. A. Y. Gunter (Knoxville: University of Tennessee Press, 1969), 297–330.
56. Schrödinger, "Elementary Particle," 203.
57. Bruce A. Shumm, *Deep Down Things: The Breathtaking Beauty of Particle Physics* (Baltimore, MD: Johns Hopkins University Press, 2004), 205–06.
58. Erwin Schrödinger, 1935; in Amir D. Aczel, *Entanglement* (New York: Four Walls Eight Windows, 2002), 55.
59. Roger Penrose, *Fashion, Faith and Fantasy in the New Physics of the Universe* (Princeton, NJ: Princeton University Press, 2016), 124. Experiments with nonlocality are recounted in Jim Baggott, *The Quantum Story* (Oxford: Oxford University Press, 2011), ch. 32.
60. A. S. Eddington, *The Nature of the Physical World* (Cambridge: Cambridge University Press, 1928), 86; Ernst Mach, "On the Principle of the Conservation of Energy," *Popular Scientific Lectures*, trans. Thomas J. McCormack (Cambridge: Cambridge University Press, 2014), 137–85; Ludwig Boltzmann, "Further Studies on the Thermal Equilibrium of Gas Molecules" (1872), in *Kinetic Theory*, ed., Steven G. Brush, 2 vols.

(Oxford: Pergamon Press, 1966), 2: 88–175. See also Hans Reichenbach, *The Direction of Time* (Berkeley: University of California Press, 1956).
61. G. N. Lewis, *The Anatomy of Science* (New Haven, CT: Yale University Press, 1926), 153.
62. Edward R. Harrison, *Cosmology: The Science of the Universe* (Cambridge: Cambridge University Press, 1981), 347.
63. Heinz R. Pagels, *Perfect Symmetry* (New York: Simon and Schuster, 1985), 237; Harrison, *Cosmology*, 356; and Joseph Silk, *Horizons of Cosmology* (West Conshohocken, PA: Templeton Press, 2009), 24. On the discovery and measurement of the cosmic background radiation, see John C. Mather and John Boslough, *The Very First Light* (New York: Basic Books, 2006).
64. Roger Penrose, *Cycles of Time* (London: Bodley Head, 2010), 75, 117.
65. See James Lovelock, *The Ages of Gaia* (Oxford: Oxford University Press, 1988). The argument has grown stronger with further research, see *Scientists Debate Gaia*, ed. Stephen Henry Schneider (Cambridge, MA: MIT Press, 2004).
66. Émile Meyerson, *Identity and Reality*, trans. Kate Loewenberg (1908; London: George Allen and Unwin, 1930), 284–85.
67. Henry B. Hollinger and Michael John Zenzen, *The Nature of Irreversibility* (Dordrecht: D. Reidel, 1985), 52, 68.
68. Ludwig Wittgenstein, *Philosophical Investigations*, 3rd ed., trans. G. E. M. Anscombe (Oxford: Blackwell, 1967), §119.
69. Albert Einstein, "Physics and Reality," *Journal of the Franklin Institute* 221, no. 3 (March 1936): 349–82; and *Letters to Solovine: 1906–1955* (New York: Open Road, 2011), letter of March 30, 1952.
70. Hesiod, *Theogony*, ll. 116–17; Plato, *Statesman*, 273a–d. This and all other citations from Plato follow *Complete Works*, ed. John M. Cooper (Indianapolis: Hackett, 1997). François Jullien says of China, "That tension between order and disorder that we already see looming in the background of the biblical creation, and starting from which Hesiod, too, organizes his whole theogony, is not encountered there." *The Book of Beginnings*, trans. Jody Gladding (2012; New Haven, CT: Yale University Press, 2015), 61.
71. Descartes, *Principles*, 3.47; in Des Chese, *Physiologia*, 395.
72. One should not be misled by the expression "chaos theory," and think there is a mathematical theory of chaos, that is, absolute disorder. The mathematics is better described as non-linear systems. See James Gleick, *Chaos: Making a New Science* (New York: Penguin, 1988).
73. Plato, *Timaeus*, 30a.

74. Spinoza, *Ethics*, I, Appendix. In *A Spinoza Reader*, Edwin Curley, ed. and trans. (Princeton, NJ: Princeton University Press, 1994), 113. On Spinoza and Bergson see Russell Ford, "Immanence and Method: Bergson's Early Reading of Spinoza," *Southern Journal of Philosophy* 42 (2004): 171–92.
75. Martin Heidegger is prominent among philosophers impressed by the question; see *Introduction to Metaphysics*, trans. Ralph Manheim (1935; New Haven, CT: Yale University Press, 1959). Leibniz discusses it; see "On the Ultimate Origination of Things," *Philosophical Essays*, ed. and trans. Roger Ariew and Daniel Garber (Indianapolis: Hackett, 1989), 149–55.
76. Francisco Suárez, in Des Chese, *Physiologia*, 27n14.
77. C. S. Peirce, *Collected Papers of Charles Sanders Peirce*, ed. Charles Hartshorne and Paul Weiss (Cambridge, MA: Harvard University Press, 1935), 5: 217.
78. Irad Kimhi, *Thinking and Being* (Cambridge, MA: Harvard University Press, 2018), 104, 147.

Chapter 3

1. Bergson, *Bulletin of the French Society for Philosophy* (1901), in A. D. Lindsay, *The Philosophy of Bergson* (London: J. M. Dent & Sons, 1911), 26.
2. On vitalism, I draw from Thomas S. Hall, *Ideas of Life and Matter: Studies in the History of General Physiology 600 BC–1900 AD*, 2 vols. (Chicago: University of Chicago Press, 1969); Jacques Roger, *The Life Sciences in Eighteenth-Century French Thought*, trans. Robert Ellrich (1963; Stanford, CA: Stanford University Press, 1997), 336–53; *Vitalism and the Scientific Image in Post-Enlightenment Life Science, 1800–2010*, ed. Sebastian Normandin and Charles T. Wolfe (Dordrecht: Springer, 2013); Peter Hanns Reill, *Vitalizing Nature in the Enlightenment* (Berkeley: University of California Press, 2005); Elizabeth A. Williams, *A Cultural History of Medical Vitalism in Enlightenment Montpellier* (London: Routledge, 2016); and E. Benton, "Vitalism in Nineteenth-Century Scientific Thought," *Studies in the History and Philosophy of Science* 5, no. 1 (1974): 17–48. On Bergson and vitalism, see *The Crisis in Modernism: Bergson and the Vitalist Controversy*, ed. Frederick Burwick and Paul Douglass (Cambridge: Cambridge University Press, 1992).
3. Charles-Louis Dumas, *Principes de physiologie* (1800–06). Williams, *Medical Vitalism*, 17, 86, 95, 242, 268–70, 276, 280.
4. Reill, *Vitalizing Nature*, 121, 136, 143, 235–36.

5. Justus von Liebig, in François Jacob, *The Logic of Life*, trans. Betty E. Spillman (1970; Princeton, NJ: Princeton University Press, 1993), 96; also Hall, *Life and Matter*, 2:266–72. An idea of *Lebenskraft* was introduced by Friedrich-Casimir Medicus, *Von der Lebenskraft* (1774), writing under the influence of Barthez. Williams, *Medical Vitalism*, 291. Alexander von Humboldt also used the term in his *Die Lebenskraft* (1795), where it named a power to suspend the "friendship and animosity of the atoms" and join material substances "that in dead nature eternally flee from each other." Reill, *Vitalizing Nature*, 21.
6. Hans Driesch, *The History and Theory of Vitalism*, trans. C. K. Ogden (1905; London: Macmillan, 1914).
7. G. W. Leibniz, *Philosophical Essays*, ed. and trans. Roger Ariew and Daniel Garber (Indianapolis, IN: Hackett, 1989), 173.
8. Driesch, *Vitalism*, 226.
9. Claude Bernard, in Georges Canguilhem, *Ideology and Rationality in the History of the Life Sciences* (Cambridge, MA: MIT Press, 1988), 133.
10. Claude Bernard, *Introduction to the Study of Experimental Medicine*, trans. Henry Copley Greene (1865; New York: Dover, 1957), 68.
11. E. S. Russell, *The Directiveness of Organic Activities* (Cambridge: Cambridge University Press, 1945), 173. On Russell and the Organicist school, see *Everything Flows: Toward a Processual Philosophy of Biology*, ed. Daniel J. Nicholson and John Dupré (New York: Oxford University Press, 2018), 3–46.
12. I discuss this acculturation to tools in *Artifice and Design: Art and Technology in Human Experience* (Ithaca, NY: Cornell University Press, 2008).
13. Charles H. Langmuir and Wally Broecker, *How to Build a Habitable Planet: The Story of Earth from the Big Bang to Humankind* (Princeton, NJ: Princeton University Press, 2012), 420–21, 454–55. "Life is a property of planets rather than individual organisms." Harold Morowitz, *Beginnings of Cellular Life* (New Haven, CT: Yale University Press, 1992), 8.
14. On pre-Platonic teleology, see David Sedley, *Creationism and Its Critics in Antiquity* (Berkeley: University of California Press, 2008). On Plato's synthesis, Thomas Kjeller Johansen, *Plato's Natural Philosophy* (Cambridge: Cambridge University Press, 2004).
15. John M. Cooper, "Aristotle on Natural Teleology," in his *Knowledge, Nature, and the Good* (Princeton, NJ: Princeton University Press, 2004), 107–29.

16. The causality of the Unmoved Mover accounts only for the fact that the acorn grows at all, not that it grows into an oak. Charles H. Kahn, "The Place of the Prime Mover in Aristotle's Teleology," in *Aristotle on Nature and Living Things*, ed. Allan Gotthelf (Bristol: Bristol Classical Press, 1985), 183–205.
17. Cicero, *De natura deorem*, 2.58, in Arthur Stanley Pease, "*Caeli enarrant*," *Harvard Theological Review* 34, no. 3 (1941): 163–200.
18. The criticism of final causes is in the Appendix to Spinoza, *Ethics*, Part One. *Conatus* is introduced in Part Three, especially Proposition 7. On *conatus* as a teleological concept, see Jeffrey K. McDonough, "The Heyday of Teleology and Early Modern Philosophy," *Midwest Studies in Philosophy* 35 (2011): 179–204.
19. Among contemporaries, Spinoza was considered to advance Stoic ideas; for instance, Leibniz describes him as the leader of a "sect of new Stoics" who hold that "things act because of [nature's] power and not due to a rational choice." Leibniz, *Philosophical Essays*, 282.
20. Emily Herring, "The Vital Impulse and Early Twentieth-Century Biology," in *The Bergsonian Mind*, ed. Mark Sinclair and Yaron Wolf (London: Routledge, 2022), 318–31.
21. E. S. Russell, in Herring, "Vital Impulse," 326.
22. J. A. Thomson, in Herring, "Vital Impulse," 327.
23. Bergson to Harald Höffding, 1915; *Reassessing Bergson*, ed. Matyáš Moravec, Frédéric Worms, and Caterina Zanfi. *Bergonsoniana* 1 (2021), 167.
24. Mathilde Tahar, "Bergson as Visionary in Evolutionary Biology," *Bergsonian Mind*, 446.
25. Steven Rose includes Bergson among "an alternative, almost underground non-reductionist tradition in biology [whose] voices were and still are drowned out by an almost universal reductionist consensus." *Lifelines: Life Beyond the Gene* (Oxford: Oxford University Press, 1997), 78–79.
26. Huxley thought Darwin exaggerated the importance of adaptation and urged a theory of nondirected saltations. See Michael Ruse, *Darwin and Design* (Cambridge, MA: Harvard University Press, 2003), 135–42. On the diversity of views among scientific evolutionists in the generations after Darwin, see Peter J. Bowler, *Evolution: The History of an Idea*, 3rd ed. (Berkeley: University of California Press, 2003).
27. T. H. Huxley, in Ruse, *Darwin and Design*, 138–39.
28. Charles Darwin, *Variations of Plants and Animals Under Domestication*, 2 vols. (London: J. Murray, 1885), 1: 236. Origin of life a pseudo-question,

Darwin, *The Origin of Species* and *The Descent of Man* (New York: Modern Library, 1936), 133, 184, 446.
29. No documented speciation by mutation: Lynn Margulis and Dorion Sagen, *Acquiring Genomes* (New York: Basic Books, 2002), 72. Miraculous: Raymond Ruyer, *Neofinalism*, trans. Alyosha Edlebi (1952; Minneapolis: University of Minnesota Press, 2016), 170–72.
30. Arlin Stoltzfus, "Mutationism and the Dual Causation of Evolutionary Change," *Evolution and Development* 8, no. 3 (2006): 304–17. See also John Beatty, "Reconsidering the Importance of Chance Variation," in *Evolution: The Extended Synthesis*, ed. Massimo Pigliucci and Gerd B. Müller (Cambridge, MA: MIT Press, 2010), 21–44.
31. Stoltzfus, "Mutationism," 315.
32. Simon Conway Morris, *Life's Solution* (Cambridge: Cambridge University Press, 2003), 151–57.
33. Research (1996) cited in Conway Morris, *Life's Solution*, 157; see also 154–55.
34. On photoreceptors, John Gerhart and Marc Kirschner, *Cells, Embryos, and Evolution* (Malden, MA: Blackwell Science, 1997), 111.
35. Conway Morris, *Life's Solution*, 309; also 119, 126–27.
36. Conway Morris, *Life's Solution*, xiii, xv, 303, 304, 306, 307. On exaptation, see Steven Jay Gould, *The Structure of Evolutionary Theory* (Cambridge, MA: Harvard University Press, 2002). Sean B. Carroll also finds evidence of natural selection in convergent evolution, see *The Making of the Fittest* (New York; Norton, 2006), 141.
37. Steven Jay Gould, *Wonderful Life: The Burgess Shale and the Nature of History* (New York: Norton, 1989), 51. See also Douglas H. Erwin, "Wonderful Life Revisited," in *Chance in Evolution*, ed. Grant Ramsey and Charles H. Pence (Chicago: University of Chicago Press, 2016), 41–75; and John H. Beatty, "Replaying Life's Tape," *Journal of Philosophy* 103, no. 7 (1984): 336–62. On "chance" in Darwin's argument, see David J. Depew, "Contingency, Chance, and Randomness in Biology," *Chance in Evolution*, 15–40.
38. Conway Morris, *Life's Solution*, 284; Charles H. Langmuir and Wally Broecker, *How to Build a Habitable Planet: The Story of Earth from the Big Bang to Humankind* (Princeton, NJ: Princeton University Press, 2012), 417–18.
39. Conway Morris, *Life's Solution*, 309–10.
40. Conway Morris, *Life's Solution*, 166.
41. For a study of the analogy, see Hisashi Fujita, "Bergson's Hand: Toward a History of (Non-Organic) Vitalism," *SubStance* 36, no. 3 (2007): 115–30.

42. I expand on the relation of technology and human evolution in *Knowledge and Civilization* (New York: Routledge, 2018).
43. See David Hume, *Dialogues on Natural Religion* (1779), Part VI. Hume's Philo argues that the evidence suggesting nature's design equally well supports the conclusion that nature is an animal or a vegetable.
44. Jean Baptiste de Lamarck, *Zoological Philosophy*, trans. Hugh Elliot (1809; London, 1914; Cambridge: Cambridge University Press, 2011). For modern reconsideration of Lamarck, see *Transformations of Lamarckism. From Subtle Fluids to Molecular Biology*, ed. Snait Gissis and Eva Jablonka (Cambridge, MA: MIT Press, 2011).
45. On cephalopods I draw from Sarah Zylinski and Daniel Osorio, "Cuttlefish Camouflage: Vision and Cognition," in *Cephalopod Cognition*, ed. A.-S. Darmaillacq, L. Dickel, and J. Mather (Cambridge: Cambridge University Press, 2014), 197–222; Sarah Zylinski and Sönke Johnsen, "Visual Cognition in Deep Sea Cephalopods," in *Cephalopod Cognition*, ed. A.-S. Darmaillacq, L. Dickel, and J. Mather (Cambridge: Cambridge University Press, 2014), 223–41; Jennifer Mather and David Scheel, "Behavior," in *Cephalopod Culture*, ed. José Iglesias, Lydia Fuentes, and Roger Villanueva (Berlin: Springer, 2014), 17–39; Sy Montgomery, *The Soul of an Octopus* (New York: Atria, 2015); and Peter Godfrey-Smith, *Other Minds: The Octopus, the Sea, and the Deep Origins of Consciousness* (New York: Farrar, Straus and Giroux, 2016).
46. Conway Morris, *Life's Solution*, 215.
47. Trajectories approach attractors asymptotically and no point of trajectory ever actually intersects one; hence attractors cannot be actual objects but only tendencies. They are real because they have specific effects, especially that of stabilizing trajectories; yet they are not actual. See Manuel Delanda, *Intensive Science and Virtual Philosophy* (London: Continuum, 2002).
48. Dan E. Nilsson and Almut Kelber, "A Functional Analysis of Compound Eye Evolution," *Arthropod Structure & Development* 36 (2007): 373–85. See also Michael F. Land, "Visual Tracking and Pursuit: Humans and Arthropods Compared," *Insect Physiology* 38, no. 12 (1992): 939–51.
49. On developmental homology, Susan Oyama, *Evolution's Eye: A Systems View of the Biology-Culture Divide* (Durham, NC: Duke University Press, 2000).
50. Gerhart and Kirschner, *Cells*, 32, 34, 114, 141; and Russell D. Fernald, "Evolution of Eyes," *Current Opinion in Neurobiology* 10 (2004): 444–50.
51. Julian Huxley, *Essays of a Biologist* (London: Chatto and Windus, 1926), 34. There's more to Huxley's relationship to Bergson than the quotation

suggests. Ten years earlier, he identified Bergson as a main influence on his first book, *The Individual and the Animal Kingdom* (1912): "It will easily be seen how much I owe to M. Bergson." Diary entries show him continuing to think highly of Bergson. "Great is Darwin and Bergson his poet." In a lecture he says, "Bergson is right when he speaks of creative evolution." Suddenly the tone changes. By 1923, Bergson is "a good poet but a bad scientist," and his name is omitted from Huxley's 1970 memoir. See Emily Herring, "'Great is Darwin and Bergson his Poet': Julian Huxley's Other Evolutionary Synthesis," *Annals of Science* 75, no. 1 (2018): 40–54.

52. On the notion of "logical space," see Ludwig Wittgenstein, *Tractatus Logico-Philosophicus*, trans. D. F. Pears and B. F. McGuinness (1921; London: Routledge & Kegan Paul, 1961), and David Lewis, *On the Plurality of Worlds* (Oxford: Basil Blackwell, 1986). Bergson expands on his argument about possibility in "The Possible and the Real" (in CM).

53. "In every wakeful *cogito*, a 'glancing ray' from the pure Ego is directed upon the 'object' of the correlate consciousness for the time being." Edmund Husserl, *Ideas*, trans. W. R. Boyce Gibson (1913; London: George Allen and Unwin, 1931), 243. On consciousness and "what it is like," Thomas Nagel, "What It is Like to be a Bat," *Mortal Questions* (Cambridge: Cambridge University Press, 1979), 165–80.

54. Bergson, in *Journal of French and Francophone Philosophy* 24, no. 2 (2016), 168. I discuss Butler's idea of evolution, including Bergson's take on it, in "Samuel Butler's Contributions to Biological Philosophy," *Common Knowledge* 29 (2023) (forthcoming).

55. On tools in human evolution, see my *Artifice and Design: Art and Technology in Human Experience* (Ithaca, NY: Cornell University Press, 2008).

56. Charles Darwin, *Action of Worms* (London: John Murray, 1881).

57. Few honeybee behaviors are fully hardwired and even comb construction skills have to be partially learned. See Lars Chittka, "Bee Cognition," *Current Biology* 27 (2017): 1037–59.

58. William Thompson, *Popular Lectures and Addresses*, 2 vols. (London: Macmillan, 1891), 1: 80.

59. William James, *Pragmatism* (1907; Cambridge, MA: Harvard University Press, 1978).

60. I discuss this explanation of truth and its career in philosophy in *Truth in Philosophy* (Cambridge, MA: Harvard University Press, 1993).

61. Arthur Schopenhauer, *The World as Will and Presentation*, vol. 2, trans. David Carus and Richard E. Aquila (1844; Upper Saddle River, NJ: Pearson

Education, 2011), 324. On Bergson and Schopenhauer, see Arnaud François, *Bergson, Schopenhauer, Nietzsche: volonté et realité* (Paris: Presses universitaires de France, 2008). In 1914, Wilhelm Wundt initiated a German controversy over Bergson's alleged plagiarism of Schopenhauer. See Caterina Zanfi, "Bergson and German Philosophy," *The Bergsonian Mind*, ed. Mark Sinclair and Yaron Wolf (London: Routledge, 2022), 305–17.
62. Schopenhauer, *World as Will and Presentation*, 2: 500.
63. Differences among biological individuals are combinatorial; not unique endowments but unique combinations of endowments. P. B. Medawar, *The Uniqueness of the Individual* (New York: Basic Books, 1957), 154–55. See also Leo W. Buss, *The Evolution of Individuality* (Princeton, NJ: Princeton University Press, 1987); and Scott F. Gilbert, Jan Sapp, and Alfred Tauber, "A Symbiotic View of Life: We Have Never Been Individuals," *Quarterly Review of Biology* 87, no. 4 (2012): 325–41. On the philosophy of individuation, see Gilbert Simondon, *Individuation in the Light of Notions of Form and Information*, trans. Taylor Adkins (1964; Minneapolis: University of Minnesota Press, 2020).
64. Gerhart and Kirschner, *Cells*, 612–13.
65. See Lynn Margulis, *Symbiotic Planet: A New Look at Evolution* (New York: Basic Books, 1998); Steven Jay Gould, *Full House* (New York: Three Rivers Press, 1996); and Lynn Margulis and Dorian Sagen, *Slanted Truths: Essays on Gaia, Symbiosis, and Evolution* (New York: Springer, 1997), 77–78.
66. Martin Rees, *Our Cosmic Habitat* (Princeton, NJ: Princeton University Press, 2001), 22.
67. What Deleuze and Guattari describe as "anorganic life" is a vital *élan* unrestricted by species. *A Thousand Plateaus*, trans. Brian Massumi (1980; Minneapolis: University of Minnesota Press, 1987), 499–503; also my "Unnatural Nuptials," *Deleuze and Evolutionary Theory*, ed., Michael Bennett and Tano Posteraro (Edinburgh: Edinburgh University Press, 2019), 23–41.
68. *Zhuangzi*, in *Readings in Classical Chinese Philosophy*, ed. Philip J. Ivanhoe and Bryan W. Van Norden (Indianapolis: Hackett, 2001), 229. I discuss this text in *Vanishing into Things: Knowledge in Chinese Tradition* (Cambridge, MA: Harvard University Press, 2015), 97–98. On Bergson and French Catholicism, R. C. Grogin, *The Bergsonian Controversy in France 1900–1914* (Calgary: University of Calgary Press, 1988).
69. Gilles Deleuze, "Bergson's Conception of Difference," *Desert Islands and Other Texts*, trans. Michael Taormina (2002; Los Angles: Semiotext(e), 2004), 47–48.

70. Lemâitre published his theory of "a homogeneous Universe of constant mass and growing radius" in 1927. Big Bang cosmology was not solely Lemaître's work and is technically referred to as the FRWL universe model, from the initials of Alexander Friedmann, H. P. Robinson, Arthur Walker, and Lemaître. See John Farrell, *The Day Without Yesterday: Lemaître, Einstein, and the Birth of Modern Cosmology* (New York: Thunder's Mouth Press, 2005). My account of Big Bang cosmology draws from James E. Lidsey, *The Bigger Bang* (Cambridge: Cambridge University Press, 2000); Martin Rees, *Before the Beginning: Our Universe and Others* (Reading, MA: Perseus Books, 1997) and *Our Cosmic Habitat* (Princeton, NJ: Princeton University Press, 2001); and Joseph Silk, *Horizons of Cosmology* (West Conshohocken, PA: Templeton Press, 2009).
71. Georges Lemaître, *The Primeval Atom: An Essay on Cosmology*, trans. Betty H. and Serge A. Korff (1946; New York: Van Nostrand, 1950), 17.
72. Lemaître, *Primeval Atom*, 18–19.
73. Attributed to Bergson in Jacques Chevalier, *Entretiens avec Bergson* (Paris, 1959), in Milič Čapek, *Bergson and Modern Physics* (Dordrecht: D. Reidel, 1971), 374.
74. Rees, *Cosmic Habitat*, 85.
75. Silk, *Cosmology*, 128.
76. Lee Smolin, *Three Roads to Quantum Gravity* (New York: Basic Books, 2001), 63.
77. Roger Penrose, *Cycles of Time* (London: Bodley Head, 2010), 182.
78. Leonard Susskind, *The Cosmic Landscape* (New York: Little, Brown, 2006), 177. Physics-existence is not mere logical possibility (noncontradiction), since elliptical planets, while logically possible, do not, in the physics sense, exist, since gravity would inevitably make them spherical.
79. Lee Smolin, *The Life of the Cosmos* (New York: Oxford University Press, 1997), 291, also 287.
80. See Svend E. Rugh and Henrik Zinkernagel, "Limits of Time in Cosmology," *The Philosophy of Cosmology*, ed. Khalil Chamcham, Joseph Silk, John D. Barrow, Simon Saunders (Cambridge: Cambridge University Press, 2017), 377–95; and Christian Wüthrich, "One Time, Two Times, or No Time?," in *Einstein vs. Bergson: An Enduring Quarrel on Time*, ed. Alessandra Campo and Simone Gazzano (Berlin: Walter de Gruyter, 2022), 209–30.
81. Carlo Rovelli, in *Einstein vs. Bergson*, vi.
82. Smolin, *Quantum Gravity*, 238, 164.

83. Richard A. Muller, *Now: The Physics of Time* (New York: W. W. Norton, 2016), 143, 293; and William Unruh, "Time, Gravity, and Quantum Mechanics," in *Time's Arrows Today*, ed. Steven F. Savitt (Cambridge: Cambridge University Press, 1995), 23–65.
84. Muller, *Now*, 293, 294–95.
85. My discussion of Bergson's German reception draws from Caterina Zanfi, *Bergson und die Deutsche Philosophie 1907–1932* (München: Verlag Karl Alber Freiburg, 2018), 270–89. I thank my colleague Johannes Steizinger for bringing this book to my attention.
86. Zanfi, *Bergson*, 270–71.
87. Zanfi, *Bergson*, 288.
88. In a 1915 paper on "French Philosophy," Bergson says of Jean-Marie Guyau, "Less famous than Nietzsche, Guyau held, before the German philosopher, in more measured terms and in a more acceptable form, that the moral ideal is to be sought in the highest possible expansion of life." In Mark Sinclair, *Bergson* (London: Routledge, 2020), 246.
89. Seilliére, in Sinclair, *Bergson*, 249.
90. Zanfi, *Bergson*, 289.
91. Arnaud François, "Life and Will in Bergson and Nietzsche," *Substance* 36, no.3 (2007): 100–14; see also François, *Bergson, Schopenhauer, Nietzsche: volonté et realité* (Paris, Presses universitaires de France, 2009); and Jeanne Delhomme, "Nietzsche et Bergson: La Représentation de la Vérité," *Les Études Bergsoniennes* 5 (1960): 37–62.
92. Nietzsche, unpublished note, in François, "Bergson and Nietzsche," 101.
93. Friedrich Nietzsche, *Thus Spoke Zarathustra*, trans. Adrian Del Caro (Cambridge: Cambridge University Press, 2006), 158; *The Will to Power*, trans. Walter Kaufmann and R. J. Hollingdale (New York: Vintage Books, 1967), §517; and *Ecce Homo*, trans. Judith Norman (Cambridge: Cambridge University Press, 2005), 110.
94. Nietzsche, *Beyond Good and Evil: Prelude to a Philosophy of the Future*, trans. Judith Norman (1886; Cambridge: Cambridge University Press, 2002), 4.
95. Spinoza, *Ethics*, 2P26; *A Spinoza Reader*, Edwin Curley, ed. and trans. (Princeton, NJ: Princeton University Press, 1994), 134.
96. Nietzsche, *Will to Power*, §616. Nietzsche was happy to rank himself with Heraclitus; see *The Pre-Platonic Philosophers*, trans. Greg Whitlock (Urbana: University of Illinois Press, 2001), ch. 10. Bergson, however, did not appreciate the comparison. In what seems to be his sole substantive reference to the Ephesian he says, "[I am] in no way setting aside *substance*. On the contrary, I affirm the persistence of existences.... How was

it ever possible to compare this doctrine with the doctrine of Heraclitus?" (см 222n23).
97. Nietzsche, *Thus Spoke Zarathustra*, 89.
98. Nietzsche, in James I. Porter, *Nietzsche and the Philology of the Future* (Stanford, CA: Stanford University Press, 2000), 142, 143.
99. Nietzsche, *Will to Power*, §1067.
100. Gilles Deleuze, *Nietzsche and Philosophy*, trans. Hugh Tomlinson (1962; New York: Columbia University Press, 2006).
101. Stoic fragment of Nemesius, in *Companion to the Stoics*, ed. Brad Inwood (Cambridge: Cambridge University Press, 2003), 141. On eternal return in ancient thought, see Richard Sorabji, *Time, Creation and the Continuum* (London: Duckworth, 1983), 182–90.
102. Deleuze, *Nietzsche and Philosophy*, xviii.
103. Nietzsche, *Thus Spoke Zarathustra*, 184.
104. Deleuze, *Nietzsche and Philosophy*, 71.
105. In *Ecce Homo*, Nietzsche mentions the Stoic idea. "The doctrine of the 'eternal return,' which is to say the unconditional and infinitely repeated cycle of all things—this is Zarathustra's doctrine, but . . . the Stoics have traces of it." Not it, but traces, implying that Zarathustra's idea is mostly not the Stoic thought. *Anti-Christ, Ecce Homo, Twilight of the Idols*, 110.
106. Perhaps I slight Kierkegaard: "The dialectic of repetition is easy, for that which is repeated has been—otherwise it could not be repeated—but the very fact that it has been makes the repetition into something new." Søren Kierkegaard, *Repetition*, trans. Howard V. Hong and Edna H. Hong (1843; Princeton, NJ: Princeton University Press, 1983), 149.
107. Nietzsche, *Twilight of the Idols*, trans. Richard Polt (1889; Indianapolis, IN: Hackett, 1997), 90–91. On time worship, Wyndham Lewis, *The Demon of Progress in the Arts* (London: Methuen, 1954).
108. Nietzsche, *Will to Power*, §636.

Chapter 4

1. Karl Popper, *The Open Society and Its Enemies* (1945; London: Routledge, 2002), 589–90.
2. Popper, *Open Society*, xl.
3. Popper, *Open Society*, 589–90.
4. See ch. 4 in Charles Darwin, *The Origin of Species and The Descent of Man* (New York: Modern Library, 1936). On morality in evolution, see

Edouard Machery and Ron Mallon, "Evolution of Morality," in *The Moral Psychology Handbook*, ed. John M. Doris et al. (Oxford: Oxford University Press, 2010); Dennis L. Krebs, *The Origin of Morality: An Evolutionary Account* (New York: Oxford University Press, 2011); and Robert J. Richards, *Darwin and the Emergence of Evolutionary Theories of Mind and Behavior* (Chicago: University of Chicago Press, 1987).

5. Alexandre Lefebvre, "Human Rights and the Leap of Love," *Journal of French and Francophone Philosophy* 24, no. 2 (2016): 21–40.
6. See Melanie White, "Habit as a Force of Life in Durkheim and Bergson," *Body and Society* 19, nos. 2–3 (2013): 240–62.
7. Alexandre Lefebvre and Nils F. Schott, "Open and Closed Societies," in *The Bergsonian Mind*, ed. Mark Sinclair and Yaron Wolf (London: Routledge, 2022), 251–63.
8. Richard Vernon, "Bergson and Political Theory," in *Interpreting Bergson*, ed. Alexandre Lefebvre and Nils F. Schott (Cambridge: Cambridge University Press, 2020), 155–71.
9. Bergson, "Psychophysical Parallelism and Positive Metaphysics" (1901), trans. Matthew Cobb, in *Continental Philosophy of Science*, ed. Gary Gutting (New York: Wiley-Blackwell, 2005), 68.
10. On the philosophy of laughter, see Ted Cohen, *Jokes: Philosophical Thoughts on Joking Matters* (Chicago: University of Chicago Press, 1999); and John Morreall, *Comic Relief: A Comprehensive Philosophy of Humor* (Malden, MA: Wiley-Blackwell, 2009). An anthropological study is Mary Douglas, "Jokes," in *Implicit Meanings* (London: Routledge and Kegan Paul, 1975), 90–114. Historical studies include Stephen Halliwell, *Greek Laughter* (Cambridge: Cambridge University Press, 2008), and Mary Beard, *Laughter in Ancient Rome* (Berkeley: University of California Press, 2014).
11. People are three times more likely to laugh when with others than when alone. Robert Provine, *Laughter: A Scientific Investigation* (Hammondsworth: Penguin, 2000), 45.
12. See Hans Blumenberg, *The Laughter of the Thracian Woman: A Protohistory of Theory*, trans. Spencer Hawkins (1987; London: Bloomsbury, 2015).
13. For a selection of his work in English, see Félix Ravaisson, *Selected Essays*, ed. Mark Sinclair (London: Bloomsbury, 2016).
14. Kant, *Critique of Judgment*, §44.
15. Arthur Koestler, *The Act of Creation* (New York: Macmillan, 1964), 47.
16. See Katherine Gilbert, "Bergson's Penal Theory of Comedy," in *Studies in Recent Aesthetic* (Durham: University of North Carolina Press, 1927);

and Bernard G. Prusak, "*Le rire à nouveau*: Rereading Bergson," *Journal of Aesthetics and Art Criticism* 62, no. 4 (2004): 377–88.
17. Frédéric Laugrand and Jarish Oosten, *Hunters, Predators, and Prey: Inuit Perceptions of Animals* (New York: Berghahn, 2014), 97.
18. Friedrich Nietzsche, *Thus Spoke Zarathustra*, trans. Adrian Del Caro (Cambridge: Cambridge University Press, 2006), 6, 9, 11.
19. Nietzsche, *Zarathustra*, 115, 117.
20. Nietzsche was received in France (for instance, by Bataille and Deleuze) as a laughing philosopher and a philosopher of laughter, which as Lydia Amir shows is not an obvious reading of Nietzsche and was for long a peculiarly French one. *The Legacy of Nietzsche's Philosophy of Laughter* (New York: Routledge, 2022).
21. Nietzsche, *Zarathustra*, 76, 93, 105, 145, 94.
22. Nietzsche, *Zarathustra*, 226, 238, 240.
23. Nietzsche, *The Gay Science*, trans. Josefine Nauckhoff (1887; Cambridge: Cambridge University Press, 2001), §1.
24. The quotations in this paragraph are from *Zarathustra*, 28, 72, 127, 239, 158, 169.
25. Nietzsche, *On the Genealogy of Morality*, Second Treatise, §2.
26. Rousseau's principal text on conscience is *Emile*, book 4.
27. See Alexandre Lefebvre, *Human Rights As a Way of Life: On Bergson's Political Philosophy* (Stanford, CA: Stanford University Press, 2013).
28. Émile Durkheim, *Moral Education*, trans. Everett Wilson and Herman Schnurer (1925; New York: Free Press, 1961), 73–74. On Bergson's implicit overthrow of Durkheim's principles, see Alexandre Lefebvre and Melanie White, "Bergson and Social Theory," in *Interpreting Bergson*, ed. Alexandre Lefebvre and Nils F. Schott (Cambridge: Cambridge University Press, 2020), 139–54.
29. See Suzanne Guerlac, "Bergson, Void, and the Politics of Life," in *Bergson, Politics, and Religion*, ed. Alexandre Lefebvre and Melanie White (Durham, NC: Duke University Press, 2012), 40–60.
30. See Paola Marrati, "Mysticism and the Foundation of the Open Society: Bergsonian Politics," in *Political Theologies*, ed. Hent de Vries and Lawrence E. Sullivan (New York: Fordham University Press, 2006), 591–601.
31. Immanuel Kant, "Idea for a Universal History with a Cosmopolitan Aim" (1784), trans. Allen W. Wood, in *Kant's Idea for a Universal History with a Cosmopolitan Aim: A Critical Guide*, ed. Amélie Oksenberg Rorty and James Schmidt (Cambridge: Cambridge University Press, 2009), 19.

32. Epicurus, *Principal Doctrines*, 31–38.
33. Immanuel Kant, "What is Enlightenment?" (1784), in *Kant on History*, trans. L. W. Beck (Indianapolis, IN: Bobbs-Merrill, 1963), 3–10.
34. Kant, *Critique of Practical Reason*, trans. T. K. Abbot (1788; London: Longman, Green, 1909), 193.
35. Plato, *Republic*, 590c; Aristotle, *Politics*, 1278a.
36. *Odyssey* 23, ll. 190–201.
37. Antiphon, in Aristotle, *Mechanical Problems* 847a; in *Minor Works*, trans. Walter S. Hett (Cambridge, MA: Harvard University Press, 1936). See also Alison Burford, *Craftsmen in Greek and Roman Society* (London: Thames and Hudson, 1972); Sarah P. Morris, *Daidalos and the Origins of Greek Art* (Princeton, NJ: Princeton University Press, 1992); and Elspeth Whitney, *Paradise Restored: The Mechanical Arts from Antiquity Through the Thirteenth Century* (Philadelphia: American Philosophical Society, 1990).
38. See Gilbert Simondon, *On the Mode of Existence of Technical Objects*, trans. Cécile Malaspina and John Rogove (1958; Minneapolis: Univocal, 2017), part 2, ch. 1.
39. Karl Marx, *Capital: A Critique of Political Economy*, trans. Samuel Moore and Edward Aveling, 3 vols. (1887; Moscow: Progress Publishers, 1954), 1:352n2. See also Robert B. Pippin, "On the Notion of Technology as Ideology," in *Technology and the Politics of Knowledge*, ed. Andrew Feenberg and Alastair Hannay (Bloomington: Indiana University Press, 1995), 43–61; and Bruce Bimber, "Three Faces of Technological Determinism," in *Does Technology Drive History?*, ed. Merritt Roe Smith and Leo Marx (Cambridge, MA: MIT Press, 1994), 79–100.
40. Jürgen Renn, *The Evolution of Knowledge: Rethinking Science for the Anthropocene* (Princeton, NJ: Princeton University Press, 2020), 229–30.
41. See André Leroi-Gourhan, *Milieu et Techniques* (Paris: Albin Michel, 1945); Simondon, *Mode of Existence of Technical Objects*; Raymond Ruyer, *Neofinalism*, trans. Alyosha Edlebi (1952; Minneapolis: University of Minnesota Press, 2016); Bernard Stiegler, *Technics and Time*, trans. Richard Beardsworth and George Collins (1994; Stanford, CA: Stanford University Press, 1998); and Bruno Latour, *Aramis, or the Love of Technology*, trans. Catherine Porter (1992; Cambridge, MA: Harvard University Press, 1996). Also, Paola Marrati, "The Natural Cyborg: The Stakes of Bergson's Philosophy of Evolution," *Southern Journal of Philosophy* 48 (2010): 3–17.
42. Bergson's vision of the nuclear future was not unique. Ten years earlier, English physicist Frederick Soddy wrote that there is "no limit to the amount of energy in the world available to support life, save only the limit

imposed by the boundaries of knowledge. . . . So far as the future is concerned, an entirely new prospect has been opened up . . . a more exalted material destiny than any which have been foretold." *The Interpretation of Radium and the Structure of the Atom* (New York: G. P. Putnam's Sons, 1922), 185.

43. John Gerhart and Marc Kirschner, *Cells, Embryos, and Evolution* (Malden, MA: Blackwell Science, 1997), 612–13.

44. Herbert Spencer, a philosopher the young Bergson studied closely, had a theory of social rhythms; for example, in religion, "long periods of exaltation and depression—generations of belief and self-mortification, following generations of indifference and laxity." *First Principles* (1862), in John Offer, *Herbert Spencer and Social Theory* (Houndmills: Palgrave Macmillan, 2010), 140.

45. On Bergson's two-fold frenzy, see Caterina Zanfi, "The Duration of History in Bergson," in *Reassessing Bergson*, ed. Matyáš Moravec, Frédéric Worms, and Caterina Zanfi, *Bergsoniana* 1 (2021): 155–72.

46. Fernand Braudel, *Capitalism and Material Life 1400–1800*, trans. Miriam Kochan (1967; New York: Harper & Row, 1975), 129. See also Christopher J. Berry, *The Idea of Luxury* (Cambridge: Cambridge University Press, 1994).

47. *Revelations of the Medieval World, A History of Private Life*, vol. 2, ed. Georges Duby, trans. Arthur Goldhammer (Cambridge, MA: Belknap Press, 1988), 408, 411.

Conclusion

1. Perhaps the most plausible idea for a concept of life is the autopoietic system, as in the self-producing and self-maintaining activities of living beings. See Lynn Margulis and Dorian Sagen, *Slanted Truths: Essays on Gaia, Symbiosis, and Evolution* (New York: Springer, 1997), 104, 267. It may be that all organisms are autopoietic systems, but it is unlikely that all autopoietic systems are organisms. Autopoiesis is a form of organization using self-referential closure and can materialize in living as well as non-living systems. Niklas Luhmann, *Essays on Self-Reference* (New York: Columbia University Press, 1990), 2.

2. Leszek Kolakowski, *Bergson* (Oxford: Oxford University Press, 1985), 102.

3. W. V. Quine, "Epistemology Naturalized," in *Ontological Relativity and Other Essays* (New York: Columbia University Press, 1969), 82; and "Existence and Existential Quantification," ibid, 126.

4. Jon Jacobs, "Naturalism," in *The Internet Encyclopedia of Philosophy*, ed. James Fieser and Bradley Dowden, https://iep.utm.edu/naturali/; David Papineau, "Naturalism," in *The Stanford Encyclopedia of Philosophy* (Winter 2016 edition), ed. Edward N. Zalta, https://plato.stanford.edu/archives/win2016/entries/naturalism/.
5. This argument is most completely spelled out in Bergson's "Introduction to Metaphysics" (1903), in CM. See also Stéphane Madelrieux, "Bergson and Naturalism," in *Interpreting Bergson*, ed. Alexandre Lefebvre and Nils F. Schott (Cambridge: Cambridge University Press, 2020), 48–66.
6. Gilles Deleuze and Félix Guattari, *A Thousand Plateaus: Capitalism and Schizophrenia*, trans. Brian Massumi (1980; Minneapolis: University of Minnesota Press, 1987), 43.
7. Alexander of Aphrodisias, paraphrasing Chryssipus, *The Hellenistic Philosophers*, ed. A. A. Long and D. N. Sedley (Cambridge: Cambridge University Press, 1987), 283. See also John Cooper, "Chrysippus on Physical Elements," in *God and Cosmos in Stoicism*, ed. Ricardo Sales (New York: Oxford University Press, 2009), 93–117.
8. Samuel Sambursky, *Physics of the Stoics* (London: Routledge and Kegan Paul, 1959), 36. *Tonos* (tension), noun, from *teino*, verb, to stretch a cord. Hippocratic texts use the term for the sinews. *Tonoi* is also a technical term for the system of ropes that holds a ship together, which Plato likened to animal *neura*, as did Aristotle, who regarded this as the most important source of corporeal integrity. The Stoic Cleanthes makes these all effects of elemental fire. David E. Hahm, *The Origins of Stoic Cosmology* (Columbus: Ohio State University Press, 1977), 155, 170. Michel Serres depicts all nature in terms of such bonds. See *The Natural Contract*, trans. Elizabeth MacArthur and William Paulson (1990; Ann Arbor: University of Michigan Press, 1995).
9. Pauline Phemister, *Leibniz and the Natural World* (Dordrecht: Springer, 2005), 45, 72.
10. The idea of a plastic force (*dunamis diaplastike, virtus formativa*) has a long history from Galen and Avicenna to Albert the Great and Ralph Cudworth, where Leibniz may have found it. See Hiro Hirai, *Medical Humanism and Natural Philosophy. Renaissance Debates on Matter, Life, and the Soul* (Leiden: Brill, 2011), 19–20.
11. Leibniz, "A New System of Nature and Communication of Substances" (1695), in *Philosophical Essays*, ed. and trans. Roger Ariew and Daniel Garber (Indianapolis: Hackett, 1989), 139.

12. Bergson's 1894–95 lecture course, in Simone Kotva, "The God of Effort: Henri Bergson and the Stoicism of Modernity," *Modern Theology* 32, no. 3 (2016): 415.
13. C. S. Peirce, *Collected Papers of Charles Sanders Peirce*, ed. Charles Hartshorne and Paul Weiss, vol. 6 (Cambridge, MA: Harvard University Press, 1935), 157.
14. This is my argument in *Empiricisms: Experience and Experiment from Antiquity to the Anthropocene* (New York: Oxford University Press, 2021).

Index

For the benefit of digital users, indexed terms that span two pages (e.g., 52–53) may, on occasion, appear on only one of those pages.

action, 4–5
actuality, 206, 208
adaptation, 130
   social, 13
affordances, 69–70
Anaxagoras, 120
anisotropy, temporal, 102–3
aphasia, 91–92
Aristotle, 114, 120–21, 126, 167–68, 192
art, 12–13, 148–49, 178–80
attention, 27
Augustine, Saint, 94–95

Bachelard, Gaston, 25–29
bacteria, 152
becoming, 98, 162–63
being, 66
Benda, Julian, 1
Bernard, Claude, 117–19
big bang, 3, 103, 155–56
   See also cosmology
biology, 58, 124–25
   Modern Synthesis, 126–27
body, and soul, 80–81
Bohr, Niels, 98–99
Boltzmann, Ludwig, 102–3
Borel, Émile, 37–38
brain, 89, 92
   See also neurology

camera, 69
capacities, 76

Čapek, Milič, 36–37
capitalism, 195, 200
Carnap, Rudolf, 82, 205
Cartwright, Nancy, 76
Cassirer, Ernst, 161, 164
chaos, 105–12
Chinese philosophy, 59–63
choice, 93
Christianity, 122, 198–99
Chrysippus, 4, 206–7
Cicero, 121–22
cinema, 13–15
Clifford, William, 81
clock, 23–24, 157
comedy, 180–81
conatus, 122–23, 203–4
concepts, 105
Confucianism, 61
consciousness, 9–10, 12–13, 24–25, 33, 45, 107, 132–33, 142–43, 144–45
   and life, 83–85
   and matter, 85–88
   plant, 84
continuity, 11–12, 16, 22–23, 25–26, 101, 111
Conway Morris, Simon, 129–31, 140, 143
cosmic background radiation, 103
cosmology, 154–56
creativity, 164

Dao, 59–63

Darwin, Charles, 113, 123–24, 171–72, 193
Darwinism, 125–28, 130–31, 203–4
De Broglie, Louis, 29
Deleuze, Gilles, 3, 4, 20–21, 56–57, 71, 154, 165–66, 205–6, 209
Democritus, 113, 114
Descartes, Rene, 35–36, 80–81, 106, 119
design, 133–34
determinism, 10–11, 43–51, 104, 191–92
Diderot, Denis, 81, 192–93
difference, 17–18, 23
discontinuity, 16, 25–26, 68, 101
   See also continuity
disorder, 106–7
   See also order
Driesch, Hans, 116–17, 118
dualism, 81
Dumas, Charles-Louis, 114
duration, 18–31
   and consciousness, 22
Durkheim, Émile, 1, 174

Eddington, Arthur, 20, 102–3
Einstein, Alfred, 2, 18, 36–37, 39–43, 101–2, 106, 107
élan vital, 140–46, 173, 190–91
empiricism, 57–58, 208–9
endosmosis, 12–13
entanglement, quantum, 101–2
entropy, 102–4
epistemology, 204–5
eternal return, 165–67
evolution, 4–5, 84–85, 113, 208–9
   convergent, 127, 128–34
   cosmic, 154–61
   human, 150–54
existence, 52–53, 71, 157
experience, 52–53, 77
extensity, 35–36
   See also space

eyes, 127, 128–30, 134–36, 137–38, 139–40

Faraday, Michael, 37–38
final cause, 113–14, 120, 122, 129–30, 168
   See also teleology
force, 207
forgetting, 61
form, 96
freedom, 10–11, 13, 49–51
free will, 43–51
Freud, Sigmund, 13, 95
future, 204

geometry, 35–36
God, 153–54, 188
Gould, Steven Jay, 130–31
Guyau, Jean-Marie, 29–30

Hamlet, 109–10
Hegel, G. W. F., 88
Heisenberg, Werner, 39, 46, 48, 72
Hesiod, 106
heterogeneity, 9–10, 23, 29–31
history, 189–90, 191
homogeneity, 17, 39
homology, 139–40
Horkheimer, Max, 28–29
Huxley, Julian, 141
Huxley, T. H., 125
Hymenoptera, 147

idealism, 81
image, 64–68, 70, 89
   mirror, 71–72
impenetrability, 12
individuality, 12–13, 37–38, 151–52, 153, 177–78, 197, 203–4
instant, 28–29, 39
instinct, 54–56
   social, 171–72
intellect, 54–55, 146–50
intelligence, 10–11
intensity, mental, 6–11

intuition, 5, 53–54, 56–57, 208–9

James, William, 2, 8, 53–54, 149–50, 208–9

Kant, Immanuel, 43–44, 51–52, 147, 189–91, 197–98
knowledge, 59–60
Koestler, Arthur, 181
Kolakowski, Leszek, 52, 204

Lamarck, Jean-Baptiste, 123–24, 135, 137
Langevin, Paul, 42–43
language, 10, 12–13, 17
Laplace, Pierre, 44, 45–46
laughter, 175–86
Leibniz, Gottfried Wilhelm, 12, 74–75, 81, 88, 151–52, 207
Lemaître, Georges, 3, 154–55
Lewis, David, 143–44
Lewis, Gilbert Newton, 102–3
Liebig, Justus von, 116, 118
life, 104, 132–33, 134, 174, 203–4, 206, 208
Lotze, Hermann, 20
Lovelock, James, 104

Mach, Ernst, 81, 102–3
machines, 119, 160–61
Maritain, Jacques, 1
Marx, Karl, 193–94
materialism, 81
mathematics, 58
matter, 38, 64–67, 74, 81–82, 104, 132–33, 142–43
McTaggart, J. M. E., 19–20
measurement, 23–24
mechanism, 113, 123–26, 133, 175–76, 177
memory, 6, 24–25, 32–33, 70, 77–81, 206
    recollection, 70–71
mental effort, 8
metaphysics, 52, 57–58

Meyerson, Émile, 17–18, 41, 104–5
Mill, J. S., 48–49, 75
morality, 171–72, 173–74
movement, 16, 25, 96–97, 163
multiplicity, 27
music, 21–22, 27–28
mysticism, 187–89, 197–98

Nagel, Thomas, 85–86
naturalism, 4–5, 204–5
natural selection, 126–27
nature, 132
negation, 28–29, 110–11
neo-Darwinism, 125–26, 127
neurology, 8, 91, 92–93, 142–43, 150–51
    See also brain
Nietzsche, Friedrich, 3–4, 51–52, 65, 161–69
    Thus Spoke Zarathustra, 182–86
nominalism, 74–75
nonbeing, 105–12, 208
now, 24, 159–60
Nozick, Robert, 48–49
nuclear energy, 196–97, 199–200

Ockham, William, 74–75, 97
octopus, 134–40
ontology, 205–8
order, 105–7

pain, 13
panpsychism, 81–88
Parmenides, 15–16, 66
past, 24–25, 31–35, 45, 94–96
Péguy, Charles, 1
Peirce, C. S., 65, 110, 202, 208–9
perception, 67–70, 90, 97–98, 163
    and memory, 77–78
perspectivism, 163
philosophy, 105–6, 148–49
photography, 64–65
physics, 98–105
    See also quantum physics
Planck, Max, 98–99

Plato, 66, 97–98, 106, 107–8, 120–21, 146–47, 192
pleasure, 13
Popper, Karl, 170–71, 172
Porzig, Walter, 17
possibility, 108–10
potential, 74, 76
pragmatism, 149–50
present, 24, 94–95
  See also now
progress, 197–98

qualia, 85–86, 87–88
quality, 79
quantification, 11–12
quantity, 11–12, 79
quantum physics, 29, 98–99, 203
  See also physics
Quine, W. V., 75, 204–5

rationalism, 5, 17–18, 149
Ravaisson, Félix, 179
relations, 82, 85
reversibility, 45, 104–5
rhythm, 27, 164
Rousseau, Jean-Jacques, 191
Rovelli, Carlo, 157–58
Russell, Bertrand, 11–12, 14–15
Russell, E. S., 119, 124

Schopenhauer, Arthur, 51–52, 81, 82–83, 150, 162
Schrödinger, Erwin, 99, 101
science, 4–5, 52, 57, 58, 82–83, 148–50
self, 13
sensation, 9
Smolin, Lee, 156, 157, 158–59
society, open and closed, 171–75, 189
Society for Psychical Research, 196
space, 35, 36–37, 102–3
  space-time, 40, 42, 43
  See also extensity
spatial thought, 11–18
Spencer, Herbert, 7, 10
Spinoza, Baruch, 12, 81, 107–8, 119, 122–24, 146, 151–52, 203–4
spirit, 88–89
Stahl, Georg Ernst, 114–15
Stoics, 4, 121–23, 146, 151–52, 165, 166–68, 206–8
Suárez, Francisco, 109
sympathy, 56

techne, 192
technology, 146–47, 187–201
teleology, 120–23, 168
  See also final cause
tendency, 36, 73–74, 76, 97, 132–33, 139, 202, 203–4, 208
Thomson, John Arthur, 124
time, 6, 18–19, 31–35, 127
  A- and B-series, 19–21, 159
  concrete and abstract, 33–34
tonos, 36, 207–8
truth, 149–50
twins paradox, 42–43

utilitarianism, 105–6, 208–9

Venn, John, 37–38
virtual, 4, 68–69, 70–76, 109, 137, 138, 202, 205–6, 208–9
  virtual image, 71
  virtual particle, 72–73
vitalism, 114–25, 133

Weismann, August, 125–26, 127, 142
Weyl, Hermann, 47
Wittgenstein, Ludwig, 105–6, 143–44

Zeno of Elea, 15–17, 97
Zhuangzi, 59–63, 153–54

www.ingramcontent.com/pod-product-compliance
Ingram Content Group UK Ltd.
Pitfield, Milton Keynes, MK11 3LW, UK
UKHW020421260326
469240UK00026B/37